SKYLANDERS SWAP FORCE

CHARACTER UPGRADE EDITION

TABLE OF CONTENTS

PORTAL MASTERY 2
MEET THE SKYLANDERS 4

MAGIC
Hoot Loop 12
Trap Shadow 14
Dune Bug 16
Super Gulp
  Pop Fizz 18
Mega Ram Spyro 20
Star Strike 22

FIRE
Blast Zone 24
Fire Kraken 26
Lava Barf Eruptor 28
Fryno 30
Fire Bone Hot Dog 32
Smolderdash 34

WATER
Freeze Blade 36
Wash Buckler 38
Blizzard Chill 40
Anchors Away
  Gill GRunt 42
Punk Shock 44
Riptide 46

Wham-Shell 48

UNDEAD
Night Shift 50
Rattle Shake 52
Twin Blade
  Chop Chop 54
Phantom Cynder 56
Grim Creeper 58
Roller Brawl 60

TECH
Magna Charge 62
Spy Rise 64
Countdown 66
Heavy Duty
  Sprocket 68
Big Bang
  Trigger Happy 70
Wind-Up 72

LIFE
Grilla Drilla 74
Stink Bomb 76
Bumble Blast 78
Thorn Horn Camo..... 80

Ninja Stealth Elf 82
Zoo Lou 84

EARTH
Doom Stone 86
Rubble Rouser 88
Flashwing 90
Hyper Beam
  Prism Break 92
Scorp 94
Slobber Tooth 96
Knockout Terrafin..... 98

AIR
Boom Jet 100
Free Ranger 102
Turbo Jet-Vac 104
Pop Thorn 106
Scratch 108
Warnado 110
Horn Blast
  Whirlwind 112

IMPROVING YOUR SKYLANDERS 114
Quests 120

BOSSES
Evil Glumshanks 124
Baron Von Shellshock
  & Evilized Whiskers 126
Fire Viper 128
Mesmeralda 130
Mr. Chompy 132
Kaos' Mon & Bubba Greebs 132
Super Evil Kaos 134
Sheep Mage 136
Cluck 137

STORY MAPS
Mount Cloudbreak 138
Cascade Glade 140
Mudwater Hollow 142
Rampant Ruins 144
Iron Jaw Gulch 146
Motleyville 148
Twisty Tunnels 150
Boney Islands 152
Winter Keep 154
Frostfest Mountains 156
Fantasm Forest 158
Kaos' Fortress 160

ACCOLADES 216
ACHIEVEMENTS AND TROPHIES 220

ADVENTURE PACK LEVELS
Sheep Wreck Islands 162
Tower of Time 164

WOODBURROW 166

SWAP ZONE CHALLENGES 168
Bounce Challenges 170
Climb Challenges 171
Dig Challenges 173
Rocket Challenges 174
Sneak Challenges 175
Speed Challenges 177
Spin Challenges 178
Teleport Challenges 179

BONUS MISSIONS 181
ARENA MODE 187
TIME ATTACK MODE 198
SCORE MODE 200

COLLECTIBLES
Hats 202
Legendary Treasures 209
Charms 212
Bonus Mission Maps 214
Story Scrolls 215

PORTAL MASTERY

Welcome back to Skylands, young Portal Master! In the midst of a vacation, Flynn stumbled upon the latest and most sinister plot Kaos has devised yet.

It is up to you to help him, and his new friend, Tessa, as they try to free her village from a Greeble invasion. What happens afterward, well, that's the adventure ahead, Portal Master. Along the way, you will face many new foes, and meet wonderful new friends, including all-new Skylanders, the *SWAP Force*. *SWAP Force*™ characters open up all new challenges, and they're all waiting for you!

WHAT'S NEW IN SKYLANDERS SWAP FORCE™?

If you are a veteran Portal Master, much of what you remember from previous games still holds true, but there are a few new and different things for you to know.

The maximum level is now 20, and while Heroic Challenges have been replaced with a new type of challenge, Arena challenges remain. Two of the biggest changes are *SWAP Force* Skylanders and Portal Master Rank.

SWAP Force™ Skylanders

The newest type of Skylander is a *SWAP Force* Skylander. These amazing Skylanders can mix and match their torsos and legs, combining abilities and elemental affinities in the process. There are other new Skylanders and new Series 2 and 3 figures as well, but *SWAP Force* Skylanders act just a bit differently.

For the most part, they work just like any other Skylander. They fight, earn XP, and complete quests. It's the top half of each *SWAP Force* character that keeps the money and XP collected, and tracks the completion of quests. The legs have one of eight special abilities that allow them to enter all-new SWAP Zone Challenges.

The top half also has two abilities (activated with the Attack 1 and Attack 3 buttons) while the Attack 2 button ability is tied to the legs. Each half has its own Upgrade Paths.

Portal Master Rank

It's no longer just Skylanders who level up! Portal Masters must now earn Stars to increase their rank. For each six Stars you earn, you gain a Portal Master Rank.

There are several ways to earn Stars, and most of them are tied to meeting specific conditions while playing through many of the game's modes.

Earning Stars with Accolades

There are four types of Accolades: Completion, Challenge, Exploration, and Collection. The conditions for completing these Accolades can be found in the Portal Master screen's sub-menus of the same name. New Accolades often become available when you complete ones that are visible, so check back each time you earn an Accolade.

⭐ Earn Stars through Special Challenge Modes

There are three types of special challenges: SWAP Zone, Bonus Mission Maps, and Survival Arena. These unique challenges take place on special maps and often include a time limit. Each challenge is worth one, two, or three stars, depending on how well you perform in them.

Earn Stars Three Ways on Story Levels

To begin gaining Portal Master Rank, you need to play through the Story Mode and the two new Adventure Packs. Each Chapter in Story Mode awards up to three Stars based on how well you played through it. After you complete the Story Mode, you also unlock Time Attack Mode and Score Mode.

Both Modes award up to three Stars. That means you can earn up to nine Stars from playing the same level in three completely different ways. The best part is that you can earn all these Stars while playing with a friend!

WHAT DO I NEED TO SEE EVERYTHING IN STORY MODE?

In order to access everything found throughout the Story Mode, you need the following:

- One Skylander figure for each of the eight elements.
- One Giant Skylander figure to open special chests found throughout the Story Levels. The Giant Skylander also counts toward covering the eight elements.
- One *Skylanders SWAP Force* figure with each of the eight special abilities: Bounce, Climb, Dig, Rocket, Sneak, Speed, Spin, Teleport. *SWAP Force* Skylanders also count toward covering the eight elements. For example that means Boom Jet counts as both an Air Skylander, and as having the Rocket ability.

You could clear the main story of *Skylanders SWAP Force* with only one Skylander figure, but the more Skylanders you have, the less trouble you run into while playing through the game. Skylanders cannot be revived once they fall in battle, and you must restart the level if you run out of healthy Skylanders. Speaking of Skylanders, turn the page to learn more about them.

MEET THE SKYLANDERS

The following pages cover the newest Skylanders, including their individual stories, stats, powers, and upgrades. Since you can still use the Skylander figures from the earlier games in the series while playing *Skylanders SWAP Force*, they are summarized first. To track your progress, select Collection on the Pause menu and go to the Skylander's tab (look for Spyro's face).

Skylander figures from different games are identified by the color of the plastic on their base. Skylander figures with a green base are from *Skylanders Spyro's Adventure™*. Skylander figures with an orange base are from *Skylanders Giants™*. The newest Skylander figures, those for *Skylanders SWAP Force*, have a blue base.

TYPES OF SKYLANDER FIGURES

There are two types of Series 2 Skylanders. Orange base Series 2 are new versions of characters for *Skylanders Giants* that first appeared in *Skylanders Spyro's Adventure*. Blue base Series 2 Skylanders are new versions of characters from either of the first two games, created for *Skylanders SWAP Force*. All Series 2 Skylanders have a special "Wow Pow!" power.

Series 3 Skylanders are new versions of characters that appeared in both of the first two games. All Series 3 Skylanders have a special "Wow Pow!" ability that is different than their Series 2 ability.

LightCore™ Skylanders are special versions of Skylanders whose figures have parts that glow. They cause a damaging shockwave when they are placed on the *Portal of Power™*.

SKYLANDER FIGURES FROM SKYLANDERS SPYRO'S ADVENTURE

When these green based Skylanders choose an Upgrade Path, the only way to select the other Upgrade Path is to reset the character in the Manage submenu on the Skylander Stats screen.

Standard Figures

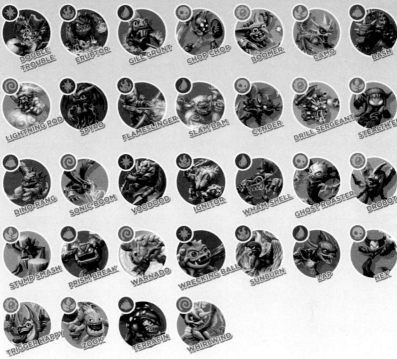

DOUBLE TROUBLE · ERUPTOR · GILL GRUNT · CHOP CHOP · BOOMER · CAMO · BASH

LIGHTNING ROD · SPYRO · FLAMESLINGER · SLAM BAM · CYNDER · DRILL SERGEANT · STEALTH ELF

DINO-RANG · SONIC BOOM · VOODOOD · IGNITOR · WHAM-SHELL · GHOST ROASTER · DROBOT

STUMP SMASH · PRISM BREAK · WARNADO · WRECKING BALL · SUNBURN · ZAP · HEX

TRIGGER HAPPY · ZOOK · TERRAFIN · WHIRLWIND

Legendary Figures

SPYRO · CHOP CHOP · TRIGGER HAPPY · BASH

Alt Deco

DARK SPYRO

OTHER FIGURES FROM *SKYLANDERS SPYRO'S ADVENTURE*

Adventure Pack Figures

There were four Adventure Packs for *Skylanders Spyro's Adventure.* While playing *Skylanders SWAP Force,* use the Adventure Packs during your regular play to execute a special attack that damages every enemy on the screen.

Adventure Packs also include two Magic Items that aid your Skylander with a special attack or a beneficial effect. The Magic Items have a timer, but it resets whenever you start a new level.

ADVENTURE PACK FIGURE	AREA OF EFFECT ATTACK
Dragon's Peak	Fireballs
Empire of Ice	Ice Shards
Darklight Crypt	Shadowy Orbs
Pirate Ship	Cannonballs

Anvil Rain

When you put this item on the Portal, anvils fall from the sky, randomly hitting enemies in the area. If an anvil hits your Skylander, it only knocks them back. It does not damage them.

Healing Elixir

This awesome item quickly heals your Skylanders while they wander around. Your Skylanders regain 30 health every second, but Healing Elixir has a short duration.

Ghost Pirate Swords

This Adventure Item spawns in two swords that float around the screen, attacking the Skylander's foes.

Hidden Treasure

When you use Hidden Treasure on a Story Level, a bonus treasure chest is generated. Use the radar at the bottom of the screen to help locate the chest. When playing on the Wii console the Hidden Treasure instead increases the gold you find for a short time.

The following table provides the areas in which the chest will spawn when the Hidden Treasure item is used on the level listed in the first column.

STORY LEVEL	CHEST 1 LOCATION	CHEST 2 LOCATION	CHEST 3 LOCATION
Mount Cloudbeak	The Overgrowth	Old Treetop Terrace	Long Worn Hollow
Cascade Glade	Luau Lagoon	Gobblepod Sanctuary	Overlook Heights
Mudwater Hollow	Billy's Bend	Big Gill Water Mill	Muddy Marsh River
Rampant Ruins	Orangutan Tower	Simian Throne Room	Western Watch
Iron Jaw Gulch	The Canteen	Sun Smoked Strand	10,000 Gallon Hat
Motleyville	Arena Overlook	Soggy Fields	Big Bang Bouncers
Twisty Tunnels	Perilous Plateau	Underground Lake	Serene Walkway
Boney Islands	Frozen Fossil Lane	Amber Alley	Glacial Gallery
Winter Keep	The Blizzard Bridges	The Frozen Curtain	Hibernal Harbor
Frostfest Mountains	Typhoon Trail	The Glacier Hills	Perilous Precipice
Fantasm Forest	Troll Toll Bridge	Fantasm Village	Birchberg
Kaos' Fortress	Sheep Tower	Glob Lobber Gangway	Chompy Churners

Sky-Iron Shield

This Adventure Item causes two rotating shields to protect your Skylander for its duration. The Sky-Iron Shield doesn't make your Skylander invulnerable, but it does make them tougher.

Time Twist Hourglass

The Time Twist Hourglass slows down time, putting the game into slow motion for the duration of the spell. The catch is, your Skylander doesn't slow down!

Sparx the Dragonfly

Sparx buzzes around, blasting enemies with his insect breath. He only stays around for about a minute, but can really help in tough fights.

Volcanic Vault

Using Volcanic Vault in *Skylanders SWAP Force* causes fire to rain down from the sky, damaging enemies for a short time.

Winged Boots

With this Adventure Item, your Skylander can run much faster than normal. This item is tremendously helpful during Time Attack.

SKYLANDER FIGURES
FROM *SKYLANDERS GIANTS*

When these orange based characters choose an Upgrade Path, the only way to select the other Upgrade Path is to reset the character in the Ownership menu. Series 2 figures are the exception. They can switch between Upgrade Paths while in a Power Pod.

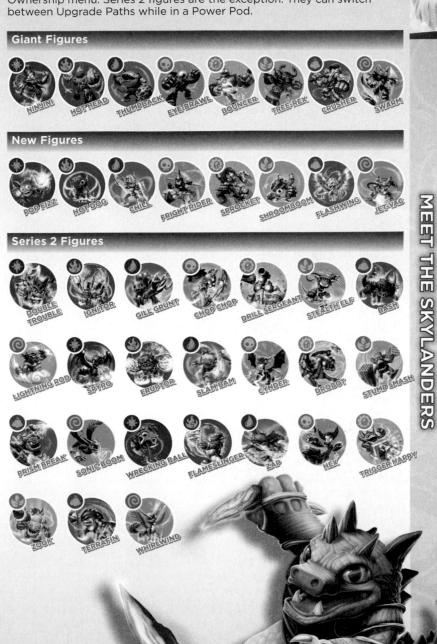

Giant Figures

NINJINI HOT HEAD THUMPBACK EYE-BRAWL BOUNCER TREE-REX CRUSHER SWARM

New Figures

POP FIZZ HOT DOG CHILL FRIGHT RIDER SPROCKET SHROOMBOOM FLASHWING JET-VAC

Series 2 Figures

DOUBLE TROUBLE IGNITOR GILL GRUNT CHOP CHOP DRILL SERGEANT STEALTH ELF BASH

LIGHTNING ROD SPYRO ERUPTOR SLAM BAM CYNDER DROBOT STUMP SMASH

PRISM BREAK SONIC BOOM WRECKING BALL FLAMESLINGER ZAP HEX TRIGGER HAPPY

ZOOK TERRAFIN WHIRLWIND

Legendary Figures

CHILL (LIGHTCORE™)

BOUNCER

JET-VAC

Series 2 Legendary Figures

IGNITOR

SLAM BAM

LightCore Figures

POP FIZZ

CHILL

SHROOMBOOM

JET-VAC

Alt Deco

PUNCH POP FIZZ

MOLTEN HOT DOG

SCARLET NINJINI

GNARLY TREE REX

GRANITE CRUSHER

POLAR WHIRLWIND

ROYAL DOUBLE TROUBLE

JADE FLASHWING

OTHER FIGURES FROM SKYLANDERS GIANTS

Two special figures were made for *Skylanders Giants*. They both can help clear out enemies and make for smoother travels.

Dragonfire Cannon

The Dragonfire Cannon blasts enemies every few seconds. It also follows Skylanders as they move through levels.

Scorpion Striker

The Scorpion Striker Catapult lobs spiked balls at enemies. If the spiked ball doesn't hit an enemy in the air, it remains on the ground and will explode if an enemy gets close.

SIDEKICKS

Sidekicks are smaller versions of Skylander figures that follow your full-sized Skylander when they are placed on the *Portal of Power*. They were made available during special promotions

after the release of both Skylanders Spyro's Adventure and Skylanders Giants. There are four sidekicks from both games. These figures are tracked under Other Toys in the Collections/Skylanders screen.

SKYLANDER FIGURES FOR
SKYLANDERS SWAP FORCE

When some characters choose an Upgrade Path, the only way to select the other Upgrade Path is to reset the character in the Ownership menu. Series 2 and Series 3 figures can switch between Upgrade Paths while in a Power Pod.

SWAP Force Figures

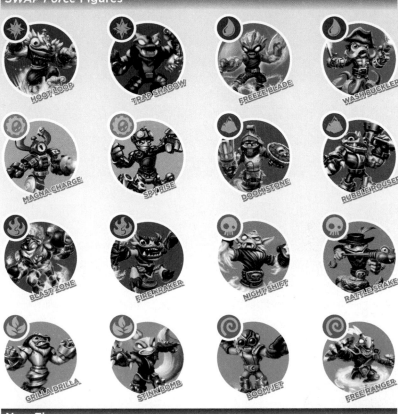

HOOT LOOP

TRAP SHADOW

FREEZE BLADE

WASH BUCKLER

MAGNA CHARGE

SPY RISE

DOOM STONE

RUBBLE ROUSER

BLAST ZONE

FIRE KRAKEN

NIGHT SHIFT

RATTLE SHAKE

GRILLA DRILLA

STINK BOMB

BOOM JET

FREE RANGER

New Figures

DUNE BUG

FRYNO

PUNK SHOCK

GRIM CREEPER

COUNTDOWN

BUMBLE BLAST

SCORP

POP THORN

STAR STRIKE

SMOLDERDASH

RIP TIDE

ROLLER BRAWL

WIND-UP

ZOO LOU

SLOBBER TOOTH

SCRATCH

Series 2 Figures

SUPER GULP POP FIZZ · FIRE BONE HOT DOG · BLIZZARD CHILL · HEAVY DUTY SPROCKET · THORN HORN CAMO · TURBO JET-VAC

Series 3 Figures

MEGA RAM SPYRO · LAVA BARF ERUPTOR · ANCHORS AWAY GILL GRUNT · TWIN BLADE CHOP CHOP · BIG BANG TRIGGER HAPPY · NINJA STEALTH ELF · HYPER BEAM PRISM BREAK

HORN BLAST WHIRLWIND · PHANTOM CYNDER · KNOCKOUT TERRAFIN

Legendary Figures

NIGHT SHIFT · ZOO LOU · FREE RANGER · GRIM CREEPER (LIGHTCORE™)

LightCore Figures

STAR STRIKE · SMOLDERDASH · WHAM-SHELL · GRIM CREEPER · COUNTDOWN · BUMBLE BLAST

FLASHWING · WARNADO

Alt Deco Figures

ENCHANTED HOOT LOOP DARK BLAST ZONE NITRO FREEZE BLADE NITRO MAGNA CHARGE DARK NINJA STEALTH ELF DARK SLOBBER TOOTH DARK MEGA RAM SPYRO

DARK WASH BUCKLER ENCHANTED STAR STRIKE (LIGHTCORE™)

OTHER FIGURES FROM *SKYLANDERS SWAP FORCE*

Tower of Time

When you place the Tower of Time figure on the *Portal of Power*, it drops gears from the sky, inflicting damage to any enemies on the screen. It also unlocks the Tower of Time Story Level and a new Ring Out Arena, the Tic Toc Terrace. The entrance for the Tower of Time is near the Yard in Woodburrow.

Fiery Forge

The Fiery Forge adds a new Battle and Ring-Out Arena of the same name. When placed on the *Portal of Power*, a cauldron floats over your Skylander's head. When enemies are near, the cauldron tips over and covers the ground with molten metal, producing an effect similar to Eruptor's attack, Eruption.

Sheep Wreck Islands

The Sheep Wreck Islands figure opens the Story Level of the same name as well as four Arenas: Vortex Banquet, Cyclops Makeover, Sheep Mage Rage, and Chunky Chompies. The entrance for Sheep Wreck Islands is at one end of The Airdocks.

Groove Machine

The Groove Machine follows Skylanders and plays music. It also makes enemies dance, preventing them from attacking.

Arkeyan Crossbow

The Arkeyan Crossbow adds a new Battle Arena called Treacherous Beach and four Survival Arenas: Sand Castle, Beach Breach, Troll Beach Attack, and Chompy Tsunami. It also generates an in-game crossbow with a lob attack. The bolt damages enemies it hits and also creates a watery wave that hits other nearby enemies.

Platinum Sheep

The Platinum Sheep disguises your Skylander as a sheep and restores health over time. Enemies ignore the sheep and allow it to recover health in peace. While you can still move around, you can't perform any other actions (like attack) until the disguise is removed.

Battle Hammer

A Battle Hammer appears over your Skylander's head. Whenever you press Attack 1, the hammer hits the ground in front of your Skylander (Skylanders still execute their normal attack, though). Nearby enemies take damage and are knocked back.

Sky Diamond

When the Sky Diamond is active, every defeated enemy drops a diamond worth 20 gold. It's a great way to earn money quickly to help pay for items and Skylander upgrades.

UFO Hat

Placing this Magic Item on the *Portal of Power* unlocks the UFO Hat.

HOOT LOOP

"Let's Ruffle Some Feathers!"

DéjàBOOM! bounces off its initial target and hits additional targets for less damage. The Dreamweaver Path turns it into a beam that remains active so long as Attack 1 is pressed. The Hypno-Owl Path is two direct upgrades to Hypnotism, an attack that slows enemies (and Hoot) while Attack 3 is pressed.

Loop the Loop begins as a great way to escape enemies but its upgrades, Infinite Loop in particular, turn it into a great offensive weapon. The Telekinesis Path boosts Loop the Loop's damage output. The Escape Artist Path adds a little damage and a wrinkle that leaves enemies guessing where Hoot Loop will appear after teleporting.

Special Quest

Wand You Like To Play A Game?

DEFEAT 50 ENEMIES WITH THE FINAL EXPLOSION OF THE FLASHBACK ATTACK.
Completing this quest calls for a touch of patience. After purchasing the Flashback upgrade, allow its explosion to finish off enemies instead of hitting them with other attacks. Large groups of Chompies are the best targets for completing this quest quickly.

Hoot Loop was raised by a guild of magicians in Skylands' most famous traveling circus. At a young age, he perfected illusions and spells that only the very best of their guild could perform, and even mastered the art of teleportation! Soon enough, he became the star of the show, known far and wide as the Amazing Hoot Loop. However, one day an army of Greebles disguised as clowns invaded, determined to destroy the popular circus. It was then that Hoot Loop gave a performance that few would ever forget. Using his incredible powers, he fought off the invaders and saved the circus—to the raucous applause of the many spectators—including Master Eon, who presented Hoot Loop with an opportunity to learn some real magic as a member of the Skylanders.

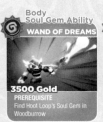

Body
Soul Gem Ability
WAND OF DREAMS

3500 Gold
PREREQUISITE
Find Hoot Loop's Soul Gem in Woodburrow

Press **Attack 1** to shoot a DéjàBOOM! and two smaller DéjàBOOM! projectiles at once.

Legs
Soul Gem Ability
INFINITE LOOP

3500 Gold
PREREQUISITE
Find Hoot Loop's Soul Gem in Woodburrow

Hold **Attack 2** to aim the portal loop, release it under Loop's body to cause a massive attack that damages enemies in a large area.

LEVEL	1	2	3	4	5	6	7	8	9	10	11	12	13	14	15	16	17	18	19	20
♥ MAX HEATH	250	275	300	325	350	375	400	425	450	500	525	550	575	600	625	650	675	700	725	750

⚡ SPEED	🛡 ARMOR	⊕ CRITICAL HIT	◎ ELEMENTAL POWER
43	24	8	25

BODY

Basic Attacks
DÉJÀBOOM!

Press **Attack 1** to shoot a magic projectile that hits enemies three times before it disappears.

Upgrades

HYPNOTISM

300 Gold
PREREQUISITE None

Hold **Attack 3** to hypnotize enemies, slowing their movement and attacks.

TRICKED YA!

800 Gold
PREREQUISITE None

Armor increased. Shiny new armor reduces damage.

FLASHBACK

1000 Gold
PREREQUISITE None

Press **Attack 1** to shoot a DéjàBOOM projectile. DéjàBOOM bounces three times and on a third bounce it explodes.

Dream-Weaver Path

DREAM BEAM

1500 Gold
PREREQUISITE
Dream-Weaver Path

Hold **Attack 1** to channel a magical beam of dreams that damages enemies.

BAD DREAMS BEAM

2000 Gold
PREREQUISITE
Purchase Dream Beam ability

Dream Beam does increased damage.

Hypno-Owl Path

MASS HYPNOSIS

1500 Gold
PREREQUISITE
Hypno-Owl Path

Hypnotism becomes more effective, slowing enemies in a larger area.

DEEP ASLEEP

2000 Gold
PREREQUISITE
Purchase Mass Hypnosis ability

Hold **Attack 3** to use a more powerful Mass Hypnosis, dealing increased damage

LEGS

Basic Attacks
LOOP THE LOOP

Press **Attack 2** to teleport forward a short distance and damage nearby enemies.

Upgrades

PORTABLE HOLE

300 Gold
PREREQUISITE None

Hold **Attack 2** to aim the portal loop. Release to teleport to that area and damage all nearby enemies.

TEMPORAL WHACK

800 Gold
PREREQUISITE None

Teleport does increased damage.

TIME SINK

1000 Gold
PREREQUISITE None

Enemies and objects are pulled towards the area where Portable Hole is aimed.

Telekinesis Path

NOW YOU SEE ME

1500 Gold
PREREQUISITE
Telekinesis Path

Hold **Attack 2** to charge Portable Hole, release to do increased damage. Damage is increased the longer it is charged.

COMPLETE CONCENTRATION

2000 Gold
PREREQUISITE
Purchase Now You See Me ability

Now You See Me does increased damage. A very impressive entrance!

Escape Artist Path

NOW YOU DON'T

1500 Gold
PREREQUISITE
Escape Artist Path

Press **Jump** after teleporting to appear back at the previous position.

TELEPORT TURBULENCE

2000 Gold
PREREQUISITE
Purchase Now You Don't ability

All teleport attacks do increased damage.

TRAP SHADOW

"Hide and Sleek!"

Once part of an elite tribe of hunters in a remote area of Skylands, Trap Shadow used his cat-like cunning, ingenious traps, and mystical stealth abilities to catch nearly everything that could be caught. As a result, his fame around Skylands grew so much that it attracted the attention of an evil cadre of wizards. They plotted to capture Trap Shadow and use his abilities to ensnare the most uncatchable thing of all—Master Eon himself. But Trap Shadow could sense them coming from miles away. Outsmarted and outmaneuvered, each of the wizards was easily captured by Trap Shadow's bewildering array of traps and snares until they were all locked away for good. Having been saved by the cunning hunter, Master Eon quickly made Trap Shadow a Skylander.

Clawing Shadow gains a nice combo addition if you choose the Feral Instincts Path. You must hold Attack 1 after the first hit to initiate the combo. Any swing after that will start up Trap Shadow's Soul Gem ability, Shadow Striker. Catch! is a great upgrade to Snap Trap, and the Trap Trickster Path turns the traps into bombs.

Shadow Kick upgrades into a stealth ability and the Prowler Path plays off that, leaving damaging footprints in Shadow's path. The Shadow Combat Path increases Shadow's direct damage potential. Shadow Kicks hit harder and from a greater distance.

Special Quest
Oh Snap!

DEFEAT 50 ENEMIES WITH YOUR TRAPS.
You can't work on this quest until you purchase Snap Trap, so as soon as it is available, start leavin traps everywhere there are enemies to complete this quest. Catch! makes completing it easier, as does choosing the Trap Trickster Path.

Body Soul Gem Ability	Legs Soul Gem Ability
SHADOW STRIKER	**LIVING SHADOW**

3500 Gold
PREREQUISITE
Find Trap Shadow's Soul Gem in Frostfest Mountains

3500 Gold
PREREQUISITE
Find Trap Shadow's Soul Gem in Frostfest Mountains

Press **Attack 1** rapidly to do quick claw attacks. Whilte doing claw attacks, hold **Attack 1** to unleash a powerful shadowy dash.

Hold **Attack 2** to prowl and become invisible. Who needs shadows to hide in? Just become one!

LEVEL	1	2	3	4	5	6	7	8	9	10	11	12	13	14	15	16	17	18	19	20
♥ MAX HEATH	c	297	324	351	378	405	432	459	486	540	567	594	621	648	675	702	729	756	783	810

⚡ SPEED	🛡 ARMOR	⊕ CRITICAL HIT	◎ ELEMENTAL POWER
43	12	8	25

BODY

Basic Attacks
CLAWING SHADOW

Press **Attack 1** to swipe shadowy claws at nearby enemies.

Upgrades

SNAP TRAP

300 Gold
PREREQUISITE None

Press **Attack 3** to throw a magically animated trap which will snap at enemies and damage them.

SHARP MAGIC

800 Gold
PREREQUISITE None

Press **Attack 1** rapidly to use powerful claw attacks that deal increased damage.

CATCH!

1000 Gold
PREREQUISITE Purchase Snap Trap

Hold **Attack 3** to aim Snap Trap, release to throw it.

Feral Instincts Path

ME-OUCH!

1500 Gold
PREREQUISITE Feral Instincts Path

Hold **Attack 1** to combo into a swipe that knocks enemies into the air.

NOCTURNAL PREDATOR

2000 Gold
PREREQUISITE Purchase Me-Ouch! ability

Me-Ouch! does increased damage. This kitty has claws...big, pointy claws!

Trap Trickster Path

GLOOM AND BOOM

1500 Gold
PREREQUISITE Trap Trickster Path

Traps will explode after a short time, damaging all enemies within a large area.

MAKE IT SNAPPY

2000 Gold
PREREQUISITE Purchase Gloom and Boom ability

All traps are now more powerful and do increased damage.

LEGS

Basic Attacks
SHADOW KICK

Press **Attack 2** to kick a wave of shadows at enemies.

Upgrades

PROWL

300 Gold
PREREQUISITE None

Hold **Attack 2** to prowl for a short time, causing any enemy touched to be damaged.

NINE LIVES

800 Gold
PREREQUISITE None

Health is increased. This cat is never done for.

OUT OF THE SHADOWS

1000 Gold
PREREQUISITE None

Hold **Attack 2** to prowl for a short time, coming out of prowl causes a large explosion that damages nearby enemies.

Shadow Combat Path

DARK MAGIC

1500 Gold
PREREQUISITE Shadow Combat Path

Press **Attack 2** to kick a wave of shadow that can damage enemies farther away.

BLACK CAT

2000 Gold
PREREQUISITE Purchase Dark Magic ability

All shadow wave attacks do even more damage.

Prowler Path

SHADE STEPS

1500 Gold
PREREQUISITE Prowler Path

Hold **Attack 2** to prowl, moving while prowling leaves behind magical pawprints that damage enemies that touch them.

BUMPS IN THE NIGHT

2000 Gold
PREREQUISITE Purchase Shade Steps ability

Shade Steps do increased damage. Huh? Whose footprints are these?

DUNE BUG

"Can't Beat the Beetle!"

Bursting Magic provides a nice boost to Mystic Missiles, allowing you to to increase the damage output of each missile, but at the cost of reduced movement speed and the attack pausing after a few seconds. Dune Ball is a great defensive weapon. Use it to roll away any enemies that get in too close.

The Scarab Sage Path is the more aggressive way to go. Each upgrade increases Dune Bug's damage output. The Dune Mage Path has defensive abilities. Dune Bomb keeps the space in front of Dune Bug clear while Sparking Wings takes care of the back.

Special Quest

That's How I Roll

ROLL YOUR DUNE BALL A TOTAL OF 5,000 FEET.

This quest only counts the distance Dune Bug rolls his Dune Ball, so you must hold Attack 2 while walking around. There's no other trick to this quest. You could even complete it while walking around Woodburrow.

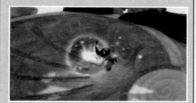

Hailing from a race of beetles changed by the powerful secrets hidden in a buried Arkeyan city, Dune Bug was next in line to become the defender of those secrets. As a small pupa, Dune Bug, along with his father, would travel to the ruins where he learned to read the ancient writings using his father's magic staff. On the day Dune Bug was to be given his own magic staff, the city fell under attack by the evil Sand Mages of Doom, who were after the secret Arkeyan tomes. Knowing what he had to do, Dune Bug used his magic to defeat the Mages and bury the city deeper into the ground until it was forever out of their reach. Dune Bug earned his magic staff that day—and a place alongside the Skylanders.

LEVEL	1	2	3	4	5	6	7	8	9	10	11	12	13	14	15	16	17	18	19	20
♥ MAX HEATH	260	286	312	338	364	390	416	442	468	520	546	572	598	624	650	676	702	728	754	780

⚡ SPEED	🛡 ARMOR	◈ CRITICAL HIT	◎ ELEMENTAL POWER
35	24	4	25

Basic Attacks

MYSTIC MISSILES

Press **Attack 1** to shoot magical beams of energy from a staff.

DUNE BALL

Hold **Attack 2** to create a large magical ball that can be rolled around and scoop up enemies.

ⓖ Soul Gem Ability
BUGGY BUDDY

4000 Gold
PREREQUISITE
Find Dune Bug's Soul Gem in Boney Islands!

Press **Attack 2** twice to summon Buggy, a little bug who rides a dune ball and rolls up nearby enemies.

Upgrades

DUNE PARADE

500 Gold
PREREQUISITE   None

Hold **Attack 2** to create a Dune Ball. Move the Dune Ball to make it grow, increasing damage, size, and how many enemies can be trapped.

DEBILITATING DUNES

700 Gold
PREREQUISITE   None

Hold **Attack 2** to create a Dune Ball. Move the Dune Ball over enemies to trap them. Press **Attack 1** to shoot enemies in the Dune Ball and do increased damage to them.

BURSTING MAGIC

900 Gold
PREREQUISITE   None

Hold **Attack 1** to fire rapid streams of powerful magic from a new staff.

BUZZING BEETLE

1200 Gold
PREREQUISITE   None

Press **Attack 3** to hover in the air. Speed is increased while hovering!

Scarab Sage Path

STUNNING SPREAD

1700 Gold
PREREQUISITE
Scarab Sage Path

Hold **Attack 1** for a short time to charge the staff, release to shoot three powerful exploding orbs of magic at enemies.

SCARAB POWER

2200 Gold
PREREQUISITE
Scarab Sage Path

Gain a new golden staff that shoots magic projectiles that do increased damage.

MAGIC SCARAB RIDE

3000 Gold
PREREQUISITE
Scarab Sage Path

Jump while hovering to create a large shockwave that damages nearby enemies.

Dune Mage Path

DUNE BOMB

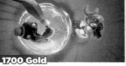

1700 Gold
PREREQUISITE
Dune Mage Path

Hold **Attack 1** for a short time to charge the staff, release to shoot a dune grenade that traps enemies and explodes.

HARDENED SHELL

2200 Gold
PREREQUISITE
Dune Mage Path

Armor is increased. A new hardened shell reduces damage taken.

SPARKING WINGS

3000 Gold
PREREQUISITE
Dune Mage Path

Press **Attack 3** to hover, causing sparks of magic to shoot out from behind.

SUPER GULP POP FIZZ

"Motion of the Potion!"

SERIES 2

When fully upgraded, Pop Fizz's potions make him a powerful ranged attacker. The yellow potion deals ranged damage. The green potion creates a pool that deals damage to any enemy that touches it. The purple potion summons minions, and gets a big boost with Pop Fizz's new Wow Pow! ability.

The Mad Scientist Path improves potions by combining their effects. The Best of the Beast Path allows Pop Fizz to stay in Beast Form longer and adds potion-based attacks. Yellow is a flame attack, green is a flailing attack that hits multiple times, and purple is a lunging ground pound.

Special Quest

Rampage

DEAL 200 DAMAGE IN A SINGLE RUN IN BEAST FORM.

The only trick to this quest is having enough enemies in the area so you can inflict 200 points of damage before they're all gone. Activate the Best of the Beast Path if your damage output is coming up short.

Nobody is quite sure who Pop Fizz was before he became an alchemist, least of all Pop Fizz himself. After many years of experimenting with magical potions, his appearance has changed quite significantly. In fact, no one even knows his original color. But it's widely known that he is a little crazy, his experiments are reckless, and the accidents they cause are too numerous to measure. Understandably, he has had a difficult time finding lab partners, or anyone that even wants to be near him. In hopes of making himself more appealing to others, he attempted to create the most effective charm potion ever—but that just turned him into a big, wild berserker. Or maybe that's just how he saw the potion working in the first place...

LEVEL	1	2	3	4	5	6	7	8	9	10	11	12	13	14	15	16	17	18	19	20
❤ MAX HEATH	270	297	324	351	378	405	432	459	486	540	567	594	621	648	675	702	729	756	783	810

⚡ SPEED	🛡 ARMOR	⊕ CRITICAL HIT	◎ ELEMENTAL POWER
43	18	6	25

Basic Attacks

POTION LOB

Press **Attack 1** to launch Pop Fizz's currently equipped potion.

BEAST FORM

Press **Attack 2** to drink a potion and temporarily change into a beasty form.

Ⓖ Soul Gem Ability
SHAKE IT!

4000 Gold
PREREQUISITE
Purchase New Concotions ability

Repeatedly press **Attack 3** to shake the potion bottle until it explodes.

Upgrades

NEW CONCOTION

500 Gold
PREREQUISITE None

Press **Attack 3** to switch to a new potion that can walk on two legs and fight by your side when thrown.

PUDDLE OF PAIN

700 Gold
PREREQUISITE
Purchase New Concotion abitlity

Press **Attack 3** again to switch to a new potion that leaves a damaging puddle of acid when thrown.

RAGING BEAST

900 Gold
PREREQUISITE None

All attacks in Beast Form do additional damage.

DEXTROUS DELIVERY

1200 Gold
PREREQUISITE None

Throw potions and grab new ones much faster.

Mad Scientist Path

MASTER CHEMIST

1700 Gold
PREREQUISITE
Mad Scientist Path

All potions do increased damage and have improved effects.

MIXOLOGIST

2200 Gold
PREREQUISITE
Mad Scientist Path

Mix the effects of different colored potions for brand new effects.

ALL IN

3000 Gold
PREREQUISITE
Mad Scientist Path

Hold **Attack 1** to pull up to three potions out and release to throw them all at once.

Best of the Beast Path

MORE BEAST!

1700 Gold
PREREQUISITE
Best of the Beast Path

Beast Form meter drains slower and recharges faster.

BERSERKER BOOST

3000 Gold
PREREQUISITE
Best of the Beast Path

In Beast Form, damaging enemies recharges the Beast Form meter.

MUTANT BEAST

2200 Gold
PREREQUISITE
Best of the Beast Path

In Beast Form, Press **Attack 3** to perform a special attack based on which potion is active.

Wow Pow!
BEAKER BUDDY

5000 Gold
PREREQUISITE
Purchase New Concoctions ability

When throwing Purple Potions, one of the bottles will grow into a giant, special pet.

A "fire-and-forget" ability that you should keep active as often as possible. Unless you're in immediate danger, switch to the purple potion and summon a Beaker Buddy whenever the previous one fades away.

MEGA RAM SPYRO
"All fired up!"

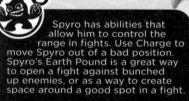

SERIES 3

Spyro has abilities that allow him to control the range in fights. Use Charge to move Spyro out of a bad position. Spyro's Earth Pound is a great way to open a fight against bunched up enemies, or as a way to create space around a good spot in a fight.

Selecting which of Spyro's upgrade paths are active boils down to your preferred method of fighting as the dragon. The Sheep Burner Path works best for Spyro players who like to stay away from the crowd. The Blitz Spyro Path is all about getting Spyro's horns dirty.

Special Quest
Full Charge

COLLECT 3 GOLD, EAT 1 FOOD ITEM, AND DEFEAT 2 ENEMIES IN 1 SPRINT CHARGE.

The best place to complete this quest is during an arena challenge where Chompies are the first enemies to appear immediately after you defeat the Food Thief. The Sprint Charge upgrade is a big help as well.

Spyro hails from a rare line of magical purple dragons that come from a faraway land few have ever traveled. It's been said that the Scrolls of the Ancients mention Spyro prominently—the old Portal Masters having chronicled his many exciting adventures and heroic deeds. Finally, it was Master Eon himself who reached out and invited him to join the Skylanders. From then on, evil faced a new enemy—and the Skylanders gained a valued ally.

LEVEL	1	2	3	4	5	6	7	8	9	10	11	12	13	14	15	16	17	18	19	20
❤ MAX HEATH	280	308	336	364	392	420	448	476	504	560	588	616	644	672	700	728	756	784	812	840

⚡ SPEED	🛡 ARMOR	⊕ CRITICAL HIT	◉ ELEMENTAL POWER
50	18	6	25

Basic Attacks

FLAMEBALL

Press **Attack 1** to breathe balls of fire at your enemies.

CHARGE

Press and hold **Attack 2** to lower your horns and charge forward, knocking over anything in your way.

Soul Gem Ability
SPYRO'S EARTH POUND

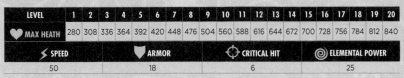

4000 Gold
PREREQUISITE
Purchase Spyro's Flight ability

This power gives Spyro a new flight attack. Press **Attack 2** while flying to dive bomb.

Upgrades

LONG RANGE RAZE

500 Gold
PREREQUISITE None

Flameball attacks travel farther.

SPYRO'S FLIGHT

700 Gold
PREREQUISITE None

Press **Attack 3** to fly. Increased speed and resistance while flying.

SPRINT CHARGE

900 Gold
PREREQUISITE None

Can perform Charge attack for increased distance.

TRIPLE FLAMEBALLS

1200 Gold
PREREQUISITE None

Shoot three Flameballs at once.

Sheep Burner Path

FIRE SHIELD

1700 Gold
PREREQUISITE
Sheep Burner Path

A fire shield appears when using the Flameball attack.

EXPLODING FIREBLAST

2200 Gold
PREREQUISITE
Sheep Burner Path

Flameballs do extra damage and the middle one explodes.

THE DAYBRINGER FLAME

3000 Gold
PREREQUISITE
Sheep Burner Path

Hold **Attack 1** to charge up Flameball attack for maximum damage.

Blitz Spyro Path

STUN CHARGE

1700 Gold
PREREQUISITE
Blitz Spyro Path

Enemies hit by Charge Attack become stunned.

COMET DASH

2200 Gold
PREREQUISITE
Blitz Spyro Path

Charge attack does increased damage.

IBEX'S WRATH CHARGE

3000 Gold
PREREQUISITE
Blitz Spyro Path

Charge longer to do extra damage.

Wow Pow!

HEAD START

5000 Gold
PREREQUISITE
None

Summon a magic worm ally at the end of your charge and send it after your enemies.

The magic worm summoned at the end of the charge explodes after making contact with an enemy. You must execute a full charge in order to fire the worm, which may not be easy to pull off in the middle of a fight. It's best to recognize a fight is just ahead and Charge into the area.

MEGA RAM SPYRO

STAR STRIKE
"Shoot For the Stars!"

Keep Star Strike clear of rough and tumble melee fights and practice using Cosmic Twirl to reflect projectiles, both the initial projectile from Star Gate and defensively to return enemy shots back at them. When you become proficient with Cosmic Twirl, Star Strike has the potential to cruise through any challenge in pristine condition.

Choose the Star Gazer Path to boost Star Strike's area of attack damage via improvements to Starfall, which works better in Arena challenges. If you're working on the Story Mode, opt for the Cosmic Reflector Path as it boosts Star Strike's armor and single target damage.

Special Quest
Deflection Master

DEFELECT THE RETURNING STAR 20 TIMES IN A ROW.

Use Star Gate to fire off a star, then press Attak 2 when the star is within range to deflect it. There's an on-screen visual cue to let you know when to press Attack 2. You can finish this quest anywhere, even Woodburrow.

Star Strike

Looking for a way to magically banish the Skylanders, Kaos poured through every dusty scroll and ancient tome he could find. Upon stumbling across a rare and extremely powerful spell, he began to recite its words. However, he sneezed midway through the incantation. As a result, instead of sending the Skylanders far away, Star Strike was plucked from her home in the distant cosmos and brought into Skylands. Surprised, Kaos thought he'd won a powerful new ally in the mysterious and reserved Star Strike. But she knew evil when she saw it and promptly unleashed her fierce magical powers on him. Word of her victory over Kaos spread quickly and she was soon asked by Master Eon to join the Skylanders.

LEVEL	1	2	3	4	5	6	7	8	9	10	11	12	13	14	15	16	17	18	19	20
♥ MAX HEATH	260	286	312	338	364	390	416	442	468	520	546	572	598	624	650	676	702	728	754	780

⚡ SPEED	🛡 ARMOR	✛ CRITICAL HIT	◎ ELEMENTAL POWER
43	12	8	25

Basic Attacks

STAR GATE

Press **Attack 1** to summon a powerful star that attacks nearby enemies then returns. Reflect the returning star with **Attack 2** to power it up and do more damage.

COSMIC TWIRL

Press **Attack 2** to perform a magical spin, reflecting any projectiles nearby.

ⓖ Soul Gem Ability
SHOOTING STARS

4000 Gold

PREREQUISITE
Find Star Strike's Soul Gem in Rampant Ruins

Press **Attack 1** rapidly to shoot many sparkling star projectiles at nearby enemies.

Upgrades

STARFALL

500 Gold

PREREQUISITE None

Press **Attack 3** to cause stars to fall and damage nearby enemies. Press **Attack 2** to deflect the stars at enemies that are farther away.

STAR FILLED SKY

700 Gold

PREREQUISITE
Purchase Starfall ability

Press **Attack 3** to cause even more stars to fall and damage nearby enemies.

YOUR BIGGEST FAN

900 Gold

PREREQUISITE None

Press **Attack 2** to spin and reflect projectiles. Spin radius is now increased, making it more likely to deflect projectiles and power up the star.

STAR POWER

1200 Gold

PREREQUISITE None

Press **Attack 1** rapidly to shoot star shards at enemies that do increased damage.

Star Gazer Path

STAR LIGHT

1700 Gold

PREREQUISITE
Star Gazer Path

Starfall now causes a massive explosive star to fall from the sky. Press **Attack 2** to deflect it at enemies.

STAR STRUCK

2200 Gold

PREREQUISITE
Star Gazer Path

Press **Attack 3** to cause powerful stars that do increased damage to fall and damage nearby enemies.

STAR BRIGHT

3000 Gold

PREREQUISITE
Star Gazer Path

Starfall can be used two times. Set up a star field blockade!

Cosmic Reflector Path

ATOM SPLITTER

1700 Gold

PREREQUISITE
Cosmic Reflector Path

Press **Attack 1** to shoot a star projectile. Press **Attack 2** when it is close to deflect it and shoot two smaller projectiles.

STAR EVASION

2200 Gold

PREREQUISITE
Cosmic Reflector Path

Armor is increased. No one would have thought a dress could be so sturdy.

SUPER STAR

3000 Gold

PREREQUISITE
Cosmic Reflector Path

Press **Attack 1** to shoot a star projectile. Press **Attack 2** when it is close to defelect it. Deflecting it four times makes it grow larger and do more damage.

BLAST ZONE

"Blast and Furious!"

As a young furnace knight, Blast Zone was part of the Skylands Bomb Squad, specializing in the safe disarming and removal of troll bombs. But it was not long before the trolls got tired of Blast Zone constantly thwarting their evil plans, so they decided to go after the furnace knight himself. Late one night, an army of trolls snuck into Blast Zone's village and threw 100 bombs down his chimney. Acting quickly, Blast Zone swallowed each bomb and then belched a jet of fire back at the invaders—sending them fleeing with their boots on fire. The tale of the attack eventually reached the ear of Master Eon, who knew the brave furnace knight had all the makings of a Skylander.

Bomb Throw is a quick, lobbed bomb that can bounce one time before exploding. The Ignition Path leads to fiery bombs doing more damage in a larger area. Flame Breath allows for spinning in place while it's active. With the Reaction Satisfaction Path, completing a circle of fire results in an explosion.

Rocket Dash begins as a quick burst but upgrades add damage and greater duration. The Fuel Injected Path ends Rocket Dash with a fiery projectile that damages enemies. The Temperatures Rising Path adds a flame shield at the end of a dash. It doesn't protect Blast Zone, but does deal damage.

Special Quest

If You Can't Stand the Heat

DEFEAT A TOTAL OF 10 ENEMIES FROM YOUR FLAME WALL IN A SINGLE USE OF YOUR FLAME BREATH.

Visit any challenge map where the main enemies are Chompies for quick completion of this quest. You can always depend on them to run directly toward your Skylander, even if it means hurling themselves into fire.

Keep Attack 3 pressed and spin in place until you complete this quest.

Body
Soul Gem Ability
BOMB PARTY

3500 Gold
PREREQUISITE
Find Blast Zone's Soul Gem in Fantasm Forest

New armor enhancements allow two Bombs to be thrown at once!

Legs
Soul Gem Ability
HOT FEET

3500 Gold
PREREQUISITE
Find Blast Zone's Soul Gem in Fantasm Forest; Purchase Fuel for the Fire ability

A fire trail is left behind while dashing that damages enemies.

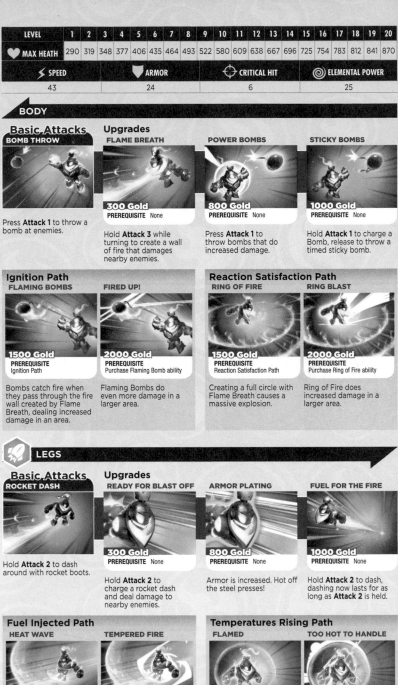

LEVEL	1	2	3	4	5	6	7	8	9	10	11	12	13	14	15	16	17	18	19	20
♥ MAX HEATH	290	319	348	377	406	435	464	493	522	580	609	638	667	696	725	754	783	812	841	870

⚡ SPEED	▽ ARMOR	⊕ CRITICAL HIT	◎ ELEMENTAL POWER
43	24	6	25

BODY

Basic Attacks
BOMB THROW

Press **Attack 1** to throw a bomb at enemies.

Upgrades

FLAME BREATH

300 Gold
PREREQUISITE None

Hold **Attack 3** while turning to create a wall of fire that damages nearby enemies.

POWER BOMBS

800 Gold
PREREQUISITE None

Press **Attack 1** to throw bombs that do increased damage.

STICKY BOMBS

1000 Gold
PREREQUISITE None

Hold **Attack 1** to charge a Bomb, release to throw a timed sticky bomb.

Ignition Path

FLAMING BOMBS

1500 Gold
PREREQUISITE Ignition Path

Bombs catch fire when they pass through the fire wall created by Flame Breath, dealing increased damage in an area.

FIRED UP!

2000 Gold
PREREQUISITE Purchase Flaming Bomb ability

Flaming Bombs do even more damage in a larger area.

Reaction Satisfaction Path

RING OF FIRE

1500 Gold
PREREQUISITE Reaction Satisfaction Path

Creating a full circle with Flame Breath causes a massive explosion.

RING BLAST

2000 Gold
PREREQUISITE Purchase Ring of Fire ability

Ring of Fire does increased damage in a larger area.

LEGS

Basic Attacks
ROCKET DASH

Hold **Attack 2** to dash around with rocket boots.

Upgrades

READY FOR BLAST OFF

300 Gold
PREREQUISITE None

Hold **Attack 2** to charge a rocket dash and deal damage to nearby enemies.

ARMOR PLATING

800 Gold
PREREQUISITE None

Armor is increased. Hot off the steel presses!

FUEL FOR THE FIRE

1000 Gold
PREREQUISITE None

Hold **Attack 2** to dash, dashing now lasts for as long as **Attack 2** is held.

Fuel Injected Path

HEAT WAVE

1500 Gold
PREREQUISITE Fuel Injected Path

A rocket-fueled fireball is shot out at the end of a dash.

TEMPERED FIRE

2000 Gold
PREREQUISITE Purchase Heave Wave ability

A more powerful Heat Wave is shot out at the end of dashing.

Temperatures Rising Path

FLAMED

1500 Gold
PREREQUISITE Temperatures Rising Path

A fiery aura appears after dashing, which damages any nearby enemy.

TOO HOT TO HANDLE

2000 Gold
PREREQUISITE Purchase Flamed ability

An even more powerful fire aura appears at the end of dashing.

FIRE KRAKEN
"Burn To Be Wild!"

An upgraded Sparkling Strikes knocks back enemies. The Showcase Path improves the staff and knockback attacks. Dragon Parade damages enemies just by running into them. The Dance of Dragons Path lets you aim and fire one Dragon Parade, then start up another. The Magnificent Parade Path adds fireworks to Dragon Parade.

Start the Show! damages nearby enemies, but the last firework blast is single-target until it's upgraded. The Big One can't be charged (watch for his tail to glow). The Stunning Sparker Path provides a speed boost as the Big One counts down. The Booming Bouncer Path includes a knockback when igniting the Big One.

Special Quest
Don't Rain On My Parade

KNOCK BACK ENEMIES 10 TIMES WITH ONE USE OF YOUR PARADE ABILITY.

Lure a group of at least five enemies tougher than Chompies, but who can't shield themselves, into a tight area. If you hit Dragon Parade just right, it should bounce each enemy twice. The enemies must be able to survive the initial hit to count to the 10 necessary to complete the quest.

Raised on a small island surrounded by a vast ocean of fire, Fire Kraken was the swiftest, most agile warrior his tribe had ever seen. When a fleet of Fire Troll ships arrived to steal the legendary Burning Heart, a huge elemental crystal that fueled the fiery seas, Fire Kraken leapt into action. Using a magical staff to control his natural ability to wield fire, he set the mighty ships ablaze, forcing the trolls into a hasty retreat. Having saved the Burning Heart as well as his homeland, Fire Kraken soon joined the Skylanders, where he knew his skills would help those in need.

Body
Soul Gem Ability
DANCE OF DRAGONS

3500 Gold
PREREQUISITE
Find Fire Kraken's Soul Gem in Twisty Tunnels

Hold **Attack 3** to start Dragon Parade, release to shoot the sparkling and explosive Dragon costume at enemies.

Legs
Soul Gem Ability
THE BIGGER ONE

3500 Gold
PREREQUISITE
Find Fire Kraken's Soul Gem in Twisty Tunnels

The Big One creates a huge colorful explosion that does increased damage in a larger radius.

LEVEL	1	2	3	4	5	6	7	8	9	10	11	12	13	14	15	16	17	18	19	20
❤ MAX HEATH	260	286	312	338	364	390	416	442	468	520	546	572	598	624	650	676	702	728	754	780

⚡ SPEED	🛡 ARMOR	🎯 CRITICAL HIT	◎ ELEMENTAL POWER
43	18	8	25

BODY

Basic Attacks
SPARKLING STRIKES

Press **Attack 1** to swing the sparkler staff, damaging nearby enemies.

Upgrades

DRAGON PARADE

300 Gold
PREREQUISITE None

Hold **Attack 3** to run around in a dragon parade costume, knocking back and damaging enemies in the way.

GLOW STICK

800 Gold
PREREQUISITE None

Press **Attack 1** to swing a new staff that does increased damage.

RISING FOUNTAIN

1000 Gold
PREREQUISITE None

Hold **Attack 1** to charge a staff attack, release to cause a large explosion that knocks up and damages nearby enemies.

The Showcase Path

RISING CHARGE

1500 Gold
PREREQUISITE
The Showcase Path

Rising Charge causes the next staff attack to cause a large explosion.

FINALE!

2000 Gold
PREREQUISITE
Purchase Rising Charge ability

Rising Fountain does increased damage in a larger area. It's showtime!

Magnificent Parade Path

YEAR OF THE DRAGON

1500 Gold
PREREQUISITE
Magnificent Parade Path

Dragon Parade does increased damage, lasts longer, and reduces damage taken while it is active.

DRAGON CANDLES

2000 Gold
PREREQUISITE
Purchase Year of the Dragon ability

Dragon Parade shoots colorful explosive fireworks at nearby enemies.

LEGS

Basic Attacks
START THE SHOW!

Press **Attack 2** up to three times to perform a firework attack on each press that damages nearby enemies.

Upgrades

SHOW-OFF

300 Gold
PREREQUISITE None

Press **Attack 2** three times to shoot three colorful projectiles at once.

KRAKEN UP

800 Gold
PREREQUISITE None

Press **Jump** to jump, throwing down fireworks and damaging nearby enemies.

THE BIG ONE

1000 Gold
PREREQUISITE None

Hold **Attack 2** for a short time to light a timed fuse that causes a massive firework attack after a short time.

Stunning Sparker Path

UNSTABLE ELEMENT

1500 Gold
PREREQUISITE
Stunning Sparker Path

Speed increases depending on how close The Big One is to exploding. The anticipation!!

SIZZLING SPARKLER

2000 Gold
PREREQUISITE
Stunning Sparker Path

Press **Attack 2** for a spin attack that does increased damage in a larger area.

Booming Bouncer Path

BIGBADABOOM

1500 Gold
PREREQUISITE
Booming Bouncer Path

Press **Attack 2** two times for a bounce attack that does increased damage in a larger area.

STRIKE THE FOES

2000 Gold
PREREQUISITE
Booming Bouncer Path

Hold **Attack 2** for a short time to light the fuse for The Big One and knock away all nearby enemies.

FIRE KRAKEN

LAVA BARF ERUPTOR

"Born to Burn!"

Eruptor is a force of nature, hailing from a species that lived deep in the underground of a floating volcanic island until a massive eruption launched their entire civilization to the surface. He's a complete hot head—steaming, fuming, and quite literally erupting over almost anything. To help control his temper, he likes to relax in lava pools, particularly because there are no crowds.

SERIES 3

Lava Lob is a fast attack, but it lacks range. It strikes enemies who are in higher areas, which is a huge advantage in many situations. Eruption takes time to charge up before it appears, which leaves Eruptor vulnerable to attack. It continues to deal damage to everything it touches, making it terrific against immobile targets.

The Magmantor Path increases the range of Lava Lob and boosts its damage output by 60%. If the Volcanor Path is more your style, get Quick Eruption immediately. The increased damage from the other abilities is great, but faster Eruptions are vital.

Special Quest
Pizza Burp

EAT 10 PIZZAS.

Pizzas appear during story mode, but the fastest way to complete this quest is in an Arena challenge that includes the Food Thief.

LEVEL	1	2	3	4	5	6	7	8	9	10	11	12	13	14	15	16	17	18	19	20
♥ MAX HEATH	290	319	348	377	406	435	464	493	522	580	609	638	667	696	725	754	783	812	841	870

⚡ SPEED	🛡 ARMOR	⊕ CRITICAL HIT	◎ ELEMENTAL POWER
35	18	6	25

Basic Attacks

LAVA LOB

Press **Attack 1** to lob blobs of lava at your enemies.

ERUPTION

Press **Attack 2** to erupt into a pool of lava, damaging enemies all around you.

Soul Gem Ability
MEGA MAGMA BALLS

4000 Gold
PREREQUISITE
Purchase Magma Ball ability

Shoot up to three Magma Balls at a time that do extra damage

Upgrades

BIG BLOB LAVA THROW

500 Gold
PREREQUISITE None

Lava Blobs get bigger and do increased damage.

FIERY REMAINS

700 Gold
PREREQUISITE None

Lava Blobs leave behind pools of flame when they hit the ground.

ERUPTION - FLYING TEPHRA

900 Gold
PREREQUISITE None

Lava balls shoot out while performing the Eruption attack.

MAGMA BALL

1200 Gold
PREREQUISITE None

Press **Attack 3** to spit out Magma Balls

Magmantor Path

HEAVY DUTY PLASMA

1700 Gold
PREREQUISITE
Magmantor Path

Lava Blobs bounce and travel further.

LAVA BLOB BOMB

2200 Gold
PREREQUISITE
Magmantor Path

Lava Blobs explode and damage nearby enemies.

BEAST OF CONFLAGRATION

3000 Gold
PREREQUISITE
Purchase Heavy Duty Plasma ability

Lava Blobs do increased damage in the form of a fiery beast.

Volcanor Path

QUICK ERUPTION

1700 Gold
PREREQUISITE
Volcanor Path

It takes much less time to perform an Eruption attack.

PYROXYSMAL SUPER ERUPTION

2200 Gold
PREREQUISITE
Volcanor Path

Eruption attack does increased damage.

REVENGE OF PROMETHEUS

3000 Gold
PREREQUISITE
Purchase Pyroxysmal Super Eruption ability

Eruption causes small volcanoes to form, shooting yet more lava balls.

Wow Pow!

LAVA BARF 2 - BARF HARDER!

5000 Gold
PREREQUISITE
Purchase Magma Ball ability

Press **Attack 3** to release Magma Balls, then hold **Attack 3** to eat them and immediately barf them back for extra damage.

Barf Harder is a tricky ability to master. You can't use this ability if any enemy is near you. You need a few seconds for the ability to charge, and the Magma Balls land a short distance away. Any close enemies can stop you and even if they fail, the attack will sail harmlessly over them. On a positive note, the spots where the lava balls land burn for a time and damage enemies that touch them.

FRYNO

"Crash and Burn!"

You shouldn't have problems in any melee fight as Fryno, but ranged enemies can be challenging. Heated deals damage to enemies near Fryno, and every third swing knocks them back. Heated also increases Fryno's heat level, which improves his damage output. Even Brawl, his other basic attack, becomes more powerful through Heated.

The Brawler Path punishes enemies limited to melee attacks even more. Fryno's Hot Shop Path is a big help when dealing with ranged opponents. The Horn and The Hog is the best way to reach ranged enemies quickly, and what's faster than throwing a motorcycle at them?

Special Quest

Frequent Frier

DELIVER A TOTAL OF 100 HEAT-IMBUED BLOWS AGAINST ENEMIES.

Use the Heated ability whenever the opportunity arises, whether before a fight starts or during one, and then use Brawl to take out enemies. There's a good chance to complete this quest during the first Story Mode chapter!

Fryno was once a member of the notorious Blazing Biker Brigade and spent most of his youth riding around Skylands with the rest of his crew. But what Fryno did not realize was that, while he enjoyed a life of freedom and adventure, his crew was responsible for acts of burglary throughout Skylands. When Fryno discovered that he had been riding around with a bunch of villains, he burned with rage and demanded that they make amends for the wrong they had done. This resulted in an epic fight, which Fryno won, and the disbanding of the Blazing Biker Brigade. Fryno was in the midst of returning the valuables his crew had stolen when he met Master Eon, who was impressed with his good character and fighting abilities, and offered him a membership to a new crew—the Skylanders.

LEVEL	1	2	3	4	5	6	7	8	9	10	11	12	13	14	15	16	17	18	19	20
♥ MAX HEATH	300	330	360	390	420	450	480	510	540	600	630	660	690	720	750	780	810	840	870	900

⚡ SPEED	🛡 ARMOR	⊕ CRITICAL HIT	◎ ELEMENTAL POWER
43	6	4	25

Basic Attacks

BRAWL

Press **Attack 1** to punch nearby enemies. Speed and damage of punches is increased depending on heat.

HEATED

Press **Attack 2** repeatedly to smash the ground and increase heat level.

🜲 Soul Gem Ability
MADNESS MAXED

4000 Gold
PREREQUISITE
Find Fryno's Soul Gem in Frostfest Mountains

Press **Attack 2** rapidly to make Fryno even more heated. So angry!

Upgrades

THE HORN AND THE HOG

500 Gold
PREREQUISITE None

Press **Attack 3** to dash forward, dealing damage to enemies in the way. When heated, Fryno jumps on a motorcycle to deal damage to nearby enemies.

BUILT TOUGH

700 Gold
PREREQUISITE None

Health is increased. Probably from punching the ground so much...

FIRED UP!

900 Gold
PREREQUISITE None

Press **Attack 2** repeatedly to throw a tantrum and become heated. Tantrums now have increased range and damage.

MOLTEN FURY

1200 Gold
PREREQUISITE None

All attacks do increased damage when heated.

Brawler Path

HOT HANDS

1700 Gold
PREREQUISITE
Brawler Path

Hold **Attack 1** to rapidly punch nearby enemies and release heat.

SPIKED UP

2200 Gold
PREREQUISITE
Purchase Hot Hands ability

New metal gloves causes Hot Hands to do increased damage.

TEMPERATURE TANTRUM

3000 Gold
PREREQUISITE
Brawler Path

Nearby enemies take damage while Fryno is heated.

Fryno's Hot Shop Path

BORN TO RIDE

1700 Gold
PREREQUISITE
Fryno's Hot Shop Path

The Horn and The Hog will always summon a molten motorcycle.

HOT ROD

2200 Gold
PREREQUISITE
Fryno's Hot Shop Path

All attacks with the motorcycle do increased damage.

CRASH AND BURN

3000 Gold
PREREQUISITE
Fryno's Hot Shop Path

Fryno throws the motorcycle at the end of a dash, causing a massive explosion that damages nearby enemies. Who's paying for that...?

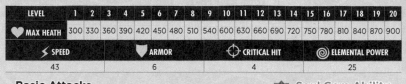

FRYNO

FIRE BONE HOT DOG

"See Spot Burn!"

Firebark is a ranged attack, but Hot Dog can still use it in multiple combos when upgaded. Wall of Fire is an effective way to control enemy position. Hold Attack 2 and Wall of Fire remains in front of Hot Dog. Release Attack 2 to send the Wall of Fire to clear the path ahead.

The Burning Bow Wow Path adds combo choices to Firebark and some offense to Comet Slam while it's charging. The Pyro Pooch Path makes Wall of Fire more powerful in every way and adds an awesome visual touch with Magmutt Battalion.

Special Quest

Animal Aggravator

EAT 10 HOT DOGS.

Hot Dogs appear throughout the Story Mode, but the fastest way to complete this quest is to run through the Bonus Mission Maps Chompy Sauce and Fishy Fishing multiple times.

Hot Dog was born in the belly of the Popcorn Volcano. While on a nearby mission, a team of Skylanders happened across the stray fire pup when the volcano erupted and Hot Dog came rocketing straight into their camp, accidentally setting Gill Grunt's tent on fire. Using his nose for danger, he helped the Skylanders complete their mission—even pouncing on a lava golem like a blazing comet when it threatened his new friends. After displaying such loyalty and bravery, Hot Dog was brought back to Eon's Citadel where he became a Skylander—and then proceeded to bury Eon's staff.

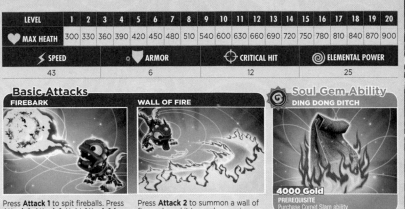

LEVEL	1	2	3	4	5	6	7	8	9	10	11	12	13	14	15	16	17	18	19	20
♥ MAX HEATH	300	330	360	390	420	450	480	510	540	600	630	660	690	720	750	780	810	840	870	900

⚡ SPEED	◇ ARMOR	⊕ CRITICAL HIT	◎ ELEMENTAL POWER
43	6	12	25

Basic Attacks

FIREBARK

Press **Attack 1** to spit fireballs. Press **Attack 1, Attack 1, Hold Attack 1** for a special combo

WALL OF FIRE

Press **Attack 2** to summon a wall of fire and send it towards enemies.

◎ Soul Gem Ability
DING DONG DITCH

4000 Gold
PREREQUISITE
Purchase Comet Slam ability

After a Comet Slam, leave a burning bag that explodes when stepped on.

Upgrades

PYRO PIERCERS

500 Gold
PREREQUISITE None

Fireballs pierce multiple targets and do increased damage.

COMET SLAM

700 Gold
PREREQUISITE None

Press **Attack 3** to flip in the air and slam down on the ground like a comet.

WALL OF MORE FIRE

900 Gold
PREREQUISITE None

Walls of Fire deal increased damage.

SUPER COMET

1200 Gold
PREREQUISITE None Purchase Comet

Hold **Attack 3** to charge up the Comet Slam and release to do increased damage.

Burning Bow Wow Path

HOT DOG COMBOS

1700 Gold
PREREQUISITE
Burning Bow Wow Path

Press **Attack 1, Attack 1, Hold Attack 2** for Burnin' Bees. Press **Attack 1, Attack 1, Hold Attack 3** for Comet Dash.

BARK BOMBS

2200 Gold
PREREQUISITE
Burning Bow Wow Path

Fireballs explode on impact and do increased damage.

PYRO PINWHEEL

3000 Gold
PREREQUISITE
Burning Bow Wow Path

While holding **Attack 3** to charge up the Comet Slam, Hot Dog shoots fireballs from all angles.

Pyro Pooch Path

BLAZING WILDFIRE

1700 Gold
PREREQUISITE
Pyro Pooch Path

Walls of Fire travel faster and do more increased damage.

GREAT WALLS OF FIRE

2200 Gold
PREREQUISITE
Pyro Pooch Path

Walls of Fire are bigger and do even MORE increased damage.

MAGMUTT BATTALION

3000 Gold
PREREQUISITE
Pyro Pooch Path

Walls of Fire are now made up of fiery dogs that do maximum damage and shoot fireballs whenever Hot Dog fires one.

Wow Pow!

BEES! BEES! BEES!

5000 Gold
PREREQUISITE
None

Hold **Attack 1** then release to fire a super powerful blast of bees.

Bees! Bees! Bees! forms a swarm of bees that eventually tracks down and damages an enemy. You don't need to worry about aiming them, just charge them up (Hot Dog can still move, just slowly) and let them fly. The downside to this attack is that you can't use it at the end of a combo. It only works on the first press of Attack 1.

SMOLDERDASH

"A Blaze of Glory!"

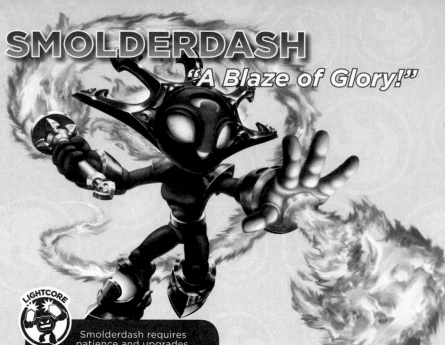

LIGHTCORE

Smolderdash requires patience and upgrades before you appreciate her potential. Flame Whip is a solid, quick hitting attack, even before upgrades. Solar Orb is a great way to hit enemies at a distance, or knock them into the air to give yourself time to move in closer. The abilities work well together.

If you choose the Sun Forger Path, practice striking Solar Orbs with Flame Whip at different distances and angles. The Sun Forged Path is more effective in situations with weaker enemies that attack in large numbers, such as Arena challenges. Eclipse boosts the damage output of everything Smolderdash does, even jumping!

Special Quest

Event Horizon

KNOCK UP A TOTAL OF 50 ENEMIES WITH YOUR EXPLODING SUN.

Exploding sun means either a second press of Attack 2 when a Solar Orb is on the screen, or striking a Solar Orb with a Flame Whip. Enemies must meet two requirements to count toward this quest. They must survive the explosion (don't expect to pad your numbers with Chompies) and they must be able to go into the air, which rules out enemies like Chompy Pods.

Smolderdash had always wanted to be a royal defender of the Fire Temple—home of the First Flame, a sacred torch that had been ignited by the original Fire Source. Unfortunately, she had been born during an eclipse and was believed by her people to be cursed, which prevented her from such an honor. But when Kaos stole the flame and used it to light the candles on his birthday cake, it was Smolderdash who went after it. Blazing like a comet, she dashed into Kaos' lair, repelled the troll security force with her flaming whip, and retrieved the sacred flame just before Kaos blew out the candles. Smolderdash returned home as a champion of her people and was finally granted the honor of becoming a royal defender. But she graciously declined, having set a new goal for herself—to help fight against Kaos as a member of the Skylanders.

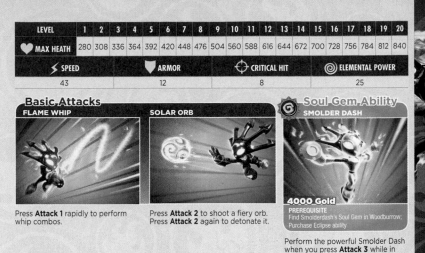

LEVEL	1	2	3	4	5	6	7	8	9	10	11	12	13	14	15	16	17	18	19	20
♥ MAX HEATH	280	308	336	364	392	420	448	476	504	560	588	616	644	672	700	728	756	784	812	840

⚡ SPEED	🛡 ARMOR	⊕ CRITICAL HIT	◎ ELEMENTAL POWER
43	12	8	25

Basic Attacks

FLAME WHIP

Press **Attack 1** rapidly to perform whip combos.

SOLAR ORB

Press **Attack 2** to shoot a fiery orb.
Press **Attack 2** again to detonate it.

🅖 Soul Gem Ability
SMOLDER DASH

4000 Gold
PREREQUISITE
Find Smolderdash's Soul Gem in Woodburrow; Purchase Eclipse ability

Perform the powerful Smolder Dash when you press **Attack 3** while in Eclipse mode!

Upgrades

ECLIPSE

500 Gold
PREREQUISITE None

Press **Attack 3** to become solar charged for a short time, making all attacks more powerful. Eclipse needs to recharge for a short time after it is used before it can be used again.

SOLAR POWERED

700 Gold
PREREQUISITE None

Speed is increased. Time to blaze through Skylands!

SUNRISE

900 Gold
PREREQUISITE None

Hold **Attack 1** to charge a sun attack, release to jump into the air and slam a huge sun into the ground.

WHIP IT!

1200 Gold
PREREQUISITE None

Press **Attack 1** to attack with more powerful whips that do increased damage. Whip it good!

Sun Forger Path

SUPER GIANT

1700 Gold
PREREQUISITE
Sun Forger Path

Hold **Attack 2** to charge a sun into a super giant sun, release to throw it forward which deals more damage and hits more enemies.

SOLAR FLARE

2200 Gold
PREREQUISITE
Sun Forger Path

Critical Hit is increased. Unleash the power of a solar flare!

SUN SPLITTER

3000 Gold
PREREQUISITE
Sun Forger Path

Press **Attack 2** to shoot a blazing sun at enemies. Press **Attack 1** to strike the sun with a whip attack causing the sun to speed up. Super Giant suns split into two smaller suns when hit.

Sun Forged Path

SOLAR BLAST

1700 Gold
PREREQUISITE
Sun Forged Path

Hold **Attack 1** to charge a sun attack, release to jump into the air and slam a huge sun into the ground, causing five smaller suns to shoot out toward enemies.

SUNNY ARMOR

2200 Gold
PREREQUISITE
Sun Forged Path

Armor is increased. So bright and cheery that enemies' attacks don't do anything to damper the mood!

SUN'S CORE

3000 Gold
PREREQUISITE
Sun Forged Path

Press **Attack 2** to shoot a blazing sun at enemies. Press **Attack 1** to strike the sun with a whip attack and gain a fiery aura that damages nearby enemies.

FREEZE BLADE
"Keeping It Cool!"

Chakram Throw is a rare ability that works equally well as a ranged attack or as a melee attack. Frigid Whirl is a great upgrade that leaves a chakram whirling around (and damaging) an enemy. The Blizzard Blade Path adds an ice attack to Frigid Whirl. Use Frostcicle to keep enemies briefly on ice. The Ice Sculptor Path turns Frostcicle into an area attack.

Speedy Skates is a damaging dash attack that upgrades to slow enemies who step on its trail. The Trail Freezer Path adds damage to the slowing effect of the trail. The Ice Skater Path lets you turn enemies into weapons.

Special Quest
Chill Out For A Second

FREEZE 100 ENEMIES WITH YOUR FROSTCICLE ATTACK.

Avoid trying for this against weaker enemies that might be defeated by the initial damage of the attack. There should be plenty of enemies who can survive, especially as you play at higher difficulties.

When he was young, Freeze Blade's family moved from the Frozen Wastelands of Vesh to the Great Lava Lakes. As it turned out, this was a very difficult adjustment for Freeze Blade. Not only was he the sole one of his kind, it was also incredibly hot and there was no ice to skate on whatsoever. But over the years, he learned to fit in with the other fire-like creatures and even discovered he had a magical ability to ice skate on any surface...even bubbling lava. One day, while out setting a new frozen lava speed record, he came across Blast Zone, who had just been ambushed by some nasty Spell Punks. After Freeze Blade stepped in to defend him, Blast Zone was so impressed by his skill in battle that he introduced him to Master Eon, who invited him to join the Skylanders.

Body
Soul Gem Ability
WINTER CHAKRAM

3500 Gold
PREREQUISITE
Find Freeze Blade's Soul Gem in Fantasm Forest

Chakram attacks have increased critical hit chance and do extra frost damage.

Legs
Soul Gem Ability
ICEBERG ENDURANCE

3500 Gold
PREREQUISITE
Find Freeze Blade's Soul Gem in Fantasm Forest

Dashing does increased damage and does not stop when attacked.

LEVEL	1	2	3	4	5	6	7	8	9	10	11	12	13	14	15	16	17	18	19	20
♥ MAX HEATH	280	308	336	364	392	420	448	476	504	532	560	588	616	644	672	700	728	756	784	812

⚡ SPEED	🛡 ARMOR	🎯 CRITICAL HIT	◎ ELEMENTAL POWER
50	6	8	25

▶ BODY

Basic Attacks
CHAKRAM THROW

Press **Attack 1** to throw anicy chakram.

Upgrades

FROSTCICLE

300 Gold
PREREQUISITE None

Press **Attack 3** to fire a shard of ice that freezes enemies.

ICICLES

800 Gold
PREREQUISITE None

Chakram gains a new layer of ice, making attacks do increased damage.

FRIGID WHIRL

1000 Gold
PREREQUISITE None

Hold **Attack 1** to charge the chakram, then release to throw it.

Blizzard Blade Path

SHAVED ICE

1500 Gold
PREREQUISITE
Blizzard Blade Path

Hold **Attack 1** to charge the chakram, release to throw the chakram and shoot ice in every direction.

WHITEOUT

2000 Gold
PREREQUISITE
Purchase Shaved Ice ability

Ice projectiles from Shaved Ice do increased damage.

Ice Sculptor Path

OH SNOW!

1500 Gold
PREREQUISITE
Ice Sculptor Path

Hold **Attack 3** to charge Frostcicle, release to freeze an entire area.

ICE TO MEET YOU

2000 Gold
PREREQUISITE
Purchase Oh Snow! ability

Frostcicle and Oh Snow! Do increased damage.

⚡ LEGS

Basic Attacks
SPEEDY SKATE

Press **Attack 2** to dash forward a short distance and damage enemies in the way.

Upgrades

ICE TRAIL

300 Gold
PREREQUISITE None

Dashing leaves behind a trail of ice that slows enemies.

GLACIAL COAT

800 Gold
PREREQUISITE None

Armor increased. As tough as a glacier!

BLADED BUTTERFLY

1000 Gold
PREREQUISITE None

Hold **Attack 2** to perform a fancy skating trick that damages all enemies nearby.

Trail Freezer Path

FLASH FREEZE

1500 Gold
PREREQUISITE
Trail Freezer Path

Press **Attack 2** to dash, dashing will now leave behind an ice trail that damages enemies.

NICE ICE

2000 Gold
PREREQUISITE
Purchase Flash Freeze ability

Flash Freeze does increased damage. A nasty case of freezer burn!

Ice Skater Path

PENALTY FROST

1500 Gold
PREREQUISITE
Iced Skater Path

Press **Attack 2** to knock back an enemy, wherever the knocked back enemy lands will cause a large freezing explosion.

ICED SKATES

2000 Gold
PREREQUISITE
Purchase Penalty Frost ability

Penalty Frost does increased damage. Don't worry, this is not a typical sports penalty.

WASH BUCKLER

"Eight Legs and No Pegs!"

Sword Slash is a touch slower than many other melee attacks, but hits harder. The Cutlass Captain Path adds a shield to Wash Buckler whenever he hits a bubble-encased enemy with a sword attack. The Bubble Buccaner Path upgrades the initial attack of Bubble Blaster, and the follow up fish attacks.

Somersaulty begins as a combination dash and attack to which Octolash adds occassional tentacle attacks while charging a Somersaulty attack. The Tentacoolest Path changes that to constant tentacle attacks. Ink Jet blinds nearby enemies while using Octolash, and the Ink Artist Path adds an ink attack in Somesaulty's wake.

Special Quest

Sleep With The Fishes

DEFEAT 50 ENEMIES WITH THE FISH IN YOUR BUBBLES.

The first step in completing this quest is purchasing the Dangerous Waters upgrade. A good second step is to choose the Bubble Buccaneer upgrades, which boost the damage done by the piranhas. Finally, pick targets that will survive the intital damage of Bubble Blaster but will fall to the follow-up fish attacks.

Wash Buckler was an orphan Mermasquid, who grew up on one of the roughest pirate ships in the Skylands. While most pirates were interested in pillaging and plundering, Wash Buckler had other ideas for the future of pirating. Over the years, he earned the respect of his crew and eventually convinced his fellow pirates that they didn't all need to be cantankerous bad guys. Thus, they set forward doing heroic deeds. Of course, this new good guy image did not sit well with other pirating crews, who attempted to sabotage Wash Buckler at every turn. But he was no ordinary pirate, and he defended his ship and his crew against the many attacking hordes. It was then that Master Eon took notice of Wash Buckler and asked him to join the Skylanders.

Body Soul Gem Ability	Legs Soul Gem Ability
ON STORMY SEAS	**TENTACLE CAROUSEL**

3500 Gold	**3500 Gold**
PREREQUISITE	PREREQUISITE
Find Wash Buckler's Soul Gem in Twisty Tunnels; Purchase Bladesail ability	Find Wash Buckler's Soul Gem in Twisty Tunnels
Hold **Attack 1** to charge Bladesail even further, release to summon a watery pirate ship that rams into enemies.	Press **Attack 2** rapidly to perform a spin attack that damages all nearby enemies.

LEVEL	1	2	3	4	5	6	7	8	9	10	11	12	13	14	15	16	17	18	19	20
♥ MAX HEATH	270	297	324	351	378	405	432	459	486	513	540	567	594	621	648	675	702	729	756	783

⚡ SPEED	🛡 ARMOR	🎯 CRITICAL HIT	◎ ELEMENTAL POWER
43	24	8	25

BODY

Basic Attacks
SWORD SLASH

Press **Attack 1** to swing a bubbly cutlass at nearby enemies.

Upgrades

BUBBLE BLASTER

300 Gold
PREREQUISITE None

Press **Attack 3** to shoot a bubble that will trap an enemy for a short time.

BLADESAIL

800 Gold
PREREQUISITE None

Sword attacks do increased damage. Hold **Attack 1** to charge the sword, release to perform a dash attack.

DANGEROUS WATERS

1000 Gold
PREREQUISITE
Purchase Bubble Blaster ability

Press **Attack 3** to shoot a piranha filled bubble at an enemy. Warning: these little fish are angry!

Cutlass Captain Path

PARLEY POOPER

1500 Gold
PREREQUISITE
Cutlass Captain Path

Popping bubbles with sword attacks will create a bubble shield that reduces damage and explodes when attacked.

FIRST MATE CUTLASS

2000 Gold
PREREQUISITE
Cutlass Captain Path

Sword attacks do even more damage. The most trusty first mate a pirate could have.

Bubble Buccaneer Path

MAROONED

1500 Gold
PREREQUISITE
Bubble Buccaneer Path

Bubble attacks do increased damage. Hold **Attack 3** to charge the Bubble Blaster, release to shoot two mega bubbles that can trap many enemies.

CAPTAIN OF PIRANHA BAY

2000 Gold
PREREQUISITE
Bubble Buccaneer Path

Piranhas do increased damage. More dangerous than your average piranha!

LEGS

Basic Attacks
SOMERSAULTY

Press **Attack 2** to dash forward and roll over enemies with powerful tentacles.

Upgrades

OCTOLASH

300 Gold
PREREQUISITE None

Hold **Attack 2** to slap enemies with two tentacles.

DEEP SKIN

800 Gold
PREREQUISITE None

Health is increased. All of the deep sea treasure hunts have really paid off!

INK JET

1000 Gold
PREREQUISITE
Purchase Octolash ability

Octolash now shoots ink that damages and temporarily causes enemies to have difficulties seeing.

Tentacoolest Path

TENTACLEVER

1500 Gold
PREREQUISITE
Tentacoolest Path

Hold **Attack 2** to slap enemies repeatedly.

SEA LEGS

2000 Gold
PREREQUISITE
Purchase Tentacleaver ability

Tentacles do increased damage. Whip those enemies into shape!

Ink Artist Path

INK TRAIL

1500 Gold
PREREQUISITE
Ink Artist Path

Press **Attack 2** to leave behind a cloud of ink.

THIS WILL NEVER COME OUT!

2000 Gold
PREREQUISITE
Purchase Ink Trail ability

Ink attacks do increased damage.

WASH BUCKLER

BLIZZARD CHILL

"Stay Cool"

SERIES 2

Javelin is a fantastic ranged attack that cuts through enemies. Improving Javelin through the Ice Lancer Path allows Chill to fill the air with icy missiles, especially if you remember to put up Ice Walls before you start throwing them. Ice Wall is a great way to keep enemies away and it can be turned into an offensive weapon with the Glacial Bash upgrade.

If you choose the Frozen Fury Path, Ice Walls improves dramatically. When enemies run into Ice Walls, they explode and form new Ice Blocks. Regardless of the path you choose with Chill, her basic attacks work together beautifully.

Special Quest

Ice Sore

DEFEAT 50 ENEMIES WITH THE CALL THE NARWHAL ATTACK.

Use Call the Narwhal against groups of Chompies whenever possible. If you want to complete this quest quickly, do Arena challenges.

Chill was the sworn guardian and personal protector of the Snow Queen. As captain of the queen's guard, her many heroic deeds had earned her the respect of the entire Ice Kingdom. But when the Cyclops army began to expand their empire into the northern realms, the Snow Queen was taken prisoner during her watch, and Chill has never forgiven herself for letting it happen. Ashamed and embarrassed, she left the Ice Kingdom behind and swore never to return until she could reclaim her honor. Now as a member of the Skylanders, she remains courageous and strong, while always on the lookout for her lost queen.

LEVEL	1	2	3	4	5	6	7	8	9	10	11	12	13	14	15	16	17	18	19	20
❤ MAX HEATH	260	286	312	338	364	390	416	442	468	494	520	546	572	598	624	650	676	702	728	754

⚡ SPEED	🛡 ARMOR	⊕ CRITICAL HIT	◎ ELEMENTAL POWER
43	24	2	25

Basic Attacks

ICE JAVELIN

Press **Attack 1** to throw a spinning ice javelin.

ICE WALL

Press **Attack 2** to summon a wall of ice blocks. Can use for protection or to knock back enemies.

🜂 Soul Gem Ability
CALL THE NARWHAL!

4000 Gold
PREREQUISITE
None

Hold **Attack 1** to charge and then release to summon a massive narwhal friend!

Upgrades

THE GREAT WALL

500 Gold
PREREQUISITE None

Hold **Attack 2** to extend the length of an ice wall.

GLACIAL BASH

700 Gold
PREREQUISITE None

Press **Attack 3** to bash enemies and ice wall blocks with your shield.

IMPERIAL ARMOR

900 Gold
PREREQUISITE None

New helmet increases Chill's Resistance.

COLD FRONT

1200 Gold
PREREQUISITE
Purchase Glacial Bash abitlity

Hold **Attack 3** to keep the shield raised and block attacks from the front.

Ice Lancer Path

BRRRR BLADE

1700 Gold
PREREQUISITE
Ice Lancer Path

New ice javelin deals increased damage.

SHATTERSPEAR

2200 Gold
PREREQUISITE
Ice Lancer Path

Javelins now split into separate ice spears when passing through an Ice Wall.

TRIPLE JAVELINS

3000 Gold
PREREQUISITE
Ice Lancer Path

Throw three javelins at once.

Frozen Fury Path

ICE BREAKER

1700 Gold
PREREQUISITE
Frozen Fury Path

Ice Wall blocks explode when struck by an ice javelin or by an enemy.

BETTER BASH

2200 Gold
PREREQUISITE
Frozen Fury Path

Glacial Blast hits multiple enemies and Ice Wall blocks in a larger area.

ON THE ROCKS

3000 Gold
PREREQUISITE
Frozen Fury Path

Exploding ice blocks freeze enemies into ice cubes of their own.

Wow Pow!

ORCASTRATION!

5000 Gold
PREREQUISITE
None

Hold **Attack 2** longer and mini orcas appear inside the ice wall, then release to shatter the wall and launch orcas.

Orcastration! does not go off until you release Attack 2. The orcas fly to the side and land at a certain distance away from the wall, but don't seek out nearby enemies. To use this ability effectively, put up a few defensive Ice Walls before you try to charge up an Ice Wall filled with orcas.

BLIZZARD CHILL

ANCHORS AWAY
GILL GRUNT
"Fear the Fish!"

Few Skylanders have abilities where you must press two buttons at the same time to activate them, but Gill Grunt now has two such abilities: his Wow Pow! ability, Anchor Management, and Neptune Gun. Gill Grunt remains the same ranged-focused fighter he has been throughout the Skylanders adventures.

Harpoon Gun is a solid attack, and improving it via the Harpooner Path makes it hit harder and strike more targets. Power Hose and Jetpack are wonderful abilities that become awesome if you choose the Water Weaver Path.

Special Quest
Anchors Away!

DEFEAT 50 ENEMIES WITH THE ANCHOR ATTACK.

Charge up Anchor Cannon when you see an upcoming fight, especially against low health enemies. Fire the Anchor Cannon into the enemies before they can approach your Skylander. Any enemies you can take out of the fight before they get in their first attack is a big help.

Gill Grunt was a brave soul who joined the Gillmen military in search of adventure. While journeying through a misty lagoon in the clouds, he met an enchanting mermaid. He vowed to return to her after his tour. Keeping his promise, he came back to the lagoon years later, only to learn a nasty band of pirates had kidnapped the mermaid. Heartbroken, Gill Grunt began searching all over Skylands. Though he had yet to find her, he joined the Skylanders to help protect others from such evil, while still keeping an ever-watchful eye for the beautiful mermaid and the pirates who took her.

LEVEL	1	2	3	4	5	6	7	8	9	10	11	12	13	14	15	16	17	18	19	20
❤ MAX HEATH	270	297	324	351	378	405	432	459	486	513	540	567	594	621	648	675	702	729	756	783

⚡ SPEED	🛡 ARMOR	⊕ CRITICAL HIT	◎ ELEMENTAL POWER
35	6	10	25

Basic Attacks

HARPOON GUN

Press **Attack 1** to shoot high-velocity harpoons at your enemies.

POWER HOSE

Press and hold **Attack 2** to spray water at your enemies to knock them back.

Soul Gem Ability

ANCHOR CANNON

4000 Gold
PREREQUISITE
None

Hold **Attack 1** to charge Anchor Cannon.

Upgrades

BARBED HARPOONS

500 Gold
PREREQUISITE None

Harpoons deal more damage.

HIGH PRESSURE HOSE

700 Gold
PREREQUISITE None

Power Hose attack does extra damage and knocks enemies back further.

HARPOON REPEATER

900 Gold
PREREQUISITE None

Harpoons reload faster.

WATER JETPACK

1200 Gold
PREREQUISITE None

Hold **Attack 3** to fly until the water jetpack runs out. Gain increased speed and resistance while flying.

Harpooner Path

QUADENT HARPOONS

1700 Gold
PREREQUISITE
Harpooner Path

Harpoons deal even MORE increased damage.

PIERCING HARPOONS

2200 Gold
PREREQUISITE
Harpooner Path

Harpoons travel straight through enemies and hit targets behind them.

TRIPLESHOT HARPOON

3000 Gold
PREREQUISITE
Harpooner Path

Shoot three Harpoons at once.

Water Weaver Path

RESERVE WATER TANK

1700 Gold
PREREQUISITE
Water Weaver Path

The Power Hose and Water Jetpack never run out of water.

BOILING WATER HOSE

2200 Gold
PREREQUISITE
Water Weaver Path

Power Hose attack deals even MORE increased damage.

NEPTUNE GUN

3000 Gold
PREREQUISITE
Water Weaver Path

When using the Power Hose, press **Attack 1** to launch exploding sea creatures.

Wow Pow!

ANCHOR MANAGEMENT!

5000 Gold
PREREQUISITE
Purchase Anchor Cannon ability

Charge up the Anchor Cannon and press **Attack 2** to do special damage.

Anchor Management turns the normally straight ahead Anchor Cannon attack into a lob attack and a blender. Where the anchor hits the ground, it sends out a large shockwave, then begins to spin. Any enemy caught by the spinning anchor is dazed for a few seconds after the spin ends. A nice benefit to Anchor Management is that you can use it to reach higher areas and soften up the enemies before taking them on directly.

PUNK SHOCK

"Amp It Up!"

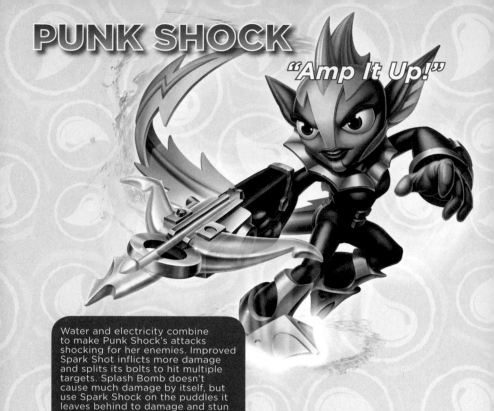

Water and electricity combine to make Punk Shock's attacks shocking for her enemies. Improved Spark Shot inflicts more damage and splits its bolts to hit multiple targets. Splash Bomb doesn't cause much damage by itself, but use Spark Shock on the puddles it leaves behind to damage and stun any enemy in the water.

The Conductor Constructor Path leads to bigger and better Splash Bomb capabilities. Bolting Blob is noteworthy because it doesn't rely on another attack to boost its damage. The Eelectrocutey Path adds some up-close options for this ranged specialist. Re-Volting Shock is great against enemies that get too close.

Special Quest

Hydrostatics

SHOCK ENEMIES WITH ELECTRIFIED WATER ZONES 100 TIMES.

Anytime you're involved in a fight that lasts more than a few seconds, you should throw down a Splash Bomb as often as possible. Use Spark Shot or Spark Splash on the resulting puddle to electrify it. Each enemy caught in the now-electrified puddle counts toward your total.

Daughter to the most royal family in Wondrous Waters, Punk Shock never really accepted her role as an undersea princess. She preferred a much more exciting life—hunting with her electric crossbow and listening to super-charged music. After journeying to the outer reaches of her kingdom to find adventure, Punk Shock returned home to discover adventure had found her. The kingdom and its people were magically frozen by the Snow Trolls, who were there to steal valuable treasure. Punk Shock used her awesomely charged crossbow to single handedly defeat the Snow Troll army and melt the ice that trapped her kingdom. Gill Grunt heard of the battle and quickly recruited Punk Shock into the Skylanders.

LEVEL	1	2	3	4	5	6	7	8	9	10	11	12	13	14	15	16	17	18	19	20
❤ MAX HEATH	270	297	324	351	378	405	432	459	486	513	540	567	594	621	648	675	702	729	756	783

⚡ SPEED	🛡 ARMOR	✛ CRITICAL HIT	◎ ELEMENTAL POWER
43	12	8	25

Basic Attacks

SPARK SHOT

Press **Attack 1** to shoot an electrified bolt. Shoot a Splash Bomb puddle to cause that area to become electrified.

SPLASH BOMB

Press **Attack 2** to throw a larger water balloon that makes a puddle where it lands. Shoot the puddle with Spark Shot to electrify it.

♥ Soul Gem Ability
EELECTROCUTE

4000 Gold
PREREQUISITE
Find Punk Shock's Soul Gem in Kaos' Fortress

Hold **Attack 1** to charge a powerful crossbow attack, release to shoot all enemies around you!

Upgrades

SPARK SPLASH

500 Gold
PREREQUISITE None

Press **Attack 3** to perform a tail attack that shocks nearby enemies. There is a short wait before this ability can be used again.

HIGH BOLTAGE

700 Gold
PREREQUISITE None

Press **Attack 1** to shoot high powered crossbolt attacks that do increased damage.

OHMG

900 Gold
PREREQUISITE None

Press **Attack 1** to shoot electric crossbow bolts that branch out and hit enemies in a larger area.

HYPERCHARGED

1200 Gold
PREREQUISITE None

Increase movement speed. Adding a spark to each step!

Conductor Constructor Path

H2THROW

1700 Gold
PREREQUISITE
Conductor Constructor Path

Press **Attack 2** to throw two additional water balloons. All water balloons last longer.

TROUBLED WATERS

2200 Gold
PREREQUISITE
Conductor Constructor Path

All water balloon attacks do increased damage. Throwing water balloons never hurt so bad!

BOLTING BLOB

3000 Gold
PREREQUISITE
Conductor Constructor Path

Hold **Attack 2** to throw a balloon into the air, release to zap it and electrify all enemies in a very large area.

Eelectrocutey Path

POSITIVELY CHARGED

1700 Gold
PREREQUISITE
Eelectrocutey Path

Gain an electric aura that sometimes shocks and damages nearby enemies.

IT HERTZ

2200 Gold
PREREQUISITE
Eelectrocutey Path

Enemies damaged by electrified water take increased damage. A perfect example of why there is no swimming during a lightning storm.

RE-VOLTING SHOCK

3000 Gold
PREREQUISITE
Eelectrocutey Path

Hold **Attack 3** to tail slap nearby enemies into the air.

PUNK SHOCK

RIP TIDE
"Go Fish!"

Where other Skylanders must choose between upgrading one attack over another, Rip Tide faces the unique challenge of deciding which fish to emphasize. Swordfish attacks are lightning quick strikes that work best against weaker enemies which appear in groups. Hammerhead attacks are meaty, deliberate swings that hit much harder and are great against powerful, solo opponents.

The Fishy Fencer and Flounder Pounder Paths emphasize one of the weapons equally. The big difference is the charge attack. Straight as an Angler is a torpedo attack that covers distance quickly. Shark Bite Bait doesn't travel as fast or far, but does more damage.

Special Quest
Whale of a Time

DAMAGE 8 ENEMIES AT ONCE WITH YOUR WHALE ON 'EM ABILITY.

The important word to note for this quest is "damage." You don't need to defeat eight enemies at once, just hit them. Any area filled with Chompies is a good choice since no other enemy swarms quite like they do. Find the right spot and use Whale On 'Em to complete the quest.

R ip Tide was known far and wide as one of the best Aqua-Fighters in Skylands. He mastered a multitude of water techniques and astonished tournament spectators with his ability to adapt his fighting style to any opponent. Amongst his repertoire were Swordfish Fencing, Hammerhead Heaving, and even the rare Blubber Whale Wallop—which he had used on numerous occasions in the legendary Rumble in the Reef. His unrivaled skill as a swordsman soon drew the attention of Master Eon. But when Kaos learned of this, he sent forth a legion of Squidface Brutes to stop Rip Tide before he could join the Skylanders...and everyone knows how that turned out, except for the Squidface Brutes, who after being knocked senseless can't remember a thing.

LEVEL	1	2	3	4	5	6	7	8	9	10	11	12	13	14	15	16	17	18	19	20
❤ MAX HEATH	300	330	360	390	420	450	480	510	540	570	600	630	660	690	720	750	780	810	840	870

⚡ SPEED	🛡 ARMOR	🎯 CRITICAL HIT	◎ ELEMENTAL POWER
43	30	4	25

Basic Attacks

TETRA ATTACK

Press **Attack 1** to swing the currently held fish at enemies. Swordfish attacks are quick while Shark attacks are slow, but more powerful.

FISH TOSS

Press **Attack 2** to toss the currently held fish at enemies. Fish Toss will also change between Swordfish and Shark.

🜲 Soul Gem Ability
REINVENTING THE WHALE

4000 Gold
PREREQUISITE
Find Rip Tide's Soul Gem in Twisty Tunnels; Purchase Whale on 'Em ability

Angry fish explode out of the whale's spout, seeking out and damaging nearby enemies.

Upgrades

WHALE ON 'EM

500 Gold
PREREQUISITE None

Press **Attack 3** to drop a large whale and smack down a large number of enemies.

BIGGER FISH TO FLY

700 Gold
PREREQUISITE None

Press **Attack 2** to throw the held fish, doing increased damage to enemies.

FRESH FISH

900 Gold
PREREQUISITE None

Press **Attack 2** to throw the currently held fish. Press **Attack 1** to attack and critically hit with the new fish.

BLISTERING BLUBBER

1200 Gold
PREREQUISITE
Purchase Whale on 'Em ability

Whale attacks do increased damage. Pocket whales are known for their helpful nature.

Fishy Fencer Path

NIPPING NEEDLE NOSE

1700 Gold
PREREQUISITE
Fishy Fencer Path

Press **Attack 2** to throw the sword fish which does damage over time to enemies that it hits.

PRACTICED PARRY

2200 Gold
PREREQUISITE
Fishy Fencer Path

Swordfish attacks do increased damage. A sword for a nose! Convenient!

STRAIGHT AS AN ANGLER

3000 Gold
PREREQUISITE
Fishy Fencer Path

Hold **Attack 1** to charge a swordfish attack, release to dash through enemies causing them to take damage and be knocked back.

Flounder Pounder Path

SHARK SURPRISE

1700 Gold
PREREQUISITE
Flounder Pounder Path

Press **Attack 2** to throw the shark which bounces off of enemies' heads before landing.

TIME TO HAMMER

2200 Gold
PREREQUISITE
Flounder Pounder Path

Hammerhead shark attacks do increased damage. There is more than one reason why they are called hammerheads.

SHARK BITE BAIT

3000 Gold
PREREQUISITE
Flounder Pounder Path

Hold **Attack 1** to charge a shark attack, release to dash forward biting any enemies in the way.

WHAM-SHELL

"Brace for the Mace!"

Wham-Shell was ruler of a kingdom deep in the oceans of Skylands that for a long time lived peacefully. That is, until his underwater utopia was invaded by a legion of oil-drilling trolls that scattered his people to the wind. Armed with a powerful mace that had been handed down from one king to the next for generations, Wham-Shell defeated the greedy trolls and drove them away. Soon after, he joined the Skylanders to help defend against this type of atrocity ever happening again.

LIGHTCORE

"Embrace the mace" should be the motto for Portal Masters using Wham-Shell. An upgraded Malacostracan Mace crushes enemies so well, it makes every other Skylander jealous. Consider Starfish Bullets as something to use while you're moving into the range of your mace attacks. The Commander Crab Path upgrades Starfish Bullets considerably, turning a single shot into three target seeking starfish that also deal damage over time. Choosing the Captain Crustacean Path opens up two new mace combos. Mace Master allows Wham-Shell to walk around and clear out tightly packed enemies. Power Slam is a great way to crush a single enemy.

Special Quest
Irate Invertebrate

DEFEAT 6 ENEMIES WITH ONE POSEIDEN STRIKE.

Since you need to defeat six enemies with one attack, Chompies from any Story Mode Chapter or Arena challenge are your best bet. If your Poseiden Strike isn't hitting hard enough, look into the Captain Crustacean Path to upgrade it.

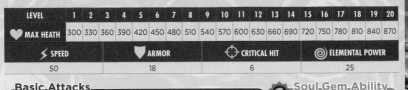

LEVEL	1	2	3	4	5	6	7	8	9	10	11	12	13	14	15	16	17	18	19	20
♥ MAX HEATH	300	330	360	390	420	450	480	510	540	570	600	630	660	690	720	750	780	810	840	870

⚡ SPEED	🛡 ARMOR	✛ CRITICAL HIT	◎ ELEMENTAL POWER
50	18	6	25

Basic Attacks

MALACOSTRACAN MACE

Press **Attack 1** to swing Wham-Shell's mace at enemies. Press **Attack 1, Attack 1**, Hold **Attack 1** for a special combo.

STARFISH BULLETS

Press **Attack 2** to fire starfish bullets from Wham-Shell's mace.

Soul Gem Ability

Ⓖ CARAPACE PLATING

4000 Gold
PREREQUISITE
None

New armor makes Wham-Shell more resistant.

Upgrades

STARFISH GIGANTICUS

500 Gold
PREREQUISITE   None

Hold **Attack 2** to charge up your Starfish Bullets attack.

KING'S MACE

700 Gold
PREREQUISITE   None

Mace attacks deal increased damage.

STARFISHICUS SUPERIORALIS

900 Gold
PREREQUISITE   None

Starfish Bullets deal increased damage.

POSEIDON STRIKE

1200 Gold
PREREQUISITE   None

Press **Attack 3** to create an electrified field that damages enemies.

Captain Crustacean Path

CRUSTACEAN COMBOS

1700 Gold
PREREQUISITE
Captain Crustacean Path

Press **Attack 1, Attack 1**, Hold **Attack 2** for Mace Master. Press **Attack 1, Attack 1**, Hold **Attack 3** for Power Slam.

MEGA TRIDENT

2200 Gold
PREREQUISITE
Captain Crustacean Path

Mace attacks deal even MORE increased damage.

MACE OF THE DEEP

3000 Gold
PREREQUISITE
Captain Crustacean Path

Hold **Attack 3** to create a more powerful Poseidon Strike.

Commander Crab Path

TRIPLICATE STARFISH

1700 Gold
PREREQUISITE
Commander Crab Path

Shoot three Starfish at once.

SEMI-ETERNAL PURSUIT

2200 Gold
PREREQUISITE
Commander Crab Path

Starfish attack homes in on enemies.

NIGHTMARE HUGGERS

3000 Gold
PREREQUISITE
Commander Crab Path

Starfish latch onto enemies, doing continuous damage.

NIGHT SHIFT

"Roll with the Punches!"

Night Shift's reach turns One-Two Punch into a ranged melee attack. The Prize Fighter Path adds damage to, and money from, enemies hit with Don't Move, Just Stick! Vampire's Bite returns a small amount of health and needs a second to recharge. The Proper Vampire Path adds damage over time and extra healing.

Ethereal Shift is a great way to escape a bad location, and the Warping Vortex Path helps in making a clean escape. A Batty Coach might be the best upgrade in the game, and it gets much better with the Underbat Path. Avoiding defeat twice is a great benefit in any situation.

Special Quest

King Of The Ring

HIT 10 ENEMIES AT ONCE WITH YOUR GIANT UPPERCUT PUNCH.

This quest requires the purchase of Night Shift's 1000 Gold upgrade, Don't Move, Just Stick! Next, find an area with 10 enemies that you can force to bunch up close to each other but that won't take out Night Shift before his move finishes charging.

From high up in the gloomy Batcrypt Mountains, Night Shift was a full-fledged baron and heir to a great fortune. But one day he decided to leave it all behind to pursue his dream as a prizefighter. It wasn't long before Night Shift became the undefeated phantom-weight champion of Skylands, famous for his massive uppercut and for having once bitten an opponent in the ring. Unfortunately, a rule change made teleportation illegal and Night Shift was forced to give up his belt, officially ending his career as a boxer. Crestfallen over being disqualified from a sport he loved so dearly, his spirits picked up when he was sought out by Master Eon, who told him that his skill as a fighter could be put to great use as a member of the Skylanders.

Body
Soul Gem Ability
GENTLEMANLY

3500 Gold
PREREQUISITE
Find Night Shift's Soul Gem in Motleyville

All attacks do increased damage at full health. Quite sporting of the enemies to miss so often, yes...quite.

Legs
Soul Gem Ability
GRAND ENTRANCE

3500 Gold
PREREQUISITE
Find Night Shift's Soul Gem in Motleyville

Slows down nearby enemies when appearing after a teleport.

LEVEL	1	2	3	4	5	6	7	8	9	10	11	12	13	14	15	16	17	18	19	20
♥ MAX HEATH	200	220	240	260	280	300	320	340	360	380	400	420	440	460	480	500	520	540	560	580

⚡ SPEED	🛡 ARMOR	⊕ CRITICAL HIT	◎ ELEMENTAL POWER
35	4	8	25

BODY

Basic Attacks
ONE-TWO PUNCH

Press **Attack 1** to punch nearby enemies with enormous boxing gloves.

Upgrades

VAMPIRE'S BITE

300 Gold
PREREQUISITE None

Press **Attack 3** to bite enemies and regain some health.

STING LIKE A BAT

800 Gold
PREREQUISITE None

Punching does increased damage. Give em' the ol' one-two combo!

DON'T MOVE, JUST STICK!

1000 Gold
PREREQUISITE None

Hold **Attack 1** to charge a punch, release to deal a massive uppercut to enemies.

Proper Vampire Path

INFECTIOUS SMILE

1500 Gold
PREREQUISITE Proper Vampire Path

Vampire's Bite deals damage over time to their targets.

HEALTHY APPETITE

2000 Gold
PREREQUISITE Proper Vampire Path

Vampire's Bite deals more damage with extra healing. Pack on the pounds!

Champion Fighter Path

PRIZE FIGHTER

1500 Gold
PREREQUISITE Champion Fighter Path

Hold **Attack 1** to charge a punch, release to do an uppercut that causes enemies that are hit to take damage and drop money.

PAY DAY

2000 Gold
PREREQUISITE Purchase Prize Fighter ability

Prize Fighter gives more money. Don't spend it all in one place like Moe Money and Moe Problems did.

✈ LEGS

Basic Attacks
ETHEREAL SHIFT

Press **Attack 2** to turn into mist and teleport a short distance forward.

Upgrades

FLOAT LIKE A VAMPIRE

300 Gold
PREREQUISITE None

Press **Attack 2** to teleport and shoot out a projectile that damages nearby enemies.

FOGGY MOVEMENT

800 Gold
PREREQUISITE None

Speed is increased. Become faster than an old fogey!

A BATTY COACH

1000 Gold
PREREQUISITE None

A bat ally prevents being defeated one time. What a great pep talk!

Warping Vortex Path

VORTEX OF DOOM

1500 Gold
PREREQUISITE Warping Vortex Path

Press **Attack 2** to teleport and create a large vortex that pull in enemies.

CLOSE TO DOOM

2000 Gold
PREREQUISITE Purchase Vortex of Doom ability

Vortex of Doom now deals damage to enemies. Dooooooom!

Underbat Path

ROUND 2

1500 Gold
PREREQUISITE Underbat Path

A Batty Coach now gives a health boost when returning from defeat. Get back in there!

LUCK OF THE UNDERBAT

2000 Gold
PREREQUISITE Underbat Path

A Batty Coach can be used twice. Okay, this time it's serious.

RATTLE SHAKE
"Go Ahead - Snake My Day!"

Some say Rattle Shake was the best tracker in the Cloudbreak Islands. Others say he could strike the center of a Gold coin at a thousand paces. But the legend of Rattle Shake was immortalized when he found himself trapped by the Black Hat Gang, the infamous group of cowboys who literally were large cows...and evil ones at that. They threatened to plunder the local village unless Rattle Shake led them inside the magical volcano Mt. Cloudbreak, where they hoped to discover enchanted treasure. Badly outnumbered, the ever calm Rattle Shake magically summoned every snake in the area and overtook the notorious bovines in an epic fight. The tale of his heroism was heard by Master Eon, who then recruited him to the Skylanders.

SWAP FORCE

Spring Loaded Snake is a big upgrade to Snake's Venom and should be an early upgrade. The Coiled Ammunition Path adds damage over time to enemies hit with Spring Loaded Snakes. Always have Deputy Snake active. It deals extra damage to enemies, and it only gets better with the Deputy's Duty Path.

Tail Sweep is a basic melee attack with two upgrades, though Ssstampede is the upgrade that is affected by the upgrade paths. The Bone Herder Path adds an attack that hits enemies near Rattle Shake. The Grave Springer Path ends with him charging into enemies and inflicting extra damage at the end of the charge.

Special Quest
Bouncing Biter

DAMAGE A TOTAL OF 100 ENEMIES WITH YOUR BOUNCING SNAKE SHOT.

You need to buy the Spring Loaded Snake ability before you can begin working on this quest. After you spend the 1000 gold, charge up the Snake Shot and fire it into groups of enemies whenever possible.

Body Soul Gem Ability	Legs Soul Gem Ability
RAISE THE SNAKES	**THE SNAKE-SKINNED KID**

3500 Gold	**3500 Gold**
PREREQUISITE Find Rattle Shake's Soul Gem in Cascade Glade	PREREQUISITE Find Rattle Shake's Soul Gem in Cascade Glade

Get a new skin which increases Critical Hit and absorbs damage. Absorbing damage causes the skin to shed then grow back after a short time.

Get a new skin which increases speed and absorbs damage. Absorbing damage causes the skin to shed then grow back after a short time.

LEVEL	1	2	3	4	5	6	7	8	9	10	11	12	13	14	15	16	17	18	19	20
♥ MAX HEATH	280	308	336	364	392	420	448	476	504	560	588	616	644	672	700	728	756	784	812	840

⚡ SPEED	🛡 ARMOR	⊕ CRITICAL HIT	◎ ELEMENTAL POWER
43	12	6	25

BODY

Basic Attacks
SNAKE'S VENOM

Press **Attack 1** to shoot snake venom at nearby enemies.

Upgrades

DEPUTY SNAKE

300 Gold
PREREQUISITE None

Press **Attack 3** to throw down a snake ally that will attack and slow nearby enemies.

FISTFUL OF SNAKES

800 Gold
PREREQUISITE None

All venom projectiles do increased damage.

SPRING LOADED SNAKE

1000 Gold
PREREQUISITE None

Hold **Attack 1** to charge a Snake Shot, release to shoot a snake that bounces between enemies and collects items along the way.

Deputy's Duty Path

NASTY SSSURPRISE

1500 Gold
PREREQUISITE Deputy's Duty Path

Deputy Snake causes an acid explosion that damages enemies where it lands.

ARMED TO THE FANGS

2000 Gold
PREREQUISITE Purchase Nasty Sssurprise ability

Nasty Sssurprise radius and Deputy Snake damage are increased.

Coiled Ammunition Path

SNAKE BITE

1500 Gold
PREREQUISITE Coiled Ammunition Path

Spring Loaded Snake poisons the first enemy it hits, dealing damage over time.

THIS BITES

2000 Gold
PREREQUISITE Purchase Snake Bite ability

Enemies poisoned by Spring Loaded Snake take more damage from Snake's Venom.

 LEGS

Basic Attacks
TAIL SWEEP

Press **Attack 2** to sweep at nearby enemies with a quick tail strike.

Upgrades

BOUNCE THE BONES

300 Gold
PREREQUISITE None

Press **Attack 2** to shoot one bouncing bone projectile.

ON BRAND

800 Gold
PREREQUISITE None

Hold **Jump** to jump and smash down into the ground, damaging and knocking enemies away.

SSSTAMPEDE

1000 Gold
PREREQUISITE Purchase Bounce the Bones ability

Press **Attack 2** to shoot three large bone projectiles at once.

Bone Herder Path

GOLIATH BONE SNAKE

1500 Gold
PREREQUISITE Bone Herder Path

Hold **Attack 2** to charge Ssstampede, release to summon a giant bone snake from the ground.

DANCES WITH SNAKES

2000 Gold
PREREQUISITE Purchase Goliath Bone Snake ability

Hold **Attack 2** while moving to charge Goliath Bone Snake, release to summon many bone snakes.

Grave Springer Path

SPURRED SPRING

1500 Gold
PREREQUISITE Grave Springer Path

Hold **Attack 2** to charge Ssstampede, release to spring forward, damaging all enemies in the way.

GRAVEYARD SMASH

2000 Gold
PREREQUISITE Purchase Spurred Spring ability

Spurred Spring causes tombstones to appear and damage enemies in a large area when landing.

TWIN BLADE
CHOP CHOP
"Slice and Dice!"

SERIES 3

Even without a ranged attack, Chop Chop is never at a disadvantage against ranged opponents. Arkeyan Shield, especially after upgrades, keeps him safe while he advances on attackers. His lightning-fast sword strokes finish off the attackers before they can get in too many more shots.

While the Undead Defender Path conveys amazing defensive capabilities, Twin Blade Chop Chop's Wow Pow! ability all but demands the Vampiric Warrior Path. They're both fantastic options and you have the luxury of tailoring your choice to the challenge. Select Vampiric Warrior for speedy destruction of enemies or Undead Defender for more dangerous opponents.

Special Quest

Stalwart Defender

DEAL 10,000 DAMAGE USING BONE BRAMBLER.

Use Bone Brambler when opportunities present themselves. Purchase Cursed Bone Brambler, or use the Arkeyan Leap combo finisher, to complete this quest even faster.

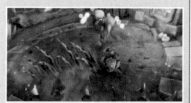

Chop Chop was once an elite warrior belonging to the ancient race of Arkeyan beings. Like many of the Arkeyans, he was created from a hybrid of elements—in his case, Undead, Magic, and Tech. Chop Chop is a relentless, highly-skilled solider who wields a sword and shield made of an indestructible metal. With the Arkeyans having vanished long ago, Chop Chop wandered Skylands for centuries looking for his creators. Eventually, he was found by Eon and recruited as a Skylander.

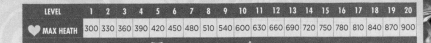

LEVEL	1	2	3	4	5	6	7	8	9	10	11	12	13	14	15	16	17	18	19	20
❤ MAX HEATH	300	330	360	390	420	450	480	510	540	600	630	660	690	720	750	780	810	840	870	900

⚡ SPEED	🛡 ARMOR	⊕ CRITICAL HIT	◎ ELEMENTAL POWER
50	24	2	25

Basic Attacks

ARKEYAN BLADE

ARKEYAN SHIELD

Press **Attack 1** to slash away at your enemies with this ancient blade. Press **Attack 1**, **Attack 1**, hold **Attack 1** for a fencing combo.

Hold **Attack 2** to absorb a limited amount of damage from most attacks, also deflects projectiles.

Soul Gem Ability
Ⓖ CURSED BONE BRAMBLER

4000 Gold
Purchase Bone Brambler ability

Bone brambles deal extra damage.

Upgrades

SPIKED SHIELD BASH

500 Gold
PREREQUISITE None

While holding **Attack 2**, press **Attack 1** to Shield Bash an enemy. Distance increases with absorbed damage.

VAMPIRIC AURA

700 Gold
PREREQUISITE None

The Arkeyan Blade does extra damage and you regain health by defeating enemies.

SHIELD SPARTAN

900 Gold
PREREQUISITE Purchase Spiked Shield Bash ability

Move faster and block more damage while holding **Attack 2**.

BONE BRAMBLER

1200 Gold
PREREQUISITE None

Press **Attack 3** to attack enemies with bone brambles.

Vampiric Warrior Path

ARKEYAN COMBAT MASTER

1700 Gold
PREREQUISITE Vampiric Warrior Path

Press **Attack 1**, **Attack 1**, Hold **Attack 2** for Arkeyan Cyclone. Press **Attack 1**, **Attack 1**, Hold **Attack 3** for Arkeyan Leap.

ARKEYAN VORPAL BLADE

2200 Gold
PREREQUISITE Vampiric Warrior Path

Sword attacks do even MORE increased damage.

DEMON BLADE OF THE UNDERWORLD

3000 Gold
PREREQUISITE Vampiric Warrior Path

Swords have longer range and do maximum damage.

Undead Defender Path

ARKEYAN SPECTRAL SHIELD

1700 Gold
PREREQUISITE Undead Defender Path

While holding **Attack 2**, press **Attack 1** to release absorbed damage on your foes.

SHIELD STUN BASH

2200 Gold
PREREQUISITE Undead Defender Path

Shield Bash attacks stun enemies.

DEMON SHIELD OF THE SHADOWS

3000 Gold
PREREQUISITE Undead Defender Path

Shield Bash does extra damage. Absorbed damage is automatically released.

Wow Pow!

DICE AND SLICE!

5000 Gold
PREREQUISITE None

Hold **Attack 1** to charge up Dual Sword Mode, then release to unleash a furious, two-sword attack.

Use Dice and Slice! when you need to deal damage in a hurry. One downside of this ability is a large charge-up time, although he can move around while charging. A meter appears near Chop Chop that fills while Attack 1 is held. As soon as you release Attack 1, Chop Chop rushes ahead with his blades carving up everything in a straight line. It's possible to turn him, but he isn't very responsive.

TWIN BLADE CHOP CHOP

PHANTOM CYNDER
"Volts and Lightning!"

While just an egg, Cynder was stolen by the henchmen of an evil dragon named Malefor and raised to do his bidding. For years, she spread fear throughout the land until she was defeated by Spyro the dragon and freed from the grip of Malefor. But dark powers still flow through her, and despite her desire to make amends for her past, most Skylanders try to keep a safe distance...just in case.

SERIES 3

Cynder is a hit and run specialist, with a great ranged attack in Spectral Lightning, and a handy escape ability called Shadow Dash. Spectral Lightning chews through enemy health while they are a safe distance away. Shadow Dash provides a way out of melee combat (not Cynder's strong suit), and leaves behind ghosts who attack nearby enemies.

The Nether Welder Path improves Spectral Lightning and is the way to go if you prefer to handle all the dirty work in combat. The Shadowdancer path boosts Cynder's Shadow Dash and Ghosts, who can take down the small fries while you focus on larger enemies.

Special Quest
On The Haunt

DEFEAT 50 ENEMIES WITH YOUR GHOST ALLY.

The only tricky part to this quest is saving up the Gold to buy Haunted Ally. After that, it is just a matter of flying around with the Ghost in tow to rack up the enemy count.

LEVEL	1	2	3	4	5	6	7	8	9	10	11	12	13	14	15	16	17	18	19	20
♥ MAX HEATH	260	286	312	338	364	390	416	442	468	520	546	572	598	624	650	676	702	728	754	780

⚡ SPEED	🛡 ARMOR	⊕ CRITICAL HIT	◎ ELEMENTAL POWER
43	18	6	25

Basic Attacks

SPECTRAL LIGHTNING

Press and hold **Attack 1** to shock enemies with bolts of lightning.

SHADOW DASH

Press **Attack 2** to dash forward in shadow mode, leaving ghostly allies in Cynder's wake.

⟡ Soul Gem Ability
HAUNTED ALLY

4000 Gold
PREREQUISITE
None

A ghost ally travels with you and damages nearby enemies.

Upgrades

CYNDER FLIGHT

500 Gold
PREREQUISITE None

Press **Attack 3** to fly. Increased speed and resistance while flying.

BLACK LIGHTNING

700 Gold
PREREQUISITE None

Spectral Lightning does increased damage.

DOUBLE SPOOKY!

900 Gold
PREREQUISITE None

Ghosts do increased damage.

SHADOW REACH

1200 Gold
PREREQUISITE None

Shadow Dash Range is increased.

Nether Welder Path

UNSTABLE FORCES

1700 Gold
PREREQUISITE
Nether Welder Path

Hitting a ghost with Spectral Lightning makes it explode, damaging enemies around.

BREATH CONTROL

2200 Gold
PREREQUISITE
Nether Welder Path

Spectral Lightning hold duration is increased

BREATH OF POWER

3000 Gold
PREREQUISITE
Nether Welder Path

Spectral Lightning damages enemies in a larger area.

Shadow Dancer Path

DEATH BOUND

1700 Gold
PREREQUISITE
Shadow Dancer Path

Enemies hit by ghosts move slower.

GHOST HAUNTER

2200 Gold
PREREQUISITE
Shadow Dancer Path

Ghosts last longer, have a greater attack range, and do even more damage.

SHADOW STRIKE

3000 Gold
PREREQUISITE
Shadow Dancer Path

Shadow Dash deals damage to enemies.

Wow Pow!
SKULL-SPLOSION!

5000 Gold
PREREQUISITE
None

While in a Shadow Dash, hold **Attack 2** to morph into a giant skull, which explodes on release.

To make it easier to track Cynder's position, the skull appears just above the ground. The best part about Skull-Splosion! is that it knocks back enemies in addition to dealing damage. That's important for Cynder, who lacks a melee attack.

PHANTOM CYNDER

GRIM CREEPER

"Your Time is Up!"

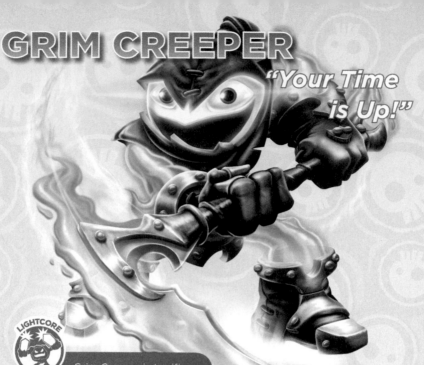

LIGHTCORE

Grim Creeper is terrific against large groups of weaker enemies, but suffers against single enemies with large health bars. Scythe Swing is a decent melee attack but it is a bit slow. The third swing is a spinning scythe attack that hits all nearby enemies. Ghost Form is where Grim Creeper's strengths lie, and it requires practice to master it.

The Spooky Specter Path focuses on Ghost Form and allows the Living Armor to defend itself while Ghost Form is flying free. The Grim Scythe Style Path has two general upgrades and a nice boost to Poltergeist Scythe.

Special Quest

Aggressive Outfit

HIT 10 ENEMIES IN A ROW WITH YOUR ARMOR WHILE IT TRAVELS BACK TO YOU.

Save this quest until Grim Creeper has advanced a few levels and upgraded Ghost Form. The amount of time required to touch 10 enemies with Ghost Form leaves him open to attacks. To give yourself additional help, set up in a narrow space (down a hall or in a single-room building) so the enemies are forced to bunch up.

When he was young, Grim Creeper visited the prestigious Grim Acres School for Ghost Wrangling, hoping to attend as a student. But when the Scaremaster interviewed him, he found that Grim didn't have any of the usual training that other students had. Because of this, he was turned away. However, as the young Grim was about to leave, a herd of rampaging ghosts suddenly flooded the school, carrying away the faculty and leaving the students to fend for themselves. Grim Creeper stood his ground, not only defending the other students, but using his amazing reaping talents to fight back the ghosts and contain them until help could arrive. Now a Skylander, Grim is considered one of the best reapers ever to swing a scythe, proving that studies alone are no substitute for bravery, passion, and true heroic spirit.

LEVEL	1	2	3	4	5	6	7	8	9	10	11	12	13	14	15	16	17	18	19	20
♥ MAX HEATH	250	275	300	325	350	375	400	425	450	500	525	550	575	600	625	650	675	700	725	750

⚡ SPEED	▽ ARMOR	◎ CRITICAL HIT	◎ ELEMENTAL POWER
43	6	8	25

Basic Attacks

SCYTHE SWING

Press **Attack 1** to swing a ghostly scythe at nearby enemies.

GHOST FORM

Press **Attack 2** to separate from the armor. Touch up to two enemies while in ghost form to mark them. Press **Attack 2** again to attack them with the living armor.

Soul Gem Ability

◎ HELP FROM BEYOND

4000 Gold
PREREQUISITE
Find Grim Creeper's Soul Gem in Iron Jaw Gulch

A ghost ally appears from defeated enemies that seeks out and attacks other nearby enemies.

Upgrades

POLTERGEIST SCYTHE

500 Gold
PREREQUISITE None

Press **Attack 3** to knock enemies into the air with a spinning spectral scythe.

SPIRIT SCYTHE

700 Gold
PREREQUISITE None

Press **Attack 1** to swing a more powerful scythe that does increased damage.

SPOOK AND DESTROY

900 Gold
PREREQUISITE None

Press **Attack 2** to go into Ghost Form and leave behind Living Armor. Touch up to five enemies while in ghost form to mark them. Press **Attack 2** again to attack them with the living armor.

ARMORED AMORE

1200 Gold
PREREQUISITE None

Living Armor does increased damage when it flies back to Grim Creeper. Those pointy boots hurt!

Grim Scythe Style Path

SPHERE OF FEAR

1700 Gold
PREREQUISITE
Grim Scythe Style Path

Hold **Attack 3** for a short time to spin the scythe in a larger area and repeatedly hit enemies into the air.

GRAVE DANGER

2200 Gold
PREREQUISITE
Grim Scythe Style Path

Critical Hit is increased. Concentrated ghost particles make it easier to do more damage to enemies.

GHASTLY DAMAGE

3000 Gold
PREREQUISITE
Grim Scythe Style Path

All attacks do more damage for a short time after enemies are hit by the Living Armor.

Spooky Specter Path

IT'S ALIVE!

1700 Gold
PREREQUISITE
Spooky Specter Path

Press **Attack 2** to go into Ghost Form and leave behind Living Armor. Living Armor attacks nearby enemies when it is attacked.

HAUNTED HELP

2200 Gold
PREREQUISITE
Spooky Specter Path

Press **Attack 2** to go into Ghost Form and leave behind Living Armor. Enemies between ghost form and the living armor take damage.

SOUL SAMPLER

3000 Gold
PREREQUISITE
Spooky Specter Path

Regain some health for each enemy hit by Spook and Destroy.

GRIM CREEPER

ROLLER BRAWL

"Let's Roll!"

What Roller Brawl lacks in defense and ranged abilities is easily made up by Derby Dash. Roller Brawl has multiple attack options while dashing, including a headbutt that, when upgraded, keeps enemies flying helplessly through the air.

The Shadow Skater Path provides a bit more defense to her, but also gives Roller Claws a nice swiping attack that hits more enemies. The Skateblade Siren Path is the more aggressive choice. It increases damage output and provides more Skateblade options. Enemies chasing Roller Blade have as much to fear as the ones she's dashing at to attack.

Special Quest

Sharp Jammer

USE YOUR DEADLY CLOTHESLINE ABILITY TO TAKE OUT 10 ENEMIES AT ONCE.

After you purchase the Deadly Clothesline ability, find a place (an Arena or a Bonus Mission Map) where you can collect 10 Chompies together. Charge up Roller Brawl's Derby Dash and run back through the pile to complete the quest.

Roller Brawl grew up with five older vampire brothers, who were all very big and overprotective. Being the smallest of her family, she learned how to use her speed and cunning to become one of the toughest jammers in the Undead Roller Derby League. It was during the championship match when she caught the eye of Kaos, who fell head-over-heels in love with her. But when her overprotective brothers stepped in, Kaos had them captured by Drow and taken prisoner. Roller Brawl swore revenge, but even with her impressive skills, she was no match for an entire Drow army. Having developed a strong distaste for evil, she joined up with the Skylanders to fight against Kaos—while never giving up on her search for her brothers.

LEVEL	1	2	3	4	5	6	7	8	9	10	11	12	13	14	15	16	17	18	19	20
♥ MAX HEATH	260	286	312	338	364	390	416	442	468	520	546	572	598	624	650	676	702	728	754	780

⚡ SPEED	🛡 ARMOR	⊕ CRITICAL HIT	◎ ELEMENTAL POWER
50	12	8	25

Basic Attacks

ROLLER CLAWS

Press **Attack 1** to slash at nearby enemies.

DERBY DASH

Press **Attack 2** to dash and damage nearby enemies when starting the dash. Press **Attack 1** or **Attack 2** to attack while dashing.

Soul Gem Ability

Ⓖ CURSED HELMET

4000 Gold
PREREQUISITE

Press **Attack 2** while dashing to head-butt an enemy and create a curse link. Touch enemies with the link to damage them!

Upgrades

SKATEBLADES

500 Gold
PREREQUISITE None

Press **Attack 3** to shoot skate blades that travel along the ground towards enemies.

IMPACT SKATER

700 Gold
PREREQUISITE None

All attacks while dashing do increased damage.

DEADLY CLOTHESLINE

900 Gold
PREREQUISITE None

Hold **Attack 2** to charge a dash, release to dash forward and clothesline any enemies in the way.

AGGRESSION

1200 Gold
PREREQUISITE None

New sharpened blades make claw attacks do increased damage.

Shadow Skater Path

PIROUETTE

1700 Gold
PREREQUISITE Shadow Skater Path

Hold **Attack 1** during a dash to do a spin attack that damages nearby enemies.

HARDENED HELM

2200 Gold
PREREQUISITE Shadow Skater Path

A new helmet increases Roller Brawl's armor, reducing damage taken.

BULLRUSH

3000 Gold
PREREQUISITE Shadow Skater Path

Hold **Attack 2** during a dash to bullrush enemies, damaging and knocking them back.

Skateblade Siren Path

SKATEBLADE TRAP

1700 Gold
PREREQUISITE Skateblade Siren Path

Press **Attack 3** while dashing to leave behind a trap that damages nearby enemies.

CRITICAL CLAWS

2200 Gold
PREREQUISITE Skateblade Siren Path

New claws increases Roller Brawl's Critical Hit chance.

SPINNING SAWS

3000 Gold
PREREQUISITE Skateblade Siren Path

Hold **Attack 3** to create saws that spin around Roller Brawl.

MAGNA CHARGE

"Attract To Attack!"

Magnet Cannon can overheat, but the Magnetic Armaments Path turns that into an advantage, and a fireball blast. Polarized Pickup grabs enemies into a powerful weapon for Magna Charge. With no enemies in range, a metallic object appears over his head. The Magnet Tuner Path adds a knock back and extra damage to Polarized Pickup.

Magneto Ball drags around an enemy caught in its electrical wake and lets you use them as a weapon. The Static Buildup Path focuses damage on enemies caught in Magneto Ball. The Drag Racer Path turns the dragged enemy into a stronger projectile.

Special Quest

Now That's Using Your Head

DEAL 5000 DAMAGE USING YOUR POLARIZED PICKUP.

Damage done to enemies being picked up and the damage done to enemies hit with the slam attack both count toward this total. Choose the Magnet Tuner Path to make this quest go faster.

Magna Charge came from the great race of Ultron robots, but was mysteriously created with a giant magnet head. This proved problematic, as his peers were all made of metal and were constantly being pulled towards him. As a result, Magna Charge was exiled to a faraway island, where he eventually learned to control his magnetic powers. After years of training, he returned to his home to demonstrate his abilities, but found everything completely destroyed. In searching for answers, Magna Charge caught the attention of Master Eon, who realized the unique Ultron soldier was a perfect candidate for the Skylanders.

Body
Soul Gem Ability

MULTI BARRELLED

3500 Gold

PREREQUISITE
Find Magna Charge's Soul Gem in Mount Cloudbreak

Upgraded Magnet Cannon that shoots three projectiles at once!

Legs
Soul Gem Ability

SUPER REPULSOR

3500 Gold

PREREQUISITE
Find Magna Charge's Soul Gem in Mount Cloudbreak

A new wheel makes thrown objects gain increased damage, range and speed.

LEVEL	1	2	3	4	5	6	7	8	9	10	11	12	13	14	15	16	17	18	19	20
♥ MAX HEATH	280	308	336	364	392	420	448	476	504	560	588	616	644	672	700	728	756	784	812	840

⚡ SPEED	🛡 ARMOR	⊕ CRITICAL HIT	◎ ELEMENTAL POWER
50	18	6	25

BODY

Basic Attacks
MAGNET CANNON

Hold **Attack 1** to rapidly fire energy projectiles. Firing for too long will cause the cannon to overheat.

Upgrades

POLARIZED PICKUP

300 Gold
PREREQUISITE None

Press **Attack 3** to pick up enemies. Press **Attack 3** again to slam them. While active, loot will be drawn in from a distance!

PLASMA SHOTS

800 Gold
PREREQUISITE None

Hold **Attack 1** to rapidly shoot a Magnet Cannon that does increased damage. Projectiles heat up after a short time, dealing extra fire damage.

MAGNETIC BUILDUP

1000 Gold
PREREQUISITE
Purchase Polarized Pickup ability

Hold an object with Polarized Pickup for a short time, release it to deal extra damage.

Magnetic Armaments Path

DISCHARGE RECHARGE

1500 Gold
PREREQUISITE
Magnetic Armaments Path

Hold **Attack 1** to overheat the Magnet Cannon, release to shoot a large fireball.

HEAVY BLASTER

2000 Gold
PREREQUISITE
Magnetic Armaments Path

Magnet Cannon does even more damage.

Magnet Tuner Path

BURST PICKUP

1200 Gold
PREREQUISITE
Magnet Tuner Path

Picking up enemies with Polarized Pickup will knock back nearby enemies.

MAGNETIC PERSONALITY

2000 Gold
PREREQUISITE
Magnet Tuner Path

Magnet attacks do increased damage. Two-Ton's Law states: if it has mass, it can be slammed.

LEGS

Basic Attacks
MAGNETO BALL

Press **Attack 2** to drag an enemy around. Press **Attack 2** again to launch them forward. Large enemies cannot be dragged.

Upgrades

EJECT

300 Gold
PREREQUISITE None

Press **Attack 3** while dragging an object or enemy to throw it behind and boost forward.

RAD WHEELS

800 Gold
PREREQUISITE None

Speed is increased. Brand new developments in magnet wheels!

DRAG CAPACITY

1000 Gold
PREREQUISITE None

Two enemies can be dragged at once while dashing.

Static Buildup Path

SHOCK STOP

1500 Gold
PREREQUISITE
Static Buildup Path

Press **Attack 1** while dragging an enemy to drop it in front of you and shock it.

CRASH TEST

2000 Gold
PREREQUISITE
Purchase Shock Stop ability

Shock Stop and Eject do increased damage.

Drag Racer Path

RAPID REPEL

1500 Gold
PREREQUISITE
Drag Racer Path

Press **Attack 1** while dragging an object or enemy to shoot it without stopping.

OPPOSITES REPEL

2000 Gold
PREREQUISITE
Purchase Rapid Repel ability

Rapid Repel does increased damage. Repulsive!

SPY RISE

"It's Classified!"

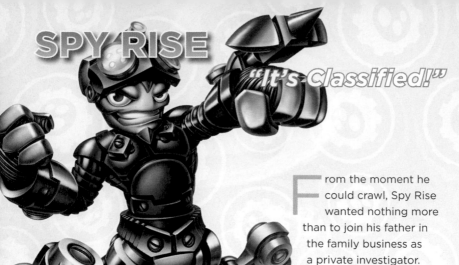

Spyder Blaster damages and slows down enemies, a big help in setting up Super Spy Scanner S3, which hits incredibly hard when charged. The Web Spinning Path allows for constant firing of Cocoon Spinner, but leaves Spy Rise stationary. The Shock Spy Path allows movement, but you must charge and aim Electroweb Pulsebomb.

Spyder Climb is a clean escape ability, going into the air where no enemies can follow. The Fire Tech Path adds a flamethrower attack that lasts as long as the button is held. The Electro Tech Path adds a cannon that requires charging each time it's used.

Special Quest

Finishing Touch

SPYDER STING 25 ENEMIES.
Spyder Sting costs 800 Gold to purchase, and it's a great way to restore health when there aren't any food drops available. Look for an icon to appear near enemies with low health. Move close to them to initiate Spyder Sting (it looks like a short blade attack) to take them out and restore some health to Spy Rise. Do it 24 more times and the quest is complete!

From the moment he could crawl, Spy Rise wanted nothing more than to join his father in the family business as a private investigator. But after being hired by a shadowy figure to gather information on the Cloudbreak Islands, his father vanished, leaving Spy Rise alone to search for answers.

He scoured the land for clues, using his immense skill in reconnaissance to track down his missing father, but all roads came up empty. Then one day, he received a tip from none other than Master Eon, which led him to a hidden lair near Mt. Cloudbreak, where he not only found his long lost father, but also uncovered an evil plot to take control of the magical volcano during the next eruption ceremony. With his father safe, Spy Rise decided to pursue a new career—as a member of the Skylanders.

Body Soul Gem Ability	Legs Soul Gem Ability
SPY WITH A GOLDEN HAND	**OMEGA SKY LASER**

3500 Gold	3500 Gold
PREREQUISITE Find Spy Rise's Soul Gem in Boney Islands	PREREQUISITE Find Spy Rise's Soul Gem in Boney Islands
Gain a new Golden blaster that shoots five projectiles at once.	Hold **Attack 1** while in the sky to shoot down a massive laser that stuns enemies.

LEVEL	1	2	3	4	5	6	7	8	9	10	11	12	13	14	15	16	17	18	19	20
♥ MAX HEATH	270	297	324	351	378	405	432	459	486	540	567	594	621	648	675	702	729	756	783	810

⚡ SPEED	🛡 ARMOR	⊕ CRITICAL HIT	◎ ELEMENTAL POWER
43	18	8	25

BODY

Basic Attacks
SPYDER BLASTER

Press **Attack 1** to shoot three spyder projectiles that slow any enemy it hits.

Upgrades

SUPER SPY SCANNER S3

300 Gold
PREREQUISITE None

Hold **Attack 3** for a short time to scan a nearby enemy, release to shoot a high-powered laser. Fully scanned enemies take additional damage.

SPYDER STING

800 Gold
PREREQUISITE None

Press **Attack 1** next to an enemy with low health to sting them and steal some health.

FUTURE TECH

1000 Gold
PREREQUISITE
Purchase Super Spy Scanner S3 ability

Super Spy Scanner S3 and Spyder Blaster do increased damage.

Web Spinner Path

COCOON SPINNER

1500 Gold
PREREQUISITE
Web Spinner Path

Hold **Attack 1** to shoot a stream of web projectiles that slow and cocoon enemies.

EXPERIMENTAL WEBS

2000 Gold
PREREQUISITE
Purchase Cocoon Spinner ability

Cocoon Spinner does increased damage. The experiment seems to be going well!

Shock Spy Path

ELECTROWEB PULSE BOMB

1500 Gold
PREREQUISITE
Shock Spy Path

Hold **Attack 1** to charge a web bomb, release to throw it, which damages and slows enemies in a large area.

IMPROVED EPD

2000 Gold
PREREQUISITE
Purchase Electroweb Pulse Bomb ability

Electroweb Pulse Bomb does increased damage and has a larger explosion.

🪜 LEGS

Basic Attacks
SPYDER CLIMB

Press **Attack 2** to climb into the air with electro web, dropping back down will damage nearby enemies.

Upgrades

SPYDER MINE

300 Gold
PREREQUISITE None

Press **Attack 2** to climb into the air and drop a spyder mine that will seek out and explode on nearby enemies.

SPYDER MINE 002

800 Gold
PREREQUISITE
Purchase Spyder Mine ability

Press **Attack 2** to climb into the air, dropping two spyder mines at once.

RAPID LASER LEGS V17

1000 Gold
PREREQUISITE None

Press **Attack 2** to climb into the air, Hold **Attack 2** while in the air to drop down and shoot electric bolts at enemies.

Fire Tech Path

FOOT-MOUNTED FLAME

1500 Gold
PREREQUISITE
Fire Tech Path

Hold **Attack 2** to shoot flames from the feet, damaging any enemies that come too close.

BLUE FLAME

2000 Gold
PREREQUISITE
Purchase Foot-Mounted Flame ability

Flamethrower deals increased damage. Experimental feet fuel turns flames blue!

Electro Tech Path

PULSE CANNON

1500 Gold
PREREQUISITE
Electro Tech Path

Hold **Attack 2** to charge a laser blast, release to shoot a massive wave of energy at enemies.

ADVANCED PULSE CANNON

2000 Gold
PREREQUISITE
Purchase Pulse Cannon ability

Increase damage of pulse cannon. At least this one isn't experimental, right?

COUNTDOWN
"I'm the Bomb!"

LIGHTCORE

There are two steps to follow when you're playing as Countdown. Step one: fill the screen with things that explode. Step two: fill the screen with explosions. Countdown fires rockets that can explode, uses his head as a timebomb, and launches mobile bomb allies that chase down enemies and explode near them. Countdown's Soul Gem ability allows him to even detonate himself!

The Boom Buddies Forever Path improves the bomb allies by allowing more of them, and increasing their damage potential. The Rocketeer Path adds two rockets to Controlled Burst and increases the radius of its explosion.

Special Quest
Out With A Bang

DEFEAT 10 ENEMIES AT ONCE WITH YOUR SELF-DESTRUCT EXPLOSION ABILITY.

Complete this quest against a large group of Chompies (an Arena or Challenge Map works best) where you can gather them in a narrow space (down a hall or in a single-room building) so the enemies are forced to group up and are caught in the explosion.

Countdown was discovered by a group of Yetis who were snowboarding one particularly chilly morning when they came across a big bomb encased in ice. After bringing it back to their cabin, they were shocked when it actually came to life. No one, not even Countdown himself, has any memory of where he came from or how he ended up frozen in the mountains. Since Countdown became a Skylander, Master Eon has been graciously trying to help piece together fragments of his past. But this has proven difficult, as Countdown loses some of his memory every time he explodes, which happens a lot. In the meantime, Countdown has enjoyed working with Master Eon and fighting alongside the Skylanders to defend their world against evil—even though he occasionally forgets what he is doing.

LEVEL	1	2	3	4	5	6	7	8	9	10	11	12	13	14	15	16	17	18	19	20
♥ MAX HEATH	290	319	348	377	406	435	464	493	522	580	609	638	667	696	725	754	783	812	841	870

⚡ SPEED	🛡 ARMOR	⊕ CRITICAL HIT	◎ ELEMENTAL POWER
43	12	8	25

Basic Attacks

ROCKET BLAST

Press **Attack 1** to fire a rocket

BOMB HEAD

Press **Attack 2** to shoot a Bomb Head that explodes and damages enemies in a large area.

Ⓖ Soul Gem Ability
SELF-DESTRUCT

4000 Gold
PREREQUISITE
Find Countdown's Soul Gem in Cascade Glade

Hold **Attack 2** for a short amount of time to cause a massive amount of damage to every enemy nearby.

Upgrades

CONTROLLED BURST

500 Gold
PREREQUISITE None

Hold **Attack 1** to charge a rocket, release to shoot a large rocket that deals increased damage.

ROARING ROCKETS

700 Gold
PREREQUISITE None

Rockets do increased damage. Kaboom!

EXPLOSIVE FRIENDSHIP

900 Gold
PREREQUISITE None

Press **Attack 3** to summon a bomb ally that explodes near enemies.

HEFTY CONCUSSION

1200 Gold
PREREQUISITE None

Press **Attack 2** to shoot a more powerful Bomb Head that does increased damage. Press **Attack 2** again to detonate the Bomb Head.

Boom Buddies Forever Path

BOOM BUDDIES

1700 Gold
PREREQUISITE
Boom Buddies Forever Path

Press **Attack 3** to summon a bomb ally that explodes near enemies. Can now have four bomb allies at once.

BOMBING BLITZERS

2200 Gold
PREREQUISITE
Boom Buddies Forever Path

Bomb allies do increased damage. Adorable and explosive.

LINGERING SPARKS

3000 Gold
PREREQUISITE
Boom Buddies Forever Path

Bomb allies shoot flames from their fuses that damage nearby enemies.

Rocketeer Path

TRIPLE THREAT

1700 Gold
PREREQUISITE
Rocketeer Path

Hold **Attack 1** to charge a rocket, release to shoot a large rocket and two smaller rockets.

WARHEAD HANDS

2200 Gold
PREREQUISITE
Rocketeer Path

All rocket attacks do even more damage. Danger! Explosive hugs!

MEGA MORTAR

3000 Gold
PREREQUISITE
Rocketeer Path

Controlled Burst does increased damage in a larger area.

HEAVY DUTY SPROCKET
"The Fix is In!"

SERIES 2

Playing as Sprocket demands patience since Turret Gun-o-Matic, one of her primary abilities, requires a bit of set up time. When the ability is completely upgraded, Sprocket can set up one turret and drive around in another one as a tank! The good news is that she can buy time to set up turrets through the use of Wrench Whack, a good melee ability, and Bouncing Betty Mines.

Go with the Operator Path when mobility is needed. It provides more versatility with her Wrench. The Gearhead Path boosts her turret (and tank), which works best when enemies come at her, like during Survival Challenges.

Special Quest
Mined Your Step

DEFEAT 50 ENEMIES USING THE LANDMINE GOLF ATTACK.

After you acquire Landmine Golf and become proficient aiming it, you should complete this quest in no time. To complete it quickly, go to any challenge that uses Chompies as the primary enemy.

Sprocket was raised with all the privileges of a rich, proper Goldling, but she cared little for fancy things. Instead, she spent most of her time growing up in her uncle's workshop, learning how to build and fix his many mechanical inventions. But everything changed on the day her uncle mysteriously vanished. When she eventually discovered that Kaos had been behind his disappearance, she constructed a battle suit and went after him, leaving the luxury and comfort of her family's wealth behind. From that moment on, Sprocket was dedicated to fighting the forces of evil, while never losing hope that she would be reunited with her beloved uncle.

LEVEL	1	2	3	4	5	6	7	8	9	10	11	12	13	14	15	16	17	18	19	20
♥ MAX HEATH	240	264	288	312	336	360	384	408	432	480	504	528	552	576	600	624	648	672	696	720

⚡ SPEED	🛡 ARMOR	◎ CRITICAL HIT	◎ ELEMENTAL POWER
43	30	2	25

Basic Attacks

WRENCH WHACK

Press **Attack 1** to swing the big wrench. Press **Attack 1**, **Attack 1**, Hold **Attack 1** to perform a combo.

TURRET GUN-O-MATIC

Press **Attack 2** to build a turret that shoots enemies. Climb inside by facing the turret and pressing **Attack 2**. Press **Jump** to exit the turret.

Soul Gem Ability

LANDMINE GOLF

4000 Gold
PREREQUISITE
Purchase Bouncing Betty Mines ability

Facing a mine, press **Attack 1** to send it flying towards enemies.

Upgrades

AUTO TURRET V2

500 Gold
PREREQUISITE None

Turret Gun-o-Matic deals increased damage and has more HP.

BOUNCING BETTY MINES

700 Gold
PREREQUISITE None

Press **Attack 3** to toss mines that explode when enemies are near.

2 TIMES THE TURRETS

900 Gold
PREREQUISITE None

Can have two active turrets at once.

TANKS A LOT!

1200 Gold
PREREQUISITE
Purchase Auto Turret V2 ability

When climbing inside a turret, it transforms into a drivable assault tank.

Gearhead Path

MINE DROP

1700 Gold
PREREQUISITE
Gearhead Path

While driving a tank, press **Attack 3** to drop mines out of the back.

EXPLODING SHELLS

2200 Gold
PREREQUISITE
Gearhead Path

Turret and Tank shells now explode on contact, doing extra damage.

SELF-DESTRUCT SYSTEM

3000 Gold
PREREQUISITE
Gearhead Path

When a Turret or Tank expires, it detonates and damages anything nearby.

Operator Path

SPROCKET COMBOS

1700 Gold
PREREQUISITE
Operator Path

Press **Attack 1**, **Attack 1**, Hold **Attack 2** for Power Surge. Press **Attack 1**, **Attack 1**, Hold **Attack 3** for Mines O' Plenty.

MONKEY WRENCH

2200 Gold
PREREQUISITE
Operator Path

Better wrench does increased damage.

ALL MINES

3000 Gold
PREREQUISITE
Operator Path

Sprocket can now deploy three Bouncing Betty Mines at once.

Wow Pow!

TANKS FOR THE NEW TOY!

5000 Gold
PREREQUISITE
Purchase Tanks a Lot! ability

While driving a tank, hold **Attack 2** to fire a Tesla Cannon. Turrets and Tank do increased damage.

Tanks For the New Toy! is a beam attack you can sweep across the field. It doesn't do much damage to a single target, but is great against large number of enemies. The downside to Tanks for the New Toy is the amount of time needed to get it up and running. Building the tank takes some time, and each Tesla Cannon blast requires charging time before it is discharged.

BIG BANG TRIGGER HAPPY

"No Gold, no Glory!"

SERIES 3

Both of Trigger Happy's basic attacks are good options. Golden Pistols doesn't do much damage per shot, but has an excellent rate of fire. Trigger Happy also lobs objects at enemies, inflicting good damage when they make contact.

The Golden Frenzy Path powers up Golden Pistols in everyway. The hit harder, can be charged longer, and its bullets bounce off walls!The Golden Money Bags path is the way to go if you prefer dealing with enemies by throwing heavy objects at them. The objects damage multiple enemies and there's a nice game of chance that could result in deploying a mine.

Special Quest

Holding Gold

SAVE UP 50,000 GOLD.

Some quests require some patience. This quest demands a great deal of it! Use everything available (such as Legendary Treasures and the Sky Diamond figure) to help boost the amount of gold you can earn on each level.

Trigger Happy is more than his name—it's his solution to every problem. Nobody knows from where he came. He just showed up one day in a small village, saving it from a group of terrorizing bandits by blasting gold coins everywhere with his custom-crafted shooters. Similar tales were soon heard from other villages, and his legend quickly grew. Now everyone in all of Skylands knows of the crazy goldslinger that will take down any bad guy...usually without bothering to aim.

LEVEL	1	2	3	4	5	6	7	8	9	10	11	12	13	14	15	16	17	18	19	20
♥ MAX HEATH	200	220	240	260	280	300	320	340	360	400	420	440	460	480	500	520	540	560	580	600

⚡ SPEED	▼ ARMOR	⊕ CRITICAL HIT	◎ ELEMENTAL POWER
50	30	10	25

Basic Attacks

GOLDEN PISTOLS

Press **Attack 1** to shoot rapid fire coins out of both Golden Pistols.

LOB GOLDEN SAFE

Press **Attack 2** to lob golden safes at your enemies.

🜲 Soul Gem Ability
INFINITE AMMO

4000 Gold
PREREQUISITE
Purchase Golden Machine Gun ability

Golden Machine Gun has unlimited Ammo.

Upgrades

GOLDEN SUPER CHARGE

500 Gold
PREREQUISITE None

Hold **Attack 1** to charge up your Golden Pistols, then release to fire a bullet that does extra damage.

POT O'GOLD

700 Gold
PREREQUISITE None

Throw a Pot of Gold, which deals increased damage.

GOLDEN MEGA CHARGE

900 Gold
PREREQUISITE
Purchase Super Charge abitlity

Charge up your Golden Pistols longer to do even MORE damage.

GOLDEN MACHINE GUN

1200 Gold
PREREQUISITE None

Hold **Attack 3** to activate Golden Machine Gun and swivel its aim using the left control stick.

Golden Frenzy Path

HAPPINESS IS A GOLDEN GUN

1700 Gold
PREREQUISITE
Golden Frenzy Path

Golden Pistols deal increased damage.

BOUNCING BULLETS

2200 Gold
PREREQUISITE
Golden Frenzy Path

Golden Pistols' bullets bounce off walls.

GOLDEN YAMATO BLAST

3000 Gold
PREREQUISITE
Purchase Happiness is a Golden Gun

Charge up your Golden Pistols even longer to do maximum damage.

Golden Money Bags Path

JUST THROWING MONEY AWAY

1700 Gold
PREREQUISITE
Golden Money Bags Path

Lob attack has longer range.

COINSPLOSION

2200 Gold
PREREQUISITE
Golden Money Bags Path

Lob attacks explode in a shower of damaging coins.

HEADS OR TAILS

3000 Gold
PREREQUISITE
Golden Money Bags Path

Toss a giant coin that deals extra damage. If it lands on heads, it turns into a mine, damaging enemies that touch it.

Wow Pow!

ROCKET RIDE!

5000 Gold
PREREQUISITE
Purchase Golden Super Charge ability

While holding **Attack 1**, press and hold **Attack 2** to charge up a golden rocket, then release to ride it as a missile.

You can't move while holding Attack 2, only change which way Trigger Happy faces. Rocket Ride! takes a few seconds to charge, and it automatically fires when it's ready. Let go of Attack 2 to jump off, although the resulting explosion does not damage Trigger Happy.

WIND-UP

"All Wound Up!"

Even experienced players may need time to feel comfortable overcranking Wind-Up and using overcranked time effectively. The increased speed and damage dealt while overcranked is offset by the time it takes to build it back up. Wind-Up is capable of demolishing enemies in a hurry, but may end up being easy pickings if the overcrank timer expires at a bad time.

The Toy Box Path is a cautious approach to Wind-Up, with a ranged attack boost, but that's only because the Winder Path includes an ability that requires taking damage. Wind-Up needs to be in the thick of fights to get the most out of it!

Special Quest

All Wound Up

DEAL A TOTAL OF 2500 DAMAGE WHILE OVERCRANKED.

As long as you remember that the Attack 2 button exists, you should complete this quest quickly. Buy a few basic upgrades to make it go even faster.

Built in the enchanted workshop of a toymaker obsessed with time, Wind-Up was created to help keep his massive collection of complicated clocks working perfectly. But when the toymaker popped out of existence in a freak accident caused by putting hot cocoa in a cross-wired Arkeyan oven, Wind-Up found himself surrounded by an invading Cyclops platoon—with an eye towards claiming the toymaker's secrets for themselves. Using split-second timing, clockwork strategy, and his totally wound up energy, Wind-Up bravely sprang into action and handily defeated the Cyclops. He later joined the Skylanders to help swing the pendulum the other way in their fight against anything that threatens Skylands.

LEVEL	1	2	3	4	5	6	7	8	9	10	11	12	13	14	15	16	17	18	19	20
♥ MAX HEATH	250	275	300	325	350	375	400	425	450	500	525	550	575	600	625	650	675	700	725	750

⚡ SPEED	🛡 ARMOR	⊕ CRITICAL HIT	◎ ELEMENTAL POWER
43	12	4	25

Basic Attacks

SHORT CIRCUIT

Press **Attack 1** to attack nearby enemies with sparking claws.

WIND UP!

Press **Attack 2** to wind up and damage nearby enemies. Winding up is needed to perform more powerful attacks.

Ⓖ Soul Gem Ability
SPRING-LOADED CRANK

4000 Gold
PREREQUISITE
Find Wind-Up's Soul Gem in Iron Jaw Gulch

Speed is increased. Automatically wind up while running.

Upgrades

OVERCRANK STABILIZER

500 Gold
PREREQUISITE None

Press **Attack 2** to rapidly fill the wind up meter. When full, press **Attack 2** again to overcrank. During overcrank press **Attack 1** to cause a large explosion that damages nearby enemies.

WINDING WEAPON
700 Gold
PREREQUISITE None

Press **Attack 2** to wind up, dealing increased damage and pulling enemies in.

SPRING SHOT

900 Gold
PREREQUISITE None

Press **Attack 3** to shoot a spring shot that launches enemies into the air. Attacking launched enemies will deal automatic critical damage!

POWER PISTONS

1200 Gold
PREREQUISITE None

Press **Attack 1** to deal increased punching damage.

Toy Box Path

CYMBALS

1700 Gold
PREREQUISITE
Toy Box Path

Hold **Attack 1** to charge a cymbal attack, release to attack all enemies in the way with a pair of cymbals.

CRASH CYMBALS

2200 Gold
PREREQUISITE
Purchase Cymbals ability

Cymbal attacks do increased damage. An easy way to crash any party!

TOY GUN

3000 Gold
PREREQUISITE
Toy Box Path

Hold **Attack 3** to shoot rapid fire suction cup projectiles at enemies.

Winder Path

WINDUP PUNCH
1700 Gold
PREREQUISITE
Winder Path

Hold **Attack 1** to charge a boxing glove punch, release to deliver a massive punch to enemies.

AUTO WIND UP
2200 Gold
PREREQUISITE
Winder Path

Taking damage automatically adds to winding up.

POWER CRANK
3000 Gold
PREREQUISITE
Winder Path

Press **Attack 2** rapidly to begin overcranking which now pulls enemies in and deals bonus damage.

GRILLA DRILLA

"If There's a Drill, There's a Way!"

I n the distant jungles of what was once the sprawling subterranean city of the Drilla Empire, Grilla Drilla served among the guards for the Drilla King. Every seven years, the king would select the bravest and strongest guard to become their leader. It was during the last selection ceremony that a troll mining operation broke through the ground above them and quickly snatched the king, wanting to know the location of the famed Drilla Diamond. Having never ventured above ground, Grilla Drilla risked everything to defeat the trolls and rescue the Drilla King. In return for his bravery, Grilla was selected as the new leader. But he instead decided to join the Skylanders, where he could protect even more residents of Skylands.

SWAP FORCE

Punchy Monkey hits multiple enemies in a straight line at the cost of a longer delay between swings. The Drilling Punches Path turns every third consecutive button press into a two-fisted punch. Monkeys summoned with Monkey Call pick their own targets and depart quickly. The Monkey Master Path doubles the number of summoned monkeys.

After purchasing every basic upgrade for Planted Turret, you can plant either a regular turret or a bomb plant depending on the situation. The Coconut Caretaker Path gives Planted Turret explosive shells that damage enemies in an area. The Banana Blaster Path increases the rate of fire for Planted Turrets.

Special Quest

Monkeys Mean Business

DEAL A TOTAL OF 2000 DAMAGE TO ENEMIES WITH SUMMONED MONKEYS.

There's rarely a bad time to summon monkeys to help you take down enemies. Choosing the Monkey Master Path helps, but you'll get this quest quickly enough without it.

Body Soul Gem Ability	Legs Soul Gem Ability
RING OF THE GOLDEN MONKEY 	**ADAPTIVE NATURE** 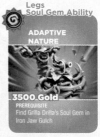
3500 Gold	**3500 Gold**
PREREQUISITE Find Grilla Drilla's Soul Gem in Iron Jaw Gulch; Purchase Silverback ability	PREREQUISITE Find Grilla Drilla's Soul Gem in Iron Jaw Gulch
Arm Drills become shiny Gold, making punch attacks do extra damage.	All plants gain thorns that damage and push back enemies that step on them.

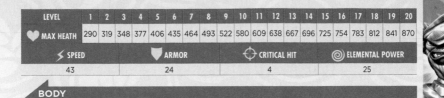

LEVEL	1	2	3	4	5	6	7	8	9	10	11	12	13	14	15	16	17	18	19	20
❤️ MAX HEATH	290	319	348	377	406	435	464	493	522	580	609	638	667	696	725	754	783	812	841	870

⚡ SPEED	🛡️ ARMOR	✛ CRITICAL HIT	◎ ELEMENTAL POWER
43	24	4	25

BODY

Basic Attacks
PUNCHY MONKEY

Press **Attack 1** to punch at nearby enemies.

Upgrades

MONKEY CALL

300 Gold
PREREQUISITE None

Press **Attack 3** to summon a pair of crazy monkeys!

SILVERBACK

800 Gold
PREREQUISITE None

Press **Attack 1** to unleash punches that deal increased damage.

REACHING MANDRILL

1000 Gold
PREREQUISITE None

Press **Attack 1** to punch at a longer range.

Monkey Master Path

TEAM MONKEY

1500 Gold
PREREQUISITE
Monkey Master Path

Monkey Call summons four monkeys at once!

KING OF THE JUNGLE

2000 Gold
PREREQUISITE
Monkey Master Path

Monkey Call does increased damage. They're going bananas!

Drilling Punches Path

DOUBLE PUNCH

1500 Gold
PREREQUISITE
Drilling Punches Path

Press **Attack 1** three times to attack with both drills.

PRIMATE POWER

2000 Gold
PREREQUISITE
Purchase Double Punch Ability

Double Punch does increased damage. POW!

LEGS

Basic Attacks
PLANTED TURRET

Press **Attack 2** to plant a coconut turret that attacks nearby enemies.

Upgrades

EXPLOSIVE GROWTH

300 Gold
PREREQUISITE None

Hold **Attack 2** to charge a turret, release to plant a bomb plant that explodes and damages enemies nearby.

SPREADING LIKE WEEDS

800 Gold
PREREQUISITE
Purchase Explosive Growth abilityExplosive Growth ability

Explosive Growth bomb plants will explode into three smaller bombs.

NATURE'S BOUNTY

1000 Gold
PREREQUISITE None

Press **Attack 2** to plant a coconut turret that shoots at nearby enemies. Press **Attack 2** again to plant another.

Coconut Caretaker Path

THIS IS COCONUTS!

1500 Gold
PREREQUISITE
Coconut Caretaker Path

Turret projectiles now explode, causing damage to enemies in a small area.

COCONUT MAYHEM

2000 Gold
PREREQUISITE
Coconut Caretaker Path

Coconuts do increased damage. Go nuts for the new and improved Coconut Blaster!

Banana Blaster Path

BANANA SPLIT

1500 Gold
PREREQUISITE
Banana Blaster Path

Coconut turret upgrades into a rapid shooting Banana turret.

GO BANANAS!

2000 Gold
PREREQUISITE
Purchase Banana Split ability

Bananas do increased damage. Delicious!

STINK BOMB

"Clear the Air!"

Stink Bomb studied martial arts under one of the greatest ninja masters in history who believed that surprise was the key to finding your true self. Thus, his master would constantly jump out and frighten him, hoping that it would scare Stink Bomb into finding his innermost strength. On one such occasion, Stink Bomb was so surprised that he instinctively released a cloud of vapor so pungent that it caused his master to disappear and never return. With this newly discovered ability, Stink Bomb developed his own form of martial arts known as Kung Fume, and wandered the land teaching it to all those who wished to learn. It was not long before the news (and smell) of this new form reached Master Eon, who sought out the young ninja at once.

Skunk-Fu Stars begins as a rapid-fire, but weak, ranged attack. The Sweeping Skunk-Fu upgrade is a charged attack that hits much harder. If you choose The Art of Skunk-Fu Path, always keep its shield active. The Art of Acorns Path adds a two-fisted ranged attack to the One-Inch Palm ability.

Skunk Cloud makes Stink Bomb invisible to enemies and upgrades boost its damaging properties. Choosing the Skunk Cloud Controller Path allows Stink Bomb to leave two damaging clouds while going into stealth. The Sneaky Tricks Path upgrades leave damaging items in Bomb's path.

Special Quest

What's That Smell?

NAUSEATE ENEMIES 50 TIMES WITH YOUR ONE-INCH PALM.

Target 50 enemies that can withstand the initial blow of One-Inch Palm for this quest. Enemies that are taken out with the initial punch aren't nauseated (they're defeated!) so they won't count.

Body Soul Gem Ability

MASTER-STAR TECHNIQUE

3500 Gold

PREREQUISITE
Find Stink Bomb's Soul Gem in Winter Keep

Press **Attack 1** to throw Master Stars that have a higher chance to critically hit!

Legs Soul Gem Ability

STEALTH SKUNK

3500 Gold

PREREQUISITE
Find Stink Bomb's Soul Gem in Winter Keep

Remain invisible even after attacking enemies.

LEVEL	1	2	3	4	5	6	7	8	9	10	11	12	13	14	15	16	17	18	19	20
♥ MAX HEATH	270	297	324	351	378	405	432	459	486	540	567	594	621	648	675	702	729	756	783	810

⚡ SPEED	🛡 ARMOR	⊕ CRITICAL HIT	◎ ELEMENTAL POWER
43	12	6	25

BODY

Basic Attacks
SKUNK-FU STARS

Press **Attack 1** to throw small stars that can damage enemies at long range.

Upgrades

ONE-INCH PALM

300 Gold
PREREQUISITE None

Press **Attack 3** to deliver a powerful palm attack that knocks away enemies.

NOXIOUS NINJA

800 Gold
PREREQUISITE None

Press **Attack 1** to throw Skunk-Fu Stars that do increased damage.

SWEEPING SKUNK-FU

1000 Gold
PREREQUISITE None

Hold **Attack 1** to charge handfuls of Skunk-Fu Stars, release to damage enemies in all directions.

The Art of Skunk-Fu Path

SKUNK-FU SHIELD

1500 Gold
PREREQUISITE
The Art of Skunk-Fu Path

Sweeping Skunk-Fu creates a whirling shield that damages nearby enemies.

SKUNK-FU MASTER

2000 Gold
PREREQUISITE
The Art of Skunk-Fu Path

Skunk-Fu Shield does increased damage.

The Art of Acorns Path

ACORN ACCURACY

1500 Gold
PREREQUISITE
The Art of Acorns Path

Hold **Attack 3** to charge a powerful poisoned acorn, release to shoot it at enemies.

SKUNK EYE

2000 Gold
PREREQUISITE
Purchase Acorn Accuracy ability

An ancient aiming technique makes acorn attacks do increased damage.

LEGS

Basic Attacks
SKUNK CLOUD

Press **Attack 2** to go invisible and damage enemies with a large obscuring cloud.

Upgrades

HIDDEN TAIL

300 Gold
PREREQUISITE None

Press **Attack 2** while invisible to perform a tail attack that does a large amount of damage to enemies.

SPORTING STRIPES

800 Gold
PREREQUISITE None

Speed is increased. The sport edition is always faster.

SKUNKING AROUND

1000 Gold
PREREQUISITE None

Press **Attack 2** to go invisible and leave a skunk cloud on the ground that damages enemies.

Skunk Cloud Controller Path

ROLLING FOG

1500 Gold
PREREQUISITE
Skunk Cloud Controller Path

Up to two skunk clouds can be active at one time.

CLOUDY CONCOCTION

2000 Gold
PREREQUISITE
Skunk Cloud Controller Path

Skunk cloud does increased damage. What a funky skunk!

Sneaky Tricks Path

SNEAKY TACTICS

1500 Gold
PREREQUISITE
Sneaky Tricks Path

Move forward slowly to cause pointy objects to be left behind that slow and damage enemies.

PAIN IN THE FOOT

2000 Gold
PREREQUISITE
Purchase Sneaky Tactics ability

Sneaky Tactics does increased damage. Tough acting sneaking action!

BUMBLE BLAST
"The Perfect Swarm!"

LIGHTCORE

The honey or the bees? That's the question for Bumble Blast's enemies since they're about to be hit by one or the other, and often both. Bumble Blast is terrific in single target fights, and improves in battles involving larger number of enemies with just a few upgrades.

The Bee Keeper Path improves Bumble Blast's damage output and gives him an option to knock back enemies with a charge up Beezooka shot. The Honey Tree Path is more about control and survival. Bumble Blast gains additional armor, and enemies covered by honey suffer from reduced movement.

Special Quest

Not the Bees!

HIT HONEY-COATED ENEMIES WITH BEES 125 TIMES.

Simply remember to alternate between Bumble Blast's two basic attacks and you should complete this quest quickly. Obtaining Bumble Blast's Soul Gem ability gets you there even faster.

Bumble Blast started life as a humble beehive in the Radiant Mountains, where for ages the bees made the sweetest, most magical honey in all of Skylands. When Kaos heard about this "super honey," he wanted it all for himself and soon launched an attack on the peaceful bees. But when his minions arrived to plunder everything the bees had created, they were met by Bumble Blast. He alone had been home to the bees and considered himself their protector. Using the power of the magic honey, Bumble Blast valiantly battled the evil minions, who felt his powerful sting that day. Afterward, Bumble Blast roamed Skylands as a protector of nature, where he soon joined with the Skylanders.

LEVEL	1	2	3	4	5	6	7	8	9	10	11	12	13	14	15	16	17	18	19	20
♥ MAX HEATH	320	352	384	416	448	480	512	544	576	640	672	704	736	768	800	832	864	896	928	960

⚡ SPEED	🛡 ARMOR	✛ CRITICAL HIT	◎ ELEMENTAL POWER
35	24	4	25

Basic Attacks

BEEZOOKA

Press **Attack 1** to shoot honey homing bees at enemies.

HONEY GLOB

Press **Attack 2** to shoot a big ball of honey that will coat enemies in honey when hit.

Soul Gem Ability

BEE-PACK BACKPACK

4000 Gold

PREREQUISITE
Find Bumble Blast's Soul Gem in Mudwater Hollow

Gain a beehive backpack that automatically launches bees at nearby foes.

Upgrades

HONEY BEECON

500 Gold

PREREQUISITE None

Bees will always target and attack enemies coated in honey.

HUNGRY BEES

700 Gold

PREREQUISITE None

Bees deal increased damage against honeyed targets.

HIVE MIND

900 Gold

PREREQUISITE None

Press **Attack 3** to shoot a beehive into the ground. The hive explodes into honey when an enemy approaches it.

PAINFUL STINGS

1200 Gold

PREREQUISITE None

Bees gain more powerful stingers, increasing their damage!

Bee Keeper Path

BEE ARMADA

1700 Gold

PREREQUISITE
Bee Keeper Path

Hold **Attack 1** to charge the Beezooka, release to shoot three bees at once.

STIRRED UP A NEST

2200 Gold

PREREQUISITE
Bee Keeper Path

A new Beezooka now shoots even more bees that do increased damage!

QUEEN BEE

3000 Gold

PREREQUISITE
Purchase Bee Armada ability

Hold **Attack 1** and charge the Beezooka even longer, release to shoot a Queen Bee that knocks enemies into the air.

Honey Tree Path

HONEY BUZZ BLAST

1700 Gold

PREREQUISITE
Honey Tree Path

Hold **Attack 2** to charge a honey attack, release to shoot a honey glob that contains angry bees.

HEAVY HONEY

2200 Gold

PREREQUISITE
Honey Tree Path

Honey attacks deal increased damage and slow enemies.

HONEYCOMB BARK

3000 Gold

PREREQUISITE
Honey Tree Path

Armor is increased. Bark skin will sometimes drip out honey that coats enemy attackers.

BUMBLE BLAST

THORN HORN CAMO
"Fruit punch!"

Hatched at the roots of the Tree of Life, Camo is half dragon and half plant—with effervescent life energy flowing through his scaly leaves. This power allows him to cultivate fruits and vegetables at a highly-accelerated rate, which causes them to explode when they ripen. Camo's unique gift caught the eye of Master Eon, initially because he was hungry and tried to eat a melon that exploded in his face. But upon realizing Camo's true power, Eon convinced him to help the Skylanders protect their world.

SERIES 2

Sun Blast begins as a strong ranged attack, and upgrades to a convneniently portable healing ability. Set up Orbiting Sun Shield whenver you have the chance. The globes that heal Camo also hurt the enemies they touch. Firecracker Vines improves quite a bit with upgrades, but remains unpredictable and hard to control. Melon Fountain takes on added importance in *SWAP Force* since it ties into Camo's Wow Pow! ability.

The Vine Virtuoso Path makes Firecracker Vines more powerful and numerous, but doesn't provide any additional control. The Melon Master Path is a strong choice, particularly after you purchase the Explosive Harvest ability.

Special Quest
Garden Gorger

EAT 10 WATERMELONS.

Watch for Watermelons throughout the Story Levels. If you aren't using Camo and you see a watermelon drop, switch to him to grab it. Bonus Mission Map Undercover Greebles is a good place to hunt for watermelons.

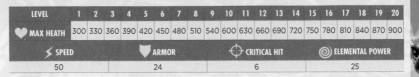

LEVEL	1	2	3	4	5	6	7	8	9	10	11	12	13	14	15	16	17	18	19	20
♥ MAX HEATH	300	330	360	390	420	450	480	510	540	600	630	660	690	720	750	780	810	840	870	900

⚡ SPEED	🛡 ARMOR	🎯 CRITICAL HIT	◎ ELEMENTAL POWER
50	24	6	25

Basic Attacks

SUN BLAST

Press **Attack 1** to blast enemies with concentrated life energy.

FIRECRACKER VINES

Press **Attack 2** to conjure up a fast-growing vine of explosive melons.

Soul Gem Ability
ORBITING SUN SHIELD

4000 Gold
PREREQUISITE
None

Hold **Attack 1** to create a Sun Blast Shield. Create three shields to gain a healing effect.

Upgrades

SEARING SUN BLAST

500 Gold
PREREQUISITE None

Sun Blast does vincreased damage.

MELON FOUNTAIN

700 Gold
PREREQUISITE None

Press **Attack 3** to send melons flying everywhere.

FIRECRACKER FOOD

900 Gold
PREREQUISITE None

Firecracker Vines do increased damage.

VIGOROUS VINES

1200 Gold
PREREQUISITE None

Firecracker Vines move quicker and farther.

Vine Virtuoso Path

MARTIAL BOUNTY

1700 Gold
PREREQUISITE
Vine Virtuoso Path

Firecracker Vines create more explosive melons.

PEPPERS OF POTENCY

2200 Gold
PREREQUISITE
Vine Virtuoso Path

Firecracker Vines do even MORE increased damage.

PROLIFERATION

3000 Gold
PREREQUISITE
Vine Virtuoso Path

Create two Firecracker Vines at once.

Melon Master Path

RING OF MIGHT

1700 Gold
PREREQUISITE
Melon Master Path

The Melon Fountain blasts out more melons.

MELON GMO

2200 Gold
PREREQUISITE
Melon Master Path

The Melon Fountain does increased damage.

MELON FORTRESS

3000 Gold
PREREQUISITE
Melon Master Path

Hold **Attack 3** to hide in the Melon Fountain and release the button to send the melons flying.

Wow Pow!

EXPLOSIVE HARVEST

5000 Gold
PREREQUISITE
None

Any melons can turn into explosive SUPERMELONS and launch at enemies.

If nothing else sways your Upgrade Path choice, then consider how much Explosive Harvest benefits all the upgrades found in the Melon Master Path and then think about how many SUPERMELONS you would be missing out on. Go Melon Master Path!

NINJA STEALTH ELF
"Silent but deadly!"

As a small child, Stealth Elf awoke one morning inside the hollow of an old tree with no memory of how she got there. She was taken in by an unusually stealthy, ninja-like forest creature in the deep forest. Under his tutelage, she has spent the majority of her life training in the art of stealth fighting. After completing her training, she became a Skylander and set out into the world to uncover the mystery behind her origins.

SERIES 3

As sneaky as she is deadly, Stealth Elf is a melee dynamo who can slip out of dangerous situations. She doesn't have a ranged attack, but she is able to reach enemies quickly when it's necessary. Stealth is far more effective against computer enemies than human opponents, but you should use it to buy time and to heal once Sylvan Regeneration is purchased.

The Pook Blade Saint Path adds combos and extra damage to Stealth Elf's bread-and-butter knife attacks. The Forest Ninja Path is a great way to take down enemies while staying relatively safe. Let the scarecrows (and a tiger) do the work.

Special Quest
Stealth Health

GAIN 1000 HP WHILE STEALTHED.
Stealth Elf must gain health for it to count for this quest. Healing done at full health does not count.

LEVEL	1	2	3	4	5	6	7	8	9	10	11	12	13	14	15	16	17	18	19	20
♥ MAX HEATH	270	297	324	351	378	405	432	459	486	540	567	594	621	648	675	702	729	756	783	810

⚡ SPEED	🛡 ARMOR	✛ CRITICAL HIT	◎ ELEMENTAL POWER
50	12	10	25

Basic Attacks

BLADE SLASH

Press **Attack 1** to slice Stealth Elf's enemies up with a pair of sharp blades. Press **Attack 1**, **Attack 1**, Hold **Attack 1** to perform a special combo.

STEALTHIER DECOY

Press **Attack 2** to have Stealth Elf disappear completely but leave behind a decoy image that enemies are drawn to.

Soul Gem Ability

SYLVAN REGENERATION

4000 Gold
PREREQUISITE
None

Regenerate health over time.

Upgrades

STRAW POOK SCARECROW

500 Gold
PREREQUISITE None

A Scarecrow appears in place of your decoy and distracts enemies.

DRAGONFANG DAGGER

700 Gold
PREREQUISITE None

Blade attacks deal increased damage.

STURDY SCARECROW

900 Gold
PREREQUISITE
Purchase Straw Pook Scarecrow abitlity

Scarecrows last longer and are more resistant

ARBOREAL ACROBATICS

1200 Gold
PREREQUISITE None

Press **Attack 3** to perform a quick acrobatic move. Hold **Attack 3** and flip in any direction using the left control stick.

Pook Blade Saint Path

ELF JITSU

1700 Gold
PREREQUISITE
Pook Blade Saint Path

Press **Attack 1**, **Attack 1**, Hold **Attack 2** for Poison Spores. Press **Attack 1**, **Attack 1**, Hold **Attack 3** for Blade Fury.

ELVEN SUNBLADE

2200 Gold
PREREQUISITE
Pook Blade Saint Path

Blade attacks deal even MORE increased damage.

SHADOWSBANE BLADE DANCE

3000 Gold
PREREQUISITE
Pook Blade Saint Path

Magical Blades fight alongside you.

Forest Ninja Path

SCARE-CRIO TRIO

1700 Gold
PREREQUISITE
Forest Ninja Path

Three Scarecrows are created in place of your decoy.

SCARECROW BOOBY TRAP

2200 Gold
PREREQUISITE
Forest Ninja Path

Scarecrows explode and damage enemies.

SCARECROW SPIN SLICER

3000 Gold
PREREQUISITE
Forest Ninja Path

Scarecrows have axes and do extra damage.

Wow Pow!

SURPRISE, TIGER!

5000 Gold
PREREQUISITE
None

While invisible, press **Attack 3** to summon a powerful tiger ally. Also unlocks Ninja costume!

The summoned tiger attacks in the same direction as Stealth Elf's eyes face. It does a nice bit of damage and knocks down the enemies it hits. The best part about this upgrade is Stealth Elf's awesome new look.

ZOO LOU

"Nature Calls!"

It would be tough to call Zoo Lou's abilities attacks since he never damages enemies directly. He instead summons jade-powered animals to take care of that for him. Wolf Call is a no-brainer. If you don't see a green wolf, summon one now! Bird Call benefits the most from upgrades, so spend your Gold there first.

The Bucking Boar Path is better against groups of enemies since it includes better armor and an attack that hits multiple targets. The Wild Wolf Path edges it out because Bird Call upgrades also help out against groups and you get extra food as a bonus.

Special Quest

Professional Boar Rider

HIT AN ENEMY WITH THE BOAR DURING 20 FULL-LENGTH BOAR RIDES.

First, you need to buy the Piggyback Ride upgrade. Each time you use the ability, hit an enemy and let the ability run its course without canceling it to get credit toward this quest.

Descended from a long line of shamans, Zoo Lou traveled far and wide to the Seven Strange Strongholds—ancient, mysterious sites of great wonder in Skylands—where he studied the wisdom and fighting styles of the Seven Strange Mages. After many years of traveling and studying, Zoo Lou returned to find an army of trolls had invaded his sacred homeland to mine its natural magic resources. Zoo Lou's warrior heart burned with fury. And having now mastered the enchanted art of communicating with nature and summoning animals, he unleashed his great mojo—attacking the trolls and single handedly freeing his lands once again. It was this heroic feat that caught the eye of Double Trouble, who then brought Zoo Lou to Master Eon and the Skylanders.

LEVEL	1	2	3	4	5	6	7	8	9	10	11	12	13	14	15	16	17	18	19	20
❤ MAX HEALTH	290	319	348	377	406	435	464	493	522	580	609	638	667	696	725	754	783	812	841	870

⚡ SPEED	🛡 ARMOR	🎯 CRITICAL HIT	◎ ELEMENTAL POWER
43	18	6	25

Basic Attacks

BIRD CALL

Press **Attack 1** to summon birds that will attack nearby enemies.

WOLF CALL

Press **Attack 2** to summon a helpful wolf ally.

⚑ Soul Gem Ability
BIRDS OF PREY

4000 Gold
PREREQUISITE
Find Zoo Lou's Soul Gem in Mudwater Hollow

Hold **Attack 1** to summon up to five birds, release to have them all swoop in on enemies, doing a devastating amount of damage.

Upgrades

PIGGYBACK RIDE

500 Gold
PREREQUISITE None

Press **Attack 3** to ride around on a wild boar, dealing damage to all nearby enemies. There is a short wait before this ability can be used again.

RAGING BOAR

700 Gold
PREREQUISITE
Purchase Piggyback Ride ability

Boar does increased damage. Riding a raging boar doesn't seem safe... for enemies!

SWOOP RE-LOOP

900 Gold
PREREQUISITE None

Press **Attack 1** to shoot spirit birds that seek out enemies and attack them twice before flying away.

BETTER BEAKS

1200 Gold
PREREQUISITE None

Bird attacks do increased damage. Caw caw caw!

The Bucking Boar Path

ROUGH RIDER

1700 Gold
PREREQUISITE
The Bucking Boar Path

Press **Attack 3** to ride around on a wild boar that kicks up damaging dust and rocks at nearby enemies.

THICKER PIGSKIN

2200 Gold
PREREQUISITE
The Bucking Boar Path

Armor is increased. Thicker skin reduces damage taken from attacks and insults.

HOG WILD

3000 Gold
PREREQUISITE
The Bucking Boar Path

Press **Attack 3** to ride around on a wild boar. After you jump off, the boar continues to trample nearby enemies for a short time.

The Wild Wolf Path

ALPHA WOLF

1700 Gold
PREREQUISITE
The Wild Wolf Path

Press **Attack 2** to summon a more powerful wolf ally that does increased damage and has more health.

HUNGER OF THE WOLF

2200 Gold
PREREQUISITE
The Wild Wolf Path

Each time the wolf attacks it gains increased attack speed.

HUNTER AND GATHERER

3000 Gold
PREREQUISITE
The Wild Wolf Path

The wolf will dig up food when health is low. Such a good little spirit!

ZOO LOU

DOOM STONE
"Another Smash Hit!"

Doom Stone was carved from the strongest and purest stone in Skylands, then magically brought to life by a wizard who was rather lazy and wanted someone strong to carry heavy things and perform other tasks around his castle. Doom Stone happily helped, and in his spare time learned the ancient ways of Stone Fighting should he ever need to protect the wizard, who became like a father to him. Sure enough the need arose when the wizard was kidnapped by his evil twin brother in order to steal his spells for himself. Doom Stone wasted no time in using the skills he learned to save his master. Afterward, the wizard knew Doom Stone had a greater calling and introduced him to Master Eon, who made him a Skylander.

Column Club is a heavy and slow melee attack that can be upgraded into a charged attack. The Column Clubber Path extends the range and damage of these attacks. Living Statue is an amazing defensive ability, blocking attacks and freezing attackers. The Jaded Fighter Path turns the frozen attackers into weapons!

Stoney Spin gains power with each button press (up to a certain point), and upgrades add to its damage and Doom Stone's speed while spinning. The Serious Spinner Path upgrades knock enemies around while spinning. The Carved Belt Path adds jade projectiles with each press of Attack 2 that results in a spin.

Special Quest
Stop Hitting Yourself

DEFEAT 50 CHOMPIES JUST BY BLOCKING.

Chompies aren't known for their self-preservation instincts, so completing this quest is a matter of buying the Living Statue upgrade and waiting for 50 Chompies to throw themselves on Doom Stone's shield.

Body Soul Gem Ability	Legs Soul Gem Ability
STONEY STARE	**SPIN THE TABLES**

3500 Gold
PREREQUISITE
Find Doom Stone's Soul Gem in Kaos' Fortress

3500 Gold
PREREQUISITE
Find Doom Stone's Soul Gem in Kaos' Fortress

Hold **Attack 3** to block and cause enchanted snakes to come alive on the shield, damaging enemies while you block.

During the fourth spin, enemies in a large radius are damaged.

LEVEL	1	2	3	4	5	6	7	8	9	10	11	12	13	14	15	16	17	18	19	20
♥ MAX HEATH	280	308	336	364	392	420	448	476	504	560	588	616	644	672	700	728	756	784	812	840

⚡ SPEED	🛡 ARMOR	✛ CRITICAL HIT	◎ ELEMENTAL POWER
35	30	6	25

BODY

Basic Attacks
COLUMN CLUB

Press **Attack 1** to swing a heavy column at nearby enemies.

Upgrades

LIVING STATUE

300 Gold
PREREQUISITE None

Hold **Attack 3** to block close attacks. Blocking attacks will cause nearby attackers to turn to jade for a short time.

REJECT AND REFLECT

800 Gold
PREREQUISITE None

Hold **Attack 3** to block projectile attacks. Blocked projectiles are hit back at enemies, turning them into jade.

COLUMN DUTY

1000 Gold
PREREQUISITE None

Hold **Attack 1** to charge the Column Club, release to cause a large area of damage. Causes more damage the longer **Attack 1** is held.

Column Clubber Path

FALLING TO PIECES

1500 Gold
PREREQUISITE
Column Clubber Path

Hold **Attack 1** to charge Column Duty, release to smash the column and break off smaller pieces of it that damage enemies in a larger area.

CLUB DOOM

2000 Gold
PREREQUISITE
Column Clubber Path

Column Duty can be charged even longer, dealing more damage in a larger area.

Jaded Fighter Path

CRACKING UP

1500 Gold
PREREQUISITE
Jaded Fighter Path

Enemies turned to jade will burst, causing small shards to damage other enemies near them.

MORE DORIC WARFARE

2000 Gold
PREREQUISITE
Jaded Fighter Path

Hold **Attack 3** to block attacks and do even more damage to blocked attackers.

LEGS

Basic Attacks
STONEY SPIN

Press **Attack 2** to rapidly attack nearby enemies and charge the stoney belt. The belt increases damage and size the more it is charged.

Upgrades

SPIN RIGHT AROUND

300 Gold
PREREQUISITE None

Hold **Attack 2** to charge a spin, release to bounce between nearby enemies.

REVOLUTIONARY BELT

800 Gold
PREREQUISITE None

Spinning does increased damage.

SPEEDY SPINNER

1000 Gold
PREREQUISITE None

Press **Attack 2** to increase the speed that the belt is spinning. Speed is increased depending on how fast the belt is spinning.

Serious Spinner Path

THE HARDER THEY FALL

1500 Gold
PREREQUISITE
Serious Spinner Path

Hold **Attack 2** to charge a spin, release to bounce between enemies and knock the last enemy hit into the air which damages them when they hit the ground.

SPINBALL KING

2000 Gold
PREREQUISITE
Serious Spinner Path

Spin Right Around does increased damage. King of the Spinball wizards!

Carved Belt Path

JADED SPIN

1500 Gold
PREREQUISITE
Carved Belt Path

Now shoot jade projectiles at enemies when spinning.

BELT PELTERS

2000 Gold
PREREQUISITE
Purchase Jaded Spin ability

Press **Attack 2** to spin and shoot powerful jade projectiles at enemies that do increased damage.

RUBBLE ROUSER

"Brace For Impact!"

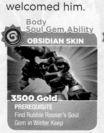

Hammer Swing hits hard, sweeping through nearby enemies, but is slow. The Drill Pitcher Path adds a combo that ends with a thrown hammer. Tools of the Trade is a hopping, overhead attack that crushes anything in front of Rubble Rouser. The Excavator Path upgrades Tools of the Trade to shower the area with bits of rubble that damage nearby enemies.

Deep Dig is an underground quick move with a great upgrade in Minor Miners. The Bolder Boulders Path flings damaging boulders while charging Deep Dig (meaning Rubble Rouser can't be hurt, it's free damage). The Miner Foreman Path doubles the number of Minor Miners and makes them stronger.

Special Quest

Oh, What a Drill!

DEAL A TOTAL OF 400 DAMAGE IN ONE DRILLING EARTHQUAKE USING THE DRILL HEAD ATTACK.

Drill Head continues to run as long as Attack 3 is pressed, but Rubble Rouser can't move until it is released. Put Rubble Rouser's back into a corner and let enemies come to attack him, only to crash into his drill.

Hailing from a race of creatures who ate rock for a living, Rubble Rouser spent most days digging his way through the vastness of Deep Mountain mouthful by mouthful alongside the rest of his people. But Rubble Rouser found he could eat up far more ground with a swing of his hammer or spin of his drill. However, the leaders of his race wanted no part of changing the way they worked. That is, until the evil Rock Lords trapped them deep within the mountain. It was then that Rubble Rouser showed everyone the power of his ways by defeating the Rock Lords with his mighty hammer and drill. Afterward, the leaders encouraged Rubble Rouser to seek out the Skylanders, who readily welcomed him.

Body
Soul Gem Ability
OBSIDIAN SKIN

3500 Gold
PREREQUISITE
Find Rubble Rouser's Soul Gem in Winter Keep

Rubble's skin becomes harder than stone, decreasing damage taken.

Legs
Soul Gem Ability
POP ROCK

3500 Gold
PREREQUISITE
Find Rubble Rouser's Soul Gem in Winter Keep

Hold **Attack 2** to drill underground, release to toss a huge boulder into the sky which comes down on enemies nearby a short time later.

LEVEL	1	2	3	4	5	6	7	8	9	10	11	12	13	14	15	16	17	18	19	20
❤ MAX HEATH	280	308	336	364	392	420	448	476	504	560	588	616	644	672	700	728	756	784	812	840

⚡ SPEED	▼ ARMOR	✛ CRITICAL HIT	◎ ELEMENTAL POWER
35	24	6	25

BODY

Basic Attacks
HAMMER SWING

Press **Attack 1** to swing a massive hammer. Hold to charge up more powerful swings!

Upgrades

TOOLS OF THE TRADE

300 Gold
PREREQUISITE None

Press **Attack 3** to smash nearby enemies with the hammer.

HAPPY HAMMERING

800 Gold
PREREQUISITE None

All hammer attacks do increased damage.

DRILL HEAD

1000 Gold
PREREQUISITE None

Hold **Attack 3** to drill into the ground, causing an earthquake!

Drill Pitcher Path

NAILED IT!

1500 Gold
PREREQUISITE Drill Pitcher Path

Press **Attack 1**, **Attack 1**, and then Hold and release **Attack 1** to throw a charged hammer attack!

SLEDGEHAMMER

2000 Gold
PREREQUISITE Purchase Nailed It! Ability

Throwing the hammer does increased damage. Don't try this indoors!

Excavator

ROCK SHARDS

1500 Gold
PREREQUISITE Excavator Path

Press **Attack 3** to send shards of rock flying out of the ground, damaging nearby enemies.

GEM QUALITY

2000 Gold
PREREQUISITE Purchase Rock Shards ability

Press **Attack 3** to unearth more powerful rock shards that damage nearby enemies.

LEGS

Basic Attacks
DEEP DIG

Press **Attack 2** to quickly dig then come out of the ground, damaging nearby enemies.

Upgrades

MINOR MINERS

300 Gold
PREREQUISITE None

Press **Attack 2** to quickly dig and burst out of the ground a short time later, damaging nearby enemies and summoning small angry miner allies.

EARTHY FORTITUDE

800 Gold
PREREQUISITE None

Health is increased. Tough as stone!

TUNNEL EXPEDITION

1000 Gold
PREREQUISITE None

Hold **Attack 2** to continue drilling while underground, release to surprise enemies from below with a devastating attack.

Bolder Boulders Path

BOULDER TOSS

1500 Gold
PREREQUISITE Bolder Boulders Path

Hold **Attack 2** to drill underground. While underground, boulders will rapidly shoot out. Aim the boulders towards enemies to damage them.

SO BOLD

2000 Gold
PREREQUISITE Purchase Boulder Toss ability

Boulders do increased damage. Getting hit with rocks really hurts.

Miner Foreman Path

MINER CRAFT

1500 Gold
PREREQUISITE Miner Foreman Path

Call up to four miner allies to help you defeat enemies! The cause is righteous.

ON STRIKE

2000 Gold
PREREQUISITE Miner Foreman Path

Miner allies do increased damage. Oh no, they won't go! Not until experience points show!

FLASHWING
"Blinded by the Light!"

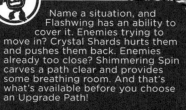

LIGHTCORE

Name a situation, and Flashwing has an ability to cover it. Enemies trying to move in? Crystal Shards hurts them and pushes them back. Enemies already too close? Shimmering Spin carves a path clear and provides some breathing room. And that's what's available before you choose an Upgrade Path!

The Super Shards Path turns Flashwing into a formidable figher in close quarters. Fully upgraded, Flashwing sticks up to three Crystal Shards into walls, which can attack enemies and heal her. The Super Spinner Path works better for open spaces. Shimmering Spin picks up extra damage, reflects projectiles, and fires lasers.

Special Quest
Let It Shine

DEFEAT 20 ENEMIES WITH ONE CRYSTAL LIGHTHOUSE.

Pick a challenge where the primary enemies are Chompies and set up Crystal Lighthouse in a crowded area.

Flashwing's true origins are a mystery. But her first appearance came when Bash made a wish that he could fly and looked up to see a shooting star streak across the sky and land in a valley below. In the center of the glowing impact crater was a large, brilliant geode—which suddenly cracked open to reveal Flashwing. Bash may not have soared that day, but his heart sure did, because Flashwing was beautiful...and lethal. As soon as Bash stepped closer, the gem dragon turned towards him. Not knowing if he was friend or foe, she blasted him off of the cliff with a full force laser pulse from her tail! Perhaps Bash flew that day after all.

LEVEL	1	2	3	4	5	6	7	8	9	10	11	12	13	14	15	16	17	18	19	20
♥ MAX HEATH	260	286	312	338	364	390	416	442	468	520	546	572	598	624	650	676	702	728	754	780

⚡ SPEED	🛡 ARMOR	✛ CRITICAL HIT	◎ ELEMENTAL POWER
43	24	2	25

Basic Attacks

CRYSTAL SHARDS

Press **Attack 1** to fire Crystal Shards.

SHIMMERING SPIN

Press **Attack 2** to spin around and damage anything in Flashwing's path.

Soul Gem Ability
CRYSTAL LIGHTHOUSE

4000 Gold
PREREQUISITE
Purchase Surrounded by Shards ability

Hold **Attack 3** to create a Crystal Lighthouse that fires laser light beams.

Upgrades

SURROUNDED BY SHARDS

500 Gold
PREREQUISITE None

Press **Attack 3** to fire Crystal Shards in all directionsbut forward.

LUMINOUS LASERS

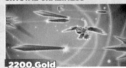

700 Gold
PREREQUISITE None

Hold **Attack 1** to charge up a powerful laser shot.

LIGHT SPEED SHARDS

900 Gold
PREREQUISITE None

Shoot Crystal Shards much faster and deal extra damage.

ARMORED AURA

1200 Gold
PREREQUISITE None

Condensed light increases your resistance.

Super Shards Path

SHOOTING SHARDS

1700 Gold
PREREQUISITE
Super Shards Path

Crystal Shards stick in walls and shoot their own crystals when **Attack 1** is pressed again.

CRYSTAL CRAZINESS

2200 Gold
PREREQUISITE
Purchase Shooting Shards ability

Up to three crystals stick in walls and shoot their own crystals when **Attack 1** is pressed again.

HEALING CRYSTALS

3000 Gold
PREREQUISITE
Purchase Shooting Shards ability

Crystals embedded in a wall heal Flashwing when she is close.

Super Spinner Path

EXTRA RADIANT ROTATION

1700 Gold
PREREQUISITE
Super Spinner Path

Shimmering Spin lasts longer and does increased damage.

REFLECTION DEFLECTION

2200 Gold
PREREQUISITE
Super Spinner Path

Gain extra armor and deflect enemies' shots back at them while spinning.

LIGHTS, CRYSTAL, ACTION!

3000 Gold
PREREQUISITE
Super Spinner Path

While spinning, press **Attack 1** to shoot beams of laser light.

FLASHWING

HYPER BEAM
PRISM BREAK
"The Beam is Supreme!"

SERIES 3

Old hands with Prism Break are familiar with the angles Energy Beam takes when they hit Crystal Shards, which is a difficult thing to master. If you're new to Prism Break, practice against the Training Dummies in Woodburrow until you get it down. You can still hold or pulse Energy Beam, but there's no way to keep Energy Beam going indefinitely.

The Crystaleer Path improves Crystal Shards and helps keep Prism Break healthy. Choose it when a challenge or level is giving you trouble. Every upgrade on the Prismancer Path improves Energy Beam's damage output, making it ideal for anything with a timer.

Special Quest
Bifurcation Sensation

DEFEAT 100 ENEMIES USING CRYSTAL ERUPTION.

Once you plunk down the 700 Gold to purchase Crystal Eruption, it should become second nature to spawn the ring of crystals when fights get hairy. You should complete this quest in a relatively short time while playing through Story Levels or completing challenges.

Prism Break was once a fearsome rock golem who didn't like to be disturbed. Then, an accidental cave-in left him buried underground. One hundred years later, a mining expedition digging for valuable jewels discovered him by chance with a well-placed blow from a pick axe—something Prism Break doesn't talk about. After 100 years of solitude, he found that the pressure of the earth had transformed him emotionally as well as physically, turning his crude rocky arms into incredible gems with powerful energy. Grateful for being free of his earthly prison, Prism Break decided to put his new abilities to good use and dedicated himself to protecting Skylands.

LEVEL	1	2	3	4	5	6	7	8	9	10	11	12	13	14	15	16	17	18	19	20
❤ MAX HEATH	290	319	348	377	406	435	464	493	522	580	609	638	667	696	725	754	783	812	841	870

⚡ SPEED	🛡 ARMOR	⊕ CRITICAL HIT	◎ ELEMENTAL POWER
35	18	6	25

Basic Attacks

ENERGY BEAM

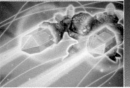

Press and hold **Attack 1** to fire a powerful energy beam.

SUMMON CRYSTAL SHARD

Press **Attack 2** to summon crystal shards to smash enemies and refract your Energy Beam.

Soul Gem Ability
SHARD SOUL PRISON

4000 Gold
PREREQUISITE None

Crystal Shards form when enemies are defeated by your Energy Beam.

Upgrades

SUPER CRYSTAL SHARD

500 Gold
PREREQUISITE None

Summoned Crystal Shards are bigger and do increased damage.

CRYSTAL ERUPTION

700 Gold
PREREQUISITE None

Press **Attack 3** to summon a damaging ring of crystals around you that pushes back enemies.

EMERALD ENERGY BEAM

900 Gold
PREREQUISITE None

Energy Beam does extra damage.

CHAINED REFRACTIONS

1200 Gold
PREREQUISITE None

Split Energy Beams divide again if they pass through a Crystal Shard.

Crystaleer Path

MASSIVE CRYSTAL EXPLOSION

1700 Gold
PREREQUISITE Crystaleer Path

Crystal Eruption attack does increased damage and covers a larger area.

TRIPLE CRYSTAL SHARD

2200 Gold
PREREQUISITE Crystaleer Path

Summon three Crystal Shards at once.

CRYSTALLINE ARMOR

3000 Gold
PREREQUISITE Crystaleer Path

A new crystal increases Prism Break's Resistance.

Prismancer Path

GOLDEN DIAMOND ENERGY BEAM

1700 Gold
PREREQUISITE Prismancer Path

Energy Beam attack does even more increased damage.

TRIPLE REFRACTED BEAM

2200 Gold
PREREQUISITE Prismancer Path

Energy Beam splits into three beams when refracted through a Crystal Shard.

FOCUSED ENERGY

3000 Gold
PREREQUISITE Prismancer Path

Energy Beam has increased range.

Wow Pow!

CRYSTAL COMRADE

5000 Gold
PREREQUISITE Purchase Super Crystal Shard ability

Press **Attack 1** to shoot Crystal Shards and gem shrapnel explode out, damaging enemies and looking cool.

Looking cool refers to both Prism Break's new, red crystal appearance and the new, red look of his Crystal Shards. Either way, Crystal Comrade must also boost Prism Break's ego. Now when he hits Crystal Shards with Energy Beam, gem bits fly off and damage enemies, and he creates a work of art dedicated to himself!

SCORP

"King of the Sting!"

Emerald Crystal and Tail Sting have odd properties that require familiarity to use them effectively. Emerald Crystal is a lob attack that attaches itself to enemies, walls, or floors. After a few seconds, its explodes and deals additional damage. Neither the crystal nor the explosion damages much, but Scorp can fire them off quickly. Tail Sting comes out in a flash and hits multiple enemies, but has a poor recovery time.

The Stinger Path boosts the damage output of Tail Sting, but doesn't help its recovery. The Crystal Venomancer Path increases both the damage done by Emerald Crystals and the area it affects.

Special Quest

Ticking Slime Bomb

DEFEAT 50 ENEMIES FROM THE POISON EXPLOSION OF YOUR MAIN ATTACK.

This is a rare quest where it's easier to finish it before you upgrade your Skylander. It isn't defeating enemies with Emerald Crystal that satisfies this quest's requirements, it's the poison explosion that takes place after the Emerald Crystal attaches itself to something. When an enemy is low on health and has an Emerald Crystal attached to it, move on to another target.

Scorp was raised in the Salt Flat Islands, an endless flat plain of rock where every day is very hot. To keep themselves entertained, the residents live for the sport of Sting Ball, an extreme game that only the strongest play to become King of Sting, a title Scorp had won numerous times. During his last championship game, the opposing team cheated by using an enchanted water gem to make it rain. But the spell got out of control and soon a raging thunderstorm flooded the land. Using his powerful claws and incredible agility, Scorp bravely battled the rising waters to retrieve the gem and hurl it far into the clouds, breaking the spell and saving everyone. Seeing how his abilities could be used for more than sport, Scorp soon sought out and joined the Skylanders.

LEVEL	1	2	3	4	5	6	7	8	9	10	11	12	13	14	15	16	17	18	19	20
MAX HEATH	260	286	312	338	364	390	416	442	468	520	546	572	598	624	650	676	702	728	754	780

⚡ SPEED	🛡 ARMOR	◎ CRITICAL HIT	◉ ELEMENTAL POWER
35	18	8	25

Basic Attacks

EMERALD CRYSTAL

Press **Attack 1** to throw a sticky explosive crystal.

TAIL STING

Press **Attack 2** to sting the ground nearby and poison enemies.

Soul Gem Ability

AVALANCHE DASH

4000 Gold
PREREQUISITE
Find Scorp's Soul Gem in Motleyville; Purchase Boulder Roll ability

Hold **Attack 3** to curl up into a ball and roll around. Dashing now lasts as long as **Attack 3** is held.

Upgrades

BOULDER ROLL

500 Gold
PREREQUISITE None

Hold **Attack 3** to curl up into a ball and roll around, damaging enemies in the way.

CHROME CARAPACE

700 Gold
PREREQUISITE None

Armor is increased. New stone plating causes enemies' attacks to do less damage.

CRYSTAL BALL

900 Gold
PREREQUISITE None

Hold **Attack 1** to charge a crystal attack, release to smash two crystals together and throw a massive sticky crystal.

EARTHLY POWER

1200 Gold
PREREQUISITE None

Press **Attack 1** to throw a sticky explosive that now does increased damage to an enemy.

Stinger Path

FUMING FISSURE

1700 Gold
PREREQUISITE
Stinger Path

Press **Attack 2** to strike the ground with a poison tail and cause a large shockwave that shoots out towards enemies.

SCORPION STRIKE

2200 Gold
PREREQUISITE
Stinger Path

Poison from tail strikes does increased damage.

POTENT POISONS

3000 Gold
PREREQUISITE
Stinger Path

Press **Attack 2** to strike with a poison tail, that now damages enemies over a longer amount of time.

Crystal Venomancer Path

CRACKED CRYSTALS

1700 Gold
PREREQUISITE
Crystal Venomancer Path

Press **Attack 1** to throw a powerful sticky explosive crystal that now does damage to enemies in a larger area.

CRYSTAL SHARDS

2200 Gold
PREREQUISITE
Crystal Venomancer Path

Emerald Crystal attacks now do even more damage. So pretty, yet so painful!

VENOMOUS CRYSTALS

3000 Gold
PREREQUISITE
Crystal Venomancer Path

When Crystal Ball explodes, it splits into two smaller crystals. Each new crystal does very powerful poison damage over time when it explodes.

SCORP

95

SLOBBER TOOTH
"Clobber and Slobber!"

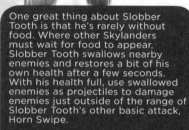

One great thing about Slobber Tooth is that he's rarely without food. Where other Skylanders must wait for food to appear, Slobber Tooth swallows nearby enemies and restores a bit of his own health after a few seconds. With his health full, use swallowed enemies as projectiles to damage enemies just outside of the range of Slobber Tooth's other basic attack, Horn Swipe.

The Food Fighter Path boosts both the healing from Chomp, and the damage done by Chuck. The Seismic Tail Path turns Slobber Tooth into a nightmare to face in close quarters. Shockwave becomes much better in every way.

Special Quest

Hungry Like a Hippo

SWALLOW 25 ENEMIES.

You must use Chomp & Chuck on 25 different enemies that can be swallowed and they must stay in Slobber Tooth's mouth until he swallows them to restore his health. Look for a heart on the screen to let you know when it's safe to swallow another enemy.

Having been asleep for thousands of years, Slobber Tooth was awakened by the fiery eruption of two volcanic islands crashing together. Immediately sought out by Kaos to become one of his minions, Slobber Tooth was promised great power. But the gruff and headstrong fighter chose to follow his own path instead. For this, Kaos attacked his ancient petrified homeland. As the only one who could protect his hibernating race, Slobber Tooth fought tooth and tail against Kaos and his minions, ultimately driving them away. For his heroism, Master Eon asked Slobber Tooth to join the Skylanders, where he could continue defending Skylands against the evil Kaos.

LEVEL	1	2	3	4	5	6	7	8	9	10	11	12	13	14	15	16	17	18	19	20
♥ MAX HEATH	300	330	360	390	420	450	480	510	540	600	630	660	690	720	750	780	810	840	870	900

⚡ SPEED	🛡 ARMOR	✛ CRITICAL HIT	◎ ELEMENTAL POWER
35	30	2	25

Basic Attacks

HORN SWIPE

Press **Attack 1** to perform a head swipe that damages nearby enemies.

CHOMP & CHUCK

Press **Attack 2** to grab enemies with a slobbery mouth attack. Press **Attack 2** again to spit them out.

ⓖ Soul Gem Ability
IRON JAW

4000 Gold
PREREQUISITE
Find Slobber Tooth's Soul Gem in Cascade Glade

Gain an iron jaw, causing all head attacks to deal increased damage.

Upgrades

UNSTOPPABLE FORCE

500 Gold
PREREQUISITE None

Hold **Attack 1** to charge forward a short distance with a powerful headbutt attack.

TOUGH HIDE

700 Gold
PREREQUISITE None

Gain bonus armor. Skin as tough as nails and rocks mixed together.

SHOCKWAVE

900 Gold
PREREQUISITE None

Press **Attack 3** to do a tail slam on the ground, damaging all enemies nearby.

LOOGEY

1200 Gold
PREREQUISITE None

Press **Attack 2** after holding an enemy with a Chomp attack to spit them out and deal increased damage.

Food Fighter Path

SNOT ROCKET

1700 Gold
PREREQUISITE
Food Fighter Path

Enemies hit with a spit attack will be covered in goo and take damage over time.

OM NOM NOM

2200 Gold
PREREQUISITE
Food Fighter Path

Press **Attack 2** to eat enemies, enemies being eaten will give more health back over a short time.

FEAST

3000 Gold
PREREQUISITE
Food Fighter Path

Hold **Attack 2** to pull enemies into a chomping mouth attack.

Seismic Tail Path

FLING

1700 Gold
PREREQUISITE
Seismic Tail Path

Press **Attack 3** to do a tail slam on the ground, press **Attack 3** again to fling all nearby enemies into the air.

WEIGHT GAIN

2200 Gold
PREREQUISITE
Seismic Tail Path

Gain a new spikey tail, causing Shockwave attacks to do increased damage.

EARTH SHAKER

3000 Gold
PREREQUISITE
Seismic Tail Path

Hold **Attack 3** to continue tail slamming the ground, causing waves of rocks to spread out and damage enemies in the way.

SLOBBER TOOTH

KNOCKOUT
TERRAFIN
"It's Feeding Time!"

Terrafin hails from The Dirt Seas, where it was common to swim, bathe, and even snorkel beneath the ground. But a powerful explosion in the sky created a blast wave that turned the ocean of sand into a vast sheet of glass, putting an end to Terrafin's duty as the local lifeguard. Not one to stay idle, the brawny dirt shark found himself training in the art of boxing, and not long after he was local champ. Fighters came from all around to challenge him, but it was a chance meeting with a great Portal Master that led him to give up his title for a greater purpose.

SERIES 3

Even before upgrades, Earth Swim is a valuable ability that allows Terrafin to pass enemies and hazards without getting hurt. Punch is exactly what it sounds like: Terrafin's fists slamming into faces and objects, breaking both. It's not fancy, but it is effective.

The Sandhog Path gives some offensive punch to Earth Swim, which helps out his Wow Pow! ability at the same time. However, Earth Swim is generally used to bring enemies in range of Punch, which is where the Brawler Path comes in. Terrafin hits harder and gets more combo options. Both make for a happy Terrafin.

Special Quest

Land Lubber

EAT 20 FOOD ITEMS WHILE BURROWING.

This quest requires the Surface Feeder upgrade. Just remember to use Earth Swim when you see a food item and you should complete this quickly. If you want to get it done even faster, go to any challenge with the Food Thief.

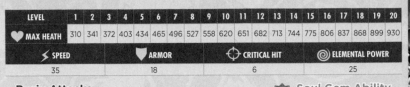

LEVEL	1	2	3	4	5	6	7	8	9	10	11	12	13	14	15	16	17	18	19	20
♥ MAX HEATH	310	341	372	403	434	465	496	527	558	620	651	682	713	744	775	806	837	868	899	930

⚡ SPEED	🛡 ARMOR	◎ CRITICAL HIT	◎ ELEMENTAL POWER
35	18	6	25

Basic Attacks

PUNCH

Press **Attack 1** to punch the enemy. Press **Attack 1**, **Attack 1**, Hold **Attack 1** to perform a combo.

EARTH SWIM

Press **Attack 2** to burrow and while underground, press **Attack 1** to perform a Belly Flop.

🅖 Soul Gem Ability
SURFACE FEEDER

4000 Gold
PREREQUISITE
None

Collect power-ups while burrowed.

Upgrades

BRASS KNUCKLES

500 Gold
PREREQUISITE None

Punch attacks do increased damage.

MEGA BELLY FLOP

700 Gold
PREREQUISITE None

Belly Flop does increased damage and affects a larger area.

FEEDING FRENZY

900 Gold
PREREQUISITE None

Press **Attack 3** to spawn mini-sharks that burrow and latch onto enemies.

MULTI TARGET PUNCHES

1200 Gold
PREREQUISITE None

Punch attack hits multiple enemies.

Sandhog Path

MASTER EARTH SWIMMER

1700 Gold
PREREQUISITE
Sandhog Path

Increased speed while burrowing.

HOMING FRENZY

2200 Gold
PREREQUISITE
Sandhog Path

Mini-sharks home in on enemies and do extra damage.

RAZORFIN

3000 Gold
PREREQUISITE
Sandhog Path

While burrowed, your dorsal fin does damage to enemies.

Brawler Path

PUGILIST

1700 Gold
PREREQUISITE
Brawler Path

Press **Attack 1**, **Attack 1**, Hold **Attack 2** for Body Slam. Press **Attack 1**, **Attack 1**, Hold **Attack 3** for Uppercut.

SPIKED KNUCKLES

2200 Gold
PREREQUISITE
Brawler Path

All punch attacks do even MORE damage.

FRENZY SHIELD

3000 Gold
PREREQUISITE
Brawler Path

You launch mini-sharks at enemies who damage you.

Wow Pow!

HAVE YOU MET MY KIDS?

5000 Gold
PREREQUISITE
Purchase Feeding Frenzy ability

While burrowed, press **Attack 3** to launch at enemies and hit them with a claw swipe move as well as with mini-shark allies.

The best part about Have You Met My Kids? is that it doesn't end Earth Swim immediately. In fact, when you get the timing down, it's possible to use this attack and follow it up immediately with a Belly Flop. That leads to a world of pain for any enemies who get hit with both attacks.

KNOCKOUT TERRAFIN

BOOM JET

"Bombs Away!"

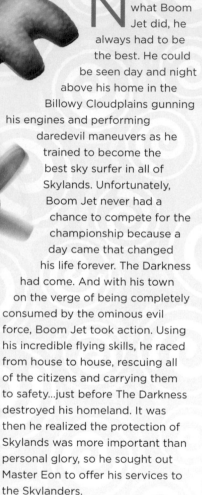

No matter what Boom Jet did, he always had to be the best. He could be seen day and night above his home in the Billowy Cloudplains gunning his engines and performing daredevil maneuvers as he trained to become the best sky surfer in all of Skylands. Unfortunately, Boom Jet never had a chance to compete for the championship because a day came that changed his life forever. The Darkness had come. And with his town on the verge of being completely consumed by the ominous evil force, Boom Jet took action. Using his incredible flying skills, he raced from house to house, rescuing all of the citizens and carrying them to safety...just before The Darkness destroyed his homeland. It was then he realized the protection of Skylands was more important than personal glory, so he sought out Master Eon to offer his services to the Skylanders.

Football Bomb becomes a much better ability when you buy the Go Long! upgrade. The Storm Bomber Path adds stationary, damaging clouds of smoke to the aftermath of a Go Long! explosion. Air Strike blasts the ground in a straight path, and the Squad Leader Path adds bombs for extra damage.

Wind Turbine needs upgrades before it does more than annoy enemies. Mach 1, for example, turns Boom Jet into a Chompy destroyer. The Sky Writer Path adds a damaging smoke trail in his wake, aiding Jet's mobility. The Ace Gunner Path is more direct damage. Two missiles are fired, and seek out targets.

Special Quest

Tactical Strikes

DEFEAT 747 ENEMIES WITH YOUR AIR STRIKE ABILITY.

Use Air Strike often in Chompy-filled areas, and to finish off low health enemies everywhere and you'll hit this quirky number in a hurry.

Body
Soul Gem Ability
SUPPLY DROP

3500 Gold
PREREQUISITE
Find Boom Jet's Soul Gem in Motleyville; Purchase Air Strike ability

Air Strike has a chance to drop health supplies if health is low.

Legs
Soul Gem Ability
MACH 2

3500 Gold
PREREQUISITE
Find Boom Jet's Soul Gem in Motleyville

Mach 1's speed is increased and a large blast damages enemies at the beginning of the dash.

LEVEL	1	2	3	4	5	6	7	8	9	10	11	12	13	14	15	16	17	18	19	20
♥ MAX HEATH	260	286	312	338	364	390	416	442	468	520	546	572	598	624	650	676	702	728	754	780

⚡ SPEED	◤ ARMOR	✛ CRITICAL HIT	◎ ELEMENTAL POWER
43	24	6	25

BODY

Basic Attacks
FOOTBALL BOMB

Press **Atttack 1** to throw a football sized bomb.

Upgrades
AIR STRIKE

300 Gold
PREREQUISITE None

Press **Attack 3** to call for help from the skies. An airstrike shoots projectiles at enemies on the ground.

TIGHT SPIRAL

800 Gold
PREREQUISITE None

Press **Attack 1** to throw a football bomb that does increased damage.

GO LONG!

1000 Gold
PREREQUISITE None

Hold **Attack 1** to charge a football bomb, release to throw a Super Bomb.

Storm Bomber Path
STORM BOMB

1500 Gold
PREREQUISITE Storm Bomber Path

Hold **Attack 1** to charge a football bomb, release to create storm clouds where the bomb lands that shock nearby enemies.

UNFRIENDLY SKIES

2000 Gold
PREREQUISITE Purchase Storm Bomb ability

Storm Bomb does increased damage. Shocking!

Squad Leader Path
BOMBERS

1500 Gold
PREREQUISITE Squad Leader Path

Air Strike now drops bombs that do damage in a large area.

TIGHT FORMATION

2000 Gold
PREREQUISITE Squad Leader Path

Press **Attack 3** to call in an Air Strike that does increased damage.

LEGS

Basic Attacks
WIND TURBINE

Hold **Attack 2** to shoot wind at nearby enemies, pushing them backwards.

Upgrades
MACH 1

300 Gold
PREREQUISITE None

Press **Attack 2** two times to dash forward. Hold **Attack 2** to continue dashing quickly.

ACE PILOT

800 Gold
PREREQUISITE None

Speed is increased. Tuned up with brand new turbo!

TURBULENCE

1000 Gold
PREREQUISITE None

Hold **Attack 2** to shoot three homing propellers at enemies.

Sky Writer Path
SKY WRITING

1500 Gold
PREREQUISITE Sky Writer Path

A smoke trail is left behind while dashing that stuns and damages enemies.

THICK SMOKE

2000 Gold
PREREQUISITE Purchase Sky Writing ability

Sky Writing does increased damage and stays around longer.

Ace Gunner Path
GUN SHIP

1500 Gold
PREREQUISITE Ace Gunner Path

Press **Attack 2** to shoot missiles from a powerful new mounted turret.

ROCKET FUEL

2000 Gold
PREREQUISITE Purchase Gun Ship ability

New turret designs make Gun Ship do increased damage.

BOOM JET

101

FREE RANGER

"Whip Up a Storm!"

Stormblade Slash is a series of melee attacks that is enhanced nicely by Gale Slash. The Wind Slasher Path adds a charged up opening attack to Stormblade Slash. Eyes of the Storm is a low powered eye beam that jumps between enemies. The Storm Focus Path turns it into a powerful, charged single shot.

Ride the Wind is an amazing ability to use against shielded enemies. They are whirled around and their shields drop. The Lightning Linguist Path adds an attack that hits enemies near Free Ranger when a tornado begins. The Tornado Thrower Path attack appears at the end and hits multiple enemies in a line.

Special Quest
Ruffled Feathers

HIT ENEMIES 25 TIMES WITHOUT STOPPING YOUR MELEE ATTACKS.

Find an area filled with enemies and keep hitting Attack 1 while avoiding the enemy attacks that can interrupt Free Ranger's swings. If you don't hit any enemies while swinging, that won't hurt anything, just keep pressing Attack 1 and hitting enemies.

F ree Ranger was hatched during a storm when a thunderous bolt of lightning struck his egg. From that very moment, his destiny was clear—he would become the greatest storm chaser ever known! He spent his entire life pursuing hurricanes, spinning inside tornados, and riding lightning. But a day came when he encountered a storm unlike any other. It was unnatural and ominous, billowing with evil, and leaving only desolation in its wake. Free Ranger was standing at its edge, moments from boldly leaping into it, when he was stopped by none other than Master Eon. The wise Portal Master told him that it was The Darkness that raged before them, and if he were up to the challenge, he could join the Skylanders to help defend against it in the Cloudbreak Islands.

Body
Soul Gem Ability
STORMING STORMBLADES

3500 Gold
PREREQUISITE
Find Free Ranger's Soul Gem in Mudwater Hollow

Press **Attack 1** to attack with more powerful Stormblades that deal extra lightning damage.

Legs
Soul Gem Ability
CHARGED WINDS

3500 Gold
PREREQUISITE
Find Free Ranger's Soul Gem in Mudwater Hollow

Hold **Attack 2** to become a tornado filled with lightning, dealing damage to all enemies in the way.

LEVEL	1	2	3	4	5	6	7	8	9	10	11	12	13	14	15	16	17	18	19	20
♥ MAX HEATH	280	308	336	364	392	420	448	476	504	560	588	616	644	672	700	728	756	784	812	840

⚡ SPEED	▽ ARMOR	⊕ CRITICAL HIT	◎ ELEMENTAL POWER
43	18	8	25

BODY

Basic Attacks
STORMBLADE SLASH

Press **Attack 1** to slash at enemies with powerful Stormblades.

Upgrades

EYES OF THE STORM

300 Gold
PREREQUISITE None

Press **Attack 3** to shoot a bolt of lightning from the eyes, stunning the first enemy and chaining to others.

CHARGED BLADES

800 Gold
PREREQUISITE None

Press **Attack 1** to slash with more powerful Stormblades that do increased damage.

GALE SLASH

1000 Gold
PREREQUISITE None

Press **Attack 1** three times to send a wave of powerful air at enemies.

Wind Slasher Path

SLICING STORM

1500 Gold
PREREQUISITE
Wind Slasher Path

Hold **Attack 1** to charge the Stormblades, release for a devastating combo attack.

FEATHERED FURY

2000 Gold
PREREQUISITE
Purchase Slicing Storm ability

Slicing Storm does increased damage. Unleash the full fury of the bird!

Storm Focus Path

LIGHTNING STRIKES THRICE

1500 Gold
PREREQUISITE
Storm Focus Path

Hold **Attack 3** to charge Eye of the Storm, release to shoot a larger bolt of lightning.

CHARGED GIGAWATT BOLT

2000 Gold
PREREQUISITE
Purchase Lightning Strikes Thrice ability

Lightning Strikes Thrice does increased damage. More powerful than lightning.

LEGS

Basic Attacks
RIDE THE WIND

Hold **Attack 2** to become a tornado and damage nearby enemies.

Upgrades

APPROACHING STORM

300 Gold
PREREQUISITE None

Hold **Attack 2** to become a tornado, speed is increasd while the tornado is active.

WIND POWERED

800 Gold
PREREQUISITE None

Becoming a tornado will last longer.

TORNADO VACUUM BOOST

1000 Gold
PREREQUISITE None

Tornadoes now pull in enemies from further away.

Lightning Linguist Path

LIGHTNING NOVA

1500 Gold
PREREQUISITE
Lightning Linguist Path

Blast all nearby enemies with a powerful lightning bolt when becoming a tornado.

NOVA FLASH

2000 Gold
PREREQUISITE
Purchase Lightning Nova ability

Lightning Nova does increased damage.

Tornado Thrower Path

WILD TORNADO

1500 Gold
PREREQUISITE
Tornado Thrower Path

When becoming a tornado ends, a powerful tornado is shot out, damaging all enemies in the way.

TWISTED TWISTER

2000 Gold
PREREQUISITE
Purchase Wild Tornado ability

More powerful tornadoes are shot forward that do increased damage to enemies.

FREE RANGER

TURBO JET-VAC
"Hawk and Awe!"

SERIES 2

Vac-Blaster blasts air out at enemies, dealing respectable damage with nice range. A flip of the switch (well, pressing the other Attack Button) results in Suction Gun sucking in enemies and dealing damage to them. Jet-Vac also uses an air-powered backpack to fly, though he can't stay aloft for long. Using Suction Gun replenishes the air that powers his backpack a bit quicker.

The Bird Blaster Path is designed to handle groups of enemies, allowing Vac-Blaster shots to damage more enemies. The Vac-Packeteer Path focuses on his Jet Pack, giving it more airtime and a new attack.

Special Quest

Bird Cleaner

TRAVEL 5000 FEET WHILE FLYING.
Flying is second nature to an eagle! To complete this quest faster, activate the Vac-Packeteer Path and purchase the ability Tank Reserves.

Jet-Vac was the greatest, most daring flying ace in all of Windham. He was given his magical wings when he was young, as was the tradition for all Sky Barons. But when his homeland was raided, he chose to sacrifice his wings to a young mother so she could fly her children to safety. This act of nobility caught the attention of Master Eon, who sought out the young Sky Baron and presented him with a gift—a powerful vacuum device that would allow him to soar through the skies once again. Jet-Vac accepted the gift with gratitude, and now daringly fights evil alongside the other Skylanders.

LEVEL	1	2	3	4	5	6	7	8	9	10	11	12	13	14	15	16	17	18	19	20
MAX HEATH	240	264	288	312	336	360	384	408	432	480	504	528	552	576	600	624	648	672	696	720

⚡ SPEED	🛡 ARMOR	⊕ CRITICAL HIT	◎ ELEMENTAL POWER
50	30	4	25

Basic Attacks

VAC-BLASTER

Press **Attack 1** to shoot enemies with a powerful blast of air.

SUCTION GUN

Hold **Attack 2** to suck enemies into the spinning fan blades.

Soul Gem Ability
EAGLE-AIR BATTLE GEAR

4000 Gold
PREREQUISITE
None

Jet-Vac gets enhanced resistances and a pretty sweet visor.

Upgrades

FEISTIER FAN

500 Gold
PREREQUISITE None

Bigger spinning fan blades on the Suction Gun do increased damage to enemies.

JET-VAC JET PACK

700 Gold
PREREQUISITE None

Press **Attack 3** to take flight. Press **Attack 1** while flying to shoot blasts of air.

VAC BLASTER 9000

900 Gold
PREREQUISITE None

Vac-Blaster does increased damage.

TURBINE SUCTION FAN

1200 Gold
PREREQUISITE
Purchase Feistier Fan ability

Suction Gun attacks do even MORE increased damage.

Bird Blaster Path

PIERCING WINDS

1700 Gold
PREREQUISITE
Bird Blaster Path

Vac-Blaster does even more increased damage and pierces multiple enemies.

VAC MASTER-BLASTER 20X

2200 Gold
PREREQUISITE
Bird Blaster Path

Vac-Blaster does maximum damage.

SUPER SUCTION AIR BLASTER

3000 Gold
PREREQUISITE
Bird Blaster Path

Suck up enemies with the Suction Gun to give the Vac-Blaster super shots.

Vac-Packeteer Path

TANK RESERVES

1700 Gold
PREREQUISITE
Vac-Packeteer Path

Can remain in flight longer and recharge faster.

THE MULCHER

2200 Gold
PREREQUISITE
Vac-Packeteer Path

Suction Gun attacks do maximum damage.

FLYING CORKSCREW

3000 Gold
PREREQUISITE
Vac-Packeteer Path

While flying, press **Attack 2** to blast forward and perform a powerful corkscrew attack.

Wow Pow!
SHOOT THE BREEZE!

5000 Gold
PREREQUISITE
None

Hold **Attack 1** to charge up the Vac Blaster, then release to release a gigantic tornado.

The fact that Shoot the Breeze! doesn't slow Jet-Vac while it's charging up makes it one of the more practical charged up attacks around. The tornado hits enemies in a straight line, so you can damage multiple enemies with one shot if you line them up correctly.

POP THORN
"Straight to the Point!"

To play Pop Thorn to his full potential, you need to learn how to control him in both his puffed state, and his popped state. Pop Thorn floats while puffed, and his primary attack fills the air with tiny spikes that seek out nearby enemies. While popped, Pop Thorn scurries around on the ground and uses a breath attack.

The Tough and Puffed Path ignores the popped state and makes Pop Thorn tougher while floating. The Controlled Breather Path boosts some of Pop Thorn's attacks, allowing them to damage more enemies in a single move.

Special Quest
Take A Deep Breath

HIT ENEMIES WITH A SINGLE STREAM OF BREATH 100 TIMES IN A ROW.

Holding Attack 2 while Pop Thorn is popped results in a continual gust of wind. You must hit enemies 100 times in a row with this gust to complete the quest. If Pop Thorn is hit, the streak ends. Go for this quest where there are no ranged enemies!

Pop Thorn hails from a race of creatures known as Pufferthorns. Often considered one of the cutest creatures in all of Skylands, they are generally quite timid and puff out sharp spines when scared. It is this ability that long ago led to the unfortunate legacy of being used as combs by giant trolls everywhere, as the sharp spines are perfect for brushing out tangles from their long, matted hair. But not long ago, one Pufferthorn took a stand. Tired of his race being used for nothing more than good grooming, Pop Thorn used his naturally thorny abilities to stand up and fight back against the giant trolls. Soon after, Master Eon made Pop Thorn a Skylander. And to this day, no trolls dare to comb their hair.

LEVEL	1	2	3	4	5	6	7	8	9	10	11	12	13	14	15	16	17	18	19	20
♥ MAX HEATH	280	308	336	364	392	420	448	476	504	560	588	616	644	672	700	728	756	784	812	840

⚡ SPEED	🛡 ARMOR	⊕ CRITICAL HIT	◎ ELEMENTAL POWER
43	24	6	25

Basic Attacks

PUFF

Press **Attack 1** to Puff and damage nearby enemies. While puffed, rapidly press **Attack 1** to shoot out homing spikes at nearby enemies.

POP

Press **Attack 2** to Pop and shoot a large wind blast. While popped, hold **Attack 2** to shoot gusts of wind at enemies.

Soul Gem Ability
TO PUFF OR NOT TO PUFF

4000 Gold
PREREQUISITE
Find Pop Thorn's Soul Gem in Mount Cloudbreak

While popped, speed is increased. While puffed, armor is increased, which reduces damage taken.

Upgrades

FRESH BREATH

500 Gold
PREREQUISITE None

Press **Attack 2** to Pop. After popping, hold **Attack 2** to shoot more powerful air projectiles for a short time.

PUFFBALL POUND

700 Gold
PREREQUISITE None

Press **Attack 1** to Puff. Press **Attack 3** while puffed to slam into the ground, damaging all nearby enemies.

POLISHED SPIKES

900 Gold
PREREQUISITE None

Press **Attack 1** to Puff. After puffing, press **Attack 1** rapidly to shoot more powerful spike projectiles for a short time.

WIND TRAP

1200 Gold
PREREQUISITE None

While popped, press **Attack 3** to leave behind a spiny mine. The mine puffs and explodes when enemies approach, launching them into the air.

Tough and Puffed Path

ROLLERPUFF

1700 Gold
PREREQUISITE
Tough and Puffed Path

While puffed, hold **Attack 3** to roll forward, damaging all enemies in the way.

BOUNCEBACK

2200 Gold
PREREQUISITE
Tough and Puffed Path

Puffing deals increased damage and reflects nearby projectiles.

PRICKLY BODY

3000 Gold
PREREQUISITE
Tough and Puffed Path

While puffed, taking damage releases a spike projectile that damages an attacker.

Controlled Breather Path

AERO TRAMPOLINE

1700 Gold
PREREQUISITE
Controlled Breather Path

While puffed, hold **Attack 3** to charge a powerful slam attack, release to bounce multiple times, damaging all enemies in the way.

DEEP BREATH

2200 Gold
PREREQUISITE
Controlled Breather Path

While puffed, press **Attack 2** to shoot three air blasts instead of one.

SCATTERED WINDS

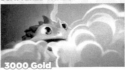

3000 Gold
PREREQUISITE
Controlled Breather Path

While popped, air beams now shoot multiple projectiles that spread.

POP THORN

SCRATCH

"The Luck of the Claw!"

She may look and sound like a playful kitten, but Scratch is a fierce Skylander. Cat Scratch is a series of rapid paw swipes that doesn't have many upgrades, but all increase her damage output. Playful Pounce is a great way to reach a spot quickly. It includes a target laser that shows you exactly where Scratch will land.

The Ruby Path is straightforward: Scratch's attacks deal more damage to more enemies. The Sapphire Path becomes more valuable against tougher enemies that don't fall quickly. After all, how much does it matter if something is slowed if it goes down in two swipes?

Special Quest

Purrfect Pounce

DEFEAT 50 ENEMIES BY POUNCING ON THEM.

Chompies are the ideal target for this quest, but you must be careful about aiming your laser. Don't hit the Chompy with the laser, just get it close enough for Scratch's Playful Pounce to do the job.

High in the peaks of the Cats Eye Mountain sits a towering city of crystal and Gold that can only be reached by creatures of the Air Element. It was here that Scratch spent her youth soaring playfully in the clouds or exploring the endless number of crystal mines. One day, an army of Pirate Greebles arrived in a fleet of airships, looking to steal ancient magic crystals buried deep in the mountain. Donning specially made armor, Scratch led an epic battle against the pirates, using her incredible fighting skills to defend the crystals and save the city. Tales of her heroism soon made their way to Jet-Vac, who traveled to Cats Eye Mountain and recruited Scratch to join the Skylanders.

LEVEL	1	2	3	4	5	6	7	8	9	10	11	12	13	14	15	16	17	18	19	20
♥ MAX HEATH	260	286	312	338	364	390	416	442	468	520	546	572	598	624	650	676	702	728	754	780

⚡ SPEED	🛡 ARMOR	⊕ CRITICAL HIT	◎ ELEMENTAL POWER
50	6	8	25

Basic Attacks

CAT SCRATCH

Press **Attack 1** to scratch at nearby enemies.

PLAYFUL POUNCE

Hold **Attack 2** to shoot a movable laser onto the ground, release to pounce where the laser was pointing.

Soul Gem Ability

GEM AFFINITY

4000 Gold
PREREQUISITE
Find Scratch's Soul Gem in Fantasm Forest

Gain health from collecting gems, coins and money.

Upgrades

WING SPARK

500 Gold
PREREQUISITE None

Press **Attack 3** to dodge an attack and knock away all enemies in an area around you.

SILVER CLAWS

700 Gold
PREREQUISITE None

Gain new silver claws that deal increased damage!

WHIRLWING

900 Gold
PREREQUISITE
Purchase Wing Spark ability

Hold **Attack 3** to pull enemies into a massive whirlwind and do damage to all of them caught inside.

SILVER MASK

1200 Gold
PREREQUISITE None

Gain a new silver mask! Hold **Attack 2** to shoot a powerful new laser at the ground, release to do a devastating pounce attack that does increased damage.

Ruby Path

SHARPENED RUBIES

1700 Gold
PREREQUISITE
Ruby Path

Sharpened rubies grant increased chance to critically hit!

RUBY RAGE

2200 Gold
PREREQUISITE
Ruby Path

Claw damage is increased. Hold **Attack 1** to charge a claw attack, release to slash through nearby enemies.

RUBY MASK

3000 Gold
PREREQUISITE
Ruby Path

Hold **Attack 2** to shoot a laser at the ground that damages enemies in a larger area.

Sapphire Path

SPEEDY SAPPHIRE

1700 Gold
PREREQUISITE
Sapphire Path

Speed is increased. Sapphires infused with the speed of wind!

SAPPHIRE SLASH

2200 Gold
PREREQUISITE
Sapphire Path

Claw damage is increased. Hold **Attack 1** to charge a wing attack, release to shoot a vortex that pulls enemies into it.

SAPPHIRE MASK

3000 Gold
PREREQUISITE
Sapphire Path

Hold **Attack 2** to shoot a laser at the ground that damages and slows enemies.

SCRATCH

WARNADO

"For the Wind!"

Warnado was hatched in the fury of a rare and powerful Enchanted Twister. Although initially frightened and quite dizzy, over the passing years he grew to enjoy his whirling surroundings and learned many abilities and secrets of the Air Element. This led to Warnado becoming a powerful force and the only known turtle of his kind. Now, the only time he gets dizzy is when standing still.

LIGHTCORE

With Spin Attack, Warnado flings his body around the area quickly, damaging multiple enemies while staying relatively safe inside his shell. Summon Tornado begins as a simple whirlwind that can trap a single enemy, but upgrades turn it into a force of nature that runs down enemies.

The Eye of the Storm path improves Spin Attack but also provides some difficult-to-use upgrades to his flight ability. The Wind Master Path turns Summon Tornado into an ability that brings forth a whirlwind that chases down enemies on its own while a second whirlwind is under your control.

Special Quest

Chompy Catcher

CATCH 100 CHOMPIES IN YOUR TORNADOES.

To find a good spot to work on this quest, pick a challenge with Chompy in the title; you can't go wrong. If you're impatient, choose the Wind Master Path and its upgrades for Summon Tornado. You'll be done in no time!

LEVEL	1	2	3	4	5	6	7	8	9	10	11	12	13	14	15	16	17	18	19	20
♥ MAX HEATH	310	341	372	403	434	465	496	527	558	620	651	682	713	744	775	806	837	868	899	930

⚡ SPEED	🛡 ARMOR	⊕ CRITICAL HIT	◎ ELEMENTAL POWER
35	30	2	25

Basic Attacks

SPIN ATTACK

Press **Attack 1** to spin Warnado's shell at enemies.

SUMMON TORNADO

Press **Attack 2** to execute a high velocity spin that generates a tornado to pick up enemies.

Soul Gem Ability

THICK SHELLED

4000 Gold
PREREQUISITE
None

This ability gives Warnado a thicker shell, reducing damage he takes from enemies.

Upgrades

SHARP SHELL

500 Gold
PREREQUISITE None

Spin Attack deals more damage.

EXTEND TORNADO

700 Gold
PREREQUISITE None

Hold **Attack 2** to extend the range of the attack.

HIGH WINDS

900 Gold
PREREQUISITE None

Tornadoes can damage multiple enemies.

WHIRLWIND FLIGHT

1200 Gold
PREREQUISITE None

Press **Attack 3** to Fly. Warnado gains increased speed and resistance while flying.

Eye of the Storm Path

LOW FRICTION SHELL

1700 Gold
PREREQUISITE
Eye of the Storm Path

Spin attack strikes father and faster.

FLYING MINI TURTLES

2200 Gold
PREREQUISITE
Eye of the Storm Path

Mini-Warnados fly with you. Press **Attack 1** to launch them at your enemies.

TURTLE SLAM

3000 Gold
PREREQUISITE
Eye of the Storm Path

While flying, hold **Attack 1** to slam down on your enemies.

Wind Master Path

GUIDED TWISTER

1700 Gold
PREREQUISITE
Wind Master Path

Hold **Attack 2** to manually control the direction of your tornado attack using the left control stick

SUMMON CYCLONE

2200 Gold
PREREQUISITE
Wind Master Path

Tornadoes are super-sized and deal more damage.

WIND ELEMENTAL

3000 Gold
PREREQUISITE
Purchase Summon Cyclone ability

Tornadoes will attack enemies on their own.

WARNADO

HORN BLAST
WHIRLWIND
"Twists of Fury!"

Rainbow of Doom hits harder than most other ranged attacks, but it has a slow rate of fire and is difficult to aim. What's great about Rainbow of Doom is that upgrading Tempest Cloud, Whirlwind's other basic attack, benefits Rainbow of Doom as well. Rainbow of Healing increases Whirlwind's value when two Skylanders are working together, but doesn't benefit Whirlwind directly.

The Ultimate Rainbower Path allows Whirlwind to fire two rainbows at once and even create a rainbow singularity. The Tempest Dragon Path allows Whirlwind to create a nice defensive ring of clouds to protect her position when necessary.

Special Quest

What Does It Mean?

DEAL 10,000 DAMAGE WITH RAINBOWS.
Unless your Attack 1 button malfunctions right after you place Whirlwind on the *Portal of Power*, you should earn this quest quickly. Rainbow of Doom should be your primary source of damage, so hitting 10,000 damage shouldn't take long.

Whirlwind is an air dragon with unicorn ancestry—two species that could not be more opposite in nature—which made her never quite fit in with either group. Other dragons were envious of her beauty, while unicorns shunned her for her ability to fly. But Whirlwind found peace within the dark and stormy clouds, where she learned to harness the tempest power within her. Despite her turbulent youth, she was the first to defend both dragons and unicorns when the trolls began hunting them, unleashing her ferocity in a brilliant and powerful rainbow that could be seen throughout many regions of Skylands. From that day forward, evil-doers would quake when dark clouds brewed, and run from the rainbow that followed the storm.

LEVEL	1	2	3	4	5	6	7	8	9	10	11	12	13	14	15	16	17	18	19	20
♥ MAX HEATH	270	297	324	351	378	405	432	459	486	540	567	594	621	648	675	702	729	756	783	810

⚡ SPEED	🛡 ARMOR	⊕ CRITICAL HIT	◎ ELEMENTAL POWER
50	18	10	25

Basic Attacks

RAINBOW OF DOOM

Press **Attack 1** to fire an arced blast of rainbow energy.

TEMPEST CLOUD

Press **Attack 2** to send forth clouds that electrocute enemies. Hold **Attack 2** to make Tempest Clouds travel farther.

Soul Gem Ability

RAINBOW OF HEALING

4000 Gold
PREREQUISITE
None

Rainbows heal your allies!

Upgrades

RAINBOW CHAIN

500 Gold
PREREQUISITE None

Rainbows do extra damage. Hit a Tempest Cloud with a Rainbow of Doom and a second rainbow chains off of it.

TRIPLE TEMPEST

700 Gold
PREREQUISITE None

Have three Tempest Clouds active at once. Tempest Clouds do extra damage.

DRAGON FLIGHT

900 Gold
PREREQUISITE None

Press **Attack 3** to fly. Whirlwind gains increased speed and resistance while flying.

DUEL RAINBOWS

1200 Gold
PREREQUISITE
Purchase Rainbow Chain ability

Hit a Tempest Cloud with a Rainbow of Doom and two rainbows will chain off of it.

Ultimate Rainbower Path

DOUBLE DOSE OF DOOM

1700 Gold
PREREQUISITE
Ultimate Rainbow Path

Shoot two Rainbows of Doom at once.

ATOMIC RAINBOW

2200 Gold
PREREQUISITE
Ultimate Rainbow Path

Rainbow of Doom attack does increased damage.

RAINBOW SINGULARITY

3000 Gold
PREREQUISITE
Ultimate Rainbow Path

Hold **Attack 1** to charge up a super powerful Rainbow of Doom black hole.

Tempest Dragon Path

TRIPLE RAINBOW, IT'S FULL ON

1700 Gold
PREREQUISITE
Tempest Dragon Path

Hit a Tempest Cloud with a Rainbow of Doom and three rainbows will chain off of it.

TEMPEST TANTRUM

2200 Gold
PREREQUISITE
Tempest Dragon Path

Bigger Tempest Cloud does increased damage with increased range.

TEMPEST MATRIX

3000 Gold
PREREQUISITE
Tempest Dragon Path

Electricity forms between Tempest Clouds that hurts enemies.

Wow Pow!

RAINBOW RUSH!

5000 Gold
PREREQUISITE
Purchase Dragon Flight ability

Hold **Attack 3** to take flight and release powerful rainbow shockwaves with each wing flap.

Rainbow Rush! is a visually impressive ability that suffers from a lack of mobility. Whirlwind hovers in place and blasts the area directly in front of her with rainbow blasts. You can spin her in place, but she can't move from the spot where she began to use the ability.

IMPROVING YOUR SKYLANDERS

As a Portal Master, one of your primary tasks is improving your Skylanders so they can stand up to their enemies throughout the Skylands. This chapter covers the many facets and methods of improving and customizing your Skylanders.

LEVELING

Whenever you defeat an enemy, they leave behind tiny XP orbs. When your Skylanders absorb these orbs, they gain experience and get closer to leveling up. You can see how close your Skylander is to leveling up by examining the XP Bar just below their health. All Skylanders can reach level 20.

STATS

Each Skylander has five Stats: Max Health, Speed, Armor, Critical Hit, and Elemental Power. Max Health is the only stat that increases when your Skylander gains a level. Elemental Power increases when you add Skylanders of the same Elemental type to your collection.

♥ Max Health

This is your Skylander's most important statistic. Whenever their health reaches zero, they are knocked out and you must place another Skylander on the portal.

Top 5 Hats for Max Health

HAT	WHERE FOUND	EFFECT
Volcano Hat	Earn this hat by completing Story Mode on Nightmare difficulty!	+15 Speed, +25 Armor, +50 Maximum Health
Runic Headband	Tuk's Emportium: Portal Master Rank 55	+9 Speed, +50 Maximum Health
Asteroid Hat	Kaos' Fortress	+50 Maximum Health
Turkey Hat	Woodburrow	+50 Maximum Health
UFO Hat	Place the UFO Hat Magic Item on the *Portal of Power*	+9 Speed, +15 Elemental Power, +40 Maximum Health

Legendary Treasures

TREASURE	WHERE FOUND	EFFECT
Crustaceous Clothes	Tuk's Emportium: Portal Master Rank 7	+20 Maximum Health
Jolly Greeble	Iron Jaw Gulch	+10 Maximum Health

Charms

CHARM	WHERE FOUND	EFFECT
Life Elixir	Tuk's Emporium: Portal Master Rank 19	+100 Maximum Health
Health Extender	Snake in the Hole arena	+50 Maximum Health
Big Pants	Beach Breach arena	+10 Maximum Health

Speed

This is how fast your Skylander can move around.

Top 5 Hats for Speed

HAT	WHERE FOUND	EFFECT
Volcano Hat	Earn this hat by completing Story Mode on Nightmare difficulty!	+15 Speed, +25 Armor, +50 Maximum Health
Great Helm	Tuk's Emporium: Portal Master Rank 80	+15 Speed, +20 Armor, +3 Critical Hit %
Four Winds Hat	Frostfest Mountains	+15 Speed
Awesome Hat	Tuk's Emporium: Portal Master Rank 48	+12 Speed, +10 Armor, +2 Critical Hit %
Winged Hat	Tuk's Emporium: Portal Master Rank 44	+12 Speed

Legendary Treasures

TREASURE	WHERE FOUND	EFFECT
Mabu Carving	Tuk's Emporium: Portal Master Rank 33	+5 Speed
Triassic Tooth	Boney Islands	+2 Speed

Charms

CHARM	WHERE FOUND	EFFECT
Rocket Propellant	Tuk's Emporium: Portal Master Rank 50	+1 Speed

Armor

Whenever a Skylander is hit by an enemy attack, it has a chance to be completely deflected by their armor. This stat reflects that chance. For every six points of armor your Skylander has, they have a 1% chance of deflecting an enemy attack. So, a Skylander with 90 Armor has a 15% chance to deflect an attack.

Top 5 Hats for Armor

HAT	WHERE FOUND	EFFECT
Crown of Frost	Winter Keep	+30 Armor
Volcano Hat	Earn this hat by completing Story Mode on Nightmare difficulty!	+15 Speed, +25 Armor, +50 Maximum Health
Teeth Top Hat	Tuk's Emporium: Portal Master Rank 75	+25 Armor, +10 Critical Hit %, +20 Elemental Power
Cactus Hat	Tuk's Emporium: Portal Master Rank 70	+9 Speed, +25 Armor
Card Shark Hat	Tuk's Emporium: Portal Master Rank 42	+25 Armor, +5 Critical Hit %

Top 7 Legendary Treasures for Armor

TREASURE	ACQUIRED	EFFECT
Buttering Blade	Tuk's Emporium: Portal Master Rank 68	+15 Armor
Snowboulder +1	Tuk's Emporium: Portal Master Rank 45	+15 Melee Armor
Spyro Duo Balloon	Tuk's Emporium: Portal Master Rank 43	+15 Melee Armor
Singing Puppet	Tuk's Emporium: Portal Master Rank 55	+15 Ranged Armor
Frozenish Flag	Tuk's Emporium: Portal Master Rank 78	+15 Ranged Armor
Masterful Disguise	Kaos' Fortress	+15 Elemental Armor Boost
Endless Cocoa Cup	Frostfest Mountains	+12 Armor

Charms

TREASURE	ACQUIRED	EFFECT
Ultimate Defense	Icicle Bombing arena	+6 Armor
Body Armor	Treble Theft bonus mission	+4 Armor
Small Shield	Sleepy Turtles bonus mission	+2 Armor
Sword Breaker	Angry Angry Plants arena	+5 Melee Armor
Impervious	Troll Beach Attack arena	+5 Ranged Armor
Mountain's Resolve	Vortex Banquet arena	+3 Elemental Armor Boost
Elemental Shield	Chompy Challenge bonus mission	+2 Elemental Armor Boost
Air Freshener	Cursed Statues bonus mission	+5 Corrupt Creature Armor
Eye Poker	Sweet Blizzard bonus mission	+5 Cyclops Armor
Element Deflect	Golem Invasion bonus mission	+5 Golem Armor
Greeble Be Gone	Chompy Sauce bonus mission	+5 Greeble Armor
Wizard Repellant	Royal Gems bonus mission	+5 Spell Punk Armor

⊕ Critical Hit

This stat determines the chance a Skylander will score a Critical Hit or "crit." A crit scores 150% of regular attack damage. For every five points in Critical Hit, the chance to score a crit increases by 1%. So a Skylander with 50 Critical Hit has a 10% chance of scoring a crit.

Top 5 Hats for Critical Hit

HAT	WHERE FOUND	EFFECT
Firefighter Helmet	Tuk's Emporium: Portal Master Rank 28	+20 Critical Hit %
Traffic Cone Hat	Tuk's Emporium: Portal Master Rank 34	+11 Critical Hit %
Teeth Top Hat	Tuk's Emporium: Portal Master Rank 75	+25 Armor, +10 Critical Hit %, +20 Elemental Power
Skullhelm	Tuk's Emporium: Portal Master Rank 56	+9 Speed, +10 Critical Hit %
Unicorn Hat	Tuk's Emporium: Portal Master Rank 60	+12 Armor, +10 Critical Hit %

Legendary Treasures

TREASURE	WHERE FOUND	EFFECT
Epic Soap of Froth	Tower of Time	+4 Critical Hit%
Bottled Warship	Tuk's Emporium: Portal Master Rank 23	+3 Critical Hit %
Expensive Souvenir	Winter Keep	+5 Critical Hit Multiplier
Elven Arrow	Winter Keep	+3 Critial Hit Multiplier
Skylander Scope	Kaos' Fortress	+2 Critial Hit Multiplier

Charms

CHARM	WHERE FOUND	EFFECT
Good Luck Charm	Cyclops Makeover areana	+1 Critical Hit %
Luck of the Mabu	Chompy Tsunami arena	+1 Critical Hit %
Pointy Spear	Pokey Pokey Spikes arena	+1 Critical Hit %
Power Blend	Sand-Pit-Fall arena	+1 Critical Hit %
Rabbit's Foot	Fishy Fishing bonus mission	+1 Critical Hit %
Cyclops Swatter	Sand Castle arena	+1 Critial Hit Multiplier
Greeble Grappler	Shellshock Curse arena	+1 Critical Hit Multiplier
Kaos Kruncher	Exploding Snowmen arena	+1 Critical Hit Multiplier
Mage Masher	Sheep Mage Rage arena	+1 Critical Hit Multiplier
Overcharged	Tuk's Emporium: Portal Master Rank 39	+1 Critical Hit Multiplier

Elemental Power

Throughout the Skylands, certain zones have favored elements. If you are using a Skylander of that element in one of these zones, they get bonus damage based on how high their Elemental Power is. Each point adds 1% to the bonus damage, so a Skylander with 100 Elemental Power will get 100% bonus damage in their favored zone

Top 5 Hats for Elemental Power

HAT	WHERE FOUND	EFFECT
Aviator's Cap	Sheep Wreck Island	+30 Elemental Power
Elephant Hat	Tuk's Emportium: Portal Master Rank 46	+10 Armor, +25 Elemental Power
Clockwork Hat	Tuk's Emportium: Portal Master Rank 75	+9 Speed, +25 Elemental Power
Crystal Hat	Tuk's Emportium: Portal Master Rank 55	+6 Speed, +25 Elemental Power
Wizard Hat	Tuk's Emportium: Portal Master Rank 40	+25 Elemental Power

Legendary Treasures

TREASURE	WHERE FOUND	EFFECT
Topiary of Doom	Fantasm Forest	+15 Elemental Power
Chieftess Figure	Tuk's Emportium: Portal Master Rank 13	+10 Elemental Power
Deputee Badge	Sheep Wreck Island	+10 Elemental Strength Boost
Cascade Bust	Cascade Glade	+5 Elemental Strength Boost

Charms

CHARM	WHERE FOUND	EFFECT
Unbridled Energy	Frigid Fight bonus mission	+10 Elemental Power
Elemental Outlet	Egg Royale bonus mission	+2 Elemental Power
Might of the Ancients	Ghost Traps bonus mission	+3 Elemental Strength Boost
Elemental Fist	Serpent Attack bonus mission	+2 Elemental Strength Boost

GENERAL BOOSTS FOR SKYLANDERS

Stats aren't the only thing you can improve through collectibles. The following Charms and Legendary Treasures provide other boosts, such as gold, or XP.

Get More Gold
Legendary Treasures

TREASURE	WHERE FOUND	EFFECT
Crooked Currency	Motleyville	+10 Gold Boost
Bubble Chest	Mudwater Hollow	+5 Gold Boost
Golden Abacus	Tuk's Emportium: Portal Master Rank 30	+5 Gold Boost
The Brass Tap	Fantasm Forest	+5 Gold Boost

Get More XP
Legendary Treasures

TREASURE	WHERE FOUND	EFFECT
Urban Art	Sheep Wreck Island	+15 XP Boost
Tik Tok Neck Clock	Iron Jaw Gulch	+10 XP Boost
Yeti Teddy	Frostfest Mountains	+5 XP Boost

Charms

CHARM	WHERE FOUND	EFFECT
Instant Experience	Perfect Captain arena	+5 XP Boost

Food Boost/Gain

Legendary Treasures

TREASURE	WHERE FOUND	EFFECT
Sweet Sasparilla	Unlock Treasure Pedestals in Woodburrow	+10 Food Gain
The Monkey's Paw	Rampant Ruins	+5 Food Gain
Moltenskin Scale	Twisty Tunnels	+10 Elemental Food Boost
The Bling Grille	Motleyville	+5 Elemental Food Boost

Charms

CHARM	WHERE FOUND	EFFECT
Delicious Food	Chomp Chomp Chompies arena	+5 Food Gain
Gourmet Meal	Boarding Party arena	+5 Food Gain
Major Meal	Master Chef bonus mission	+5 Food Gain
Tasty Food	Fruit Fight bonus mission	+5 Food Gain
Vitamin Supplements	Froezen Delight bonus mission	+15 Elemental Food Boost
Elemental Noms	Super Hungry Gobble Pods arena	+5 Elemental Food Boost

Have More Luck

Legendary Treasures

TREASURE	WHERE FOUND	EFFECT
Bonnie Bonsai	Tuk's Emportium: Portal Master Rank 37	+15 Luck
Major Award Monkey	Rampart Ruins	+10 Luck
Refurbished Engine	Tuk's Emportium: Portal Master Rank 27	+10 Elemental Luck Boost
Crystal Fire Hearth	Twisty Tunnels	+5 Elemental Luck Boost

Charms

CHARM	WHERE FOUND	EFFECT
Power Clover	Chunky Chmopies arena	+6 Luck
Eight Leaf Clover	Beware the Bird arena	+4 Luck
Four Leaf Clover	Plants Vs Cakes bonus mission	+2 Luck
Charmed Actions	Thief on the Run bonus mission	+3 Elemental Luck Boost
Elemental Fortune	Undercover Greebles bonus mission	+2 Elemental Luck Boost

Pickup Range

Legendary Treasures

TREASURE	ACQUIRED	EFFECT
Whizzing Whatsit	Complete 36 SWAP Zone Challenges on Nightmare difficulty	+30 Pickup Range
Glowy Mushroom	Fantasm Forest	+15 Pickup Range

Charms

CHARM	WHERE FOUND	EFFECT
Electro Magnet	Magic Cells bonus mission	+5 Pickup Range

POWERS & UPGRADES

Each non-*SWAP Force* Skylander starts out with two Powers. For more details on what powers your individual Skylanders start out with, check out The Skylanders chapter. *SWAP Force* Skylanders begin with one power for their body, and another power for their legs. In addition to these starting powers, each regular Skylander and *SWAP Force* body can also purchase an additional power in the Power Pod, but it costs gold.

The remaining Power Upgrades are all purchased from Power Pods. There is one Power Pod in Woodburrow, and others are found at Checkpoints in most Story Levels.

Upgrade Paths

Skylanders must also choose a Path. This Path represents the Skylander choosing to develop one power or ability over another.

Most Skylanders must permanently commit to one path once they have unlocked their first four power upgrades. *SWAP Force* Skylanders have Upgrade Path choices for both their body and their legs.

The exceptions to this rule are the Series 2 and Series 3 figures. After committing to a path, these Skylanders may switch paths while inside a Power Pod.

Wow-Pow! Powers

Series 2 and Series 3 figures have new Wow-Pow! powers that are expensive, but significantly improve an existing power. For more details on Series 2 and 3 Wow Pow! powers, check out The Skylanders chapter.

Soul Gem Ability

All characters introduced in *Skylanders SWAP Force* must find their Soul Gem before they can purchase their Soul Gem Ability. The walkthrough contains more information on where to find each Soul Gem, or check out The Skylanders section of the guide. Skylanders from the previous games may purchase their Soul Gem Power without the need to find a Soul Gem.

HATS

Each Skylander can wear one magic hat which provides bonuses to stats. Hats are available for purchase from Tuk's Emporium, and found throughout Story Mode Levels. Use Hats to supplement your Skylander's weaker Stats. For instance, if your Skylander has low armor, look for a hat that provides additional armor! You can change your Skylander's Hat at any time via the Skylanders menu. Once you find a Hat, you can put it on as many Skylanders as you like. See our Collectibles chapter for more information on individual Hats.

LEGENDARY TREASURES

After Tibbet unlocks Legendary Treasure Pedestals, you have a new way to boost your Skylanders. Placing a Legendary Treasure on one of these Pedestals conveys a bonus that applies to every aspect of the game. The best part about Legendary Treasures is that you can tailor the ones in use to your needs. If you have a new Skylander and want to hit level 20 as quickly as possible, opt for Tik Tok Neck Clock or Urban Art which boost your XP. If you're short on gold because of all the Hats you need to buy, put The Brass Tap and Bubble Chest on the Pedestals to increase the gold you find.

Some of the bonuses are oddly specific, but they could be a tremendous help for you when you're shooting to complete certain Challenges, whether it's in the Arena, Time Attack, or just finishing off Kaos for the first time.

CHARMS

Except for a few Tuk sells, you must earn Charms by completing Bonus Mission Maps and Arena challenges. Each Charm is active as soon as you acquire it. All the effects are cumulative and the bonuses from Charms are active at all times.

QUESTS

All Skylanders have nine Quests to complete. You can check your Skylander's progress on any of these quests at any time by entering the Skylander menu and selecting Quests. Completing these quests improves their rank. Also when a Skylander receives a Quest medal, they receive +25 of Max Health Bonus. So completing all the Quests earns a Skylander +75 of their Max. Health. Improving a Skylander's rank gives them a medal next to their name and also works toward Portal Master Accolades.

BRONZE TOY QUEST MEDAL	SILVER TOY QUEST MEDAL	GOLD TOY QUEST MEDAL
Complete 3 Quests	Complete 7 Quests	Complete 10 Quests

Every Skylander shares six quests, and each Skylander of the same Element shares another two. Elementalist appears as an Elemental quest, but the condition for completing it is the same for every character. Each Skylander has a unique quest as well. For more information about unique quests, check out the individual Skylanders sections found earlier in this guide.

General Quests

BADGUY BASHER
Objective: Defeat 1000 enemies.

Every enemy defeated by your Skylander counts here, even if it's 1000 Chompies. To get through this quest quickly, run challenges where Chompies appear in large numbers.

FRUIT FRONTIERSMAN
Objective: Eat 15 fruits in Story Levels or Arenas.

Eat every piece of fruit you see while playing in Story Levels and Arenas. If your current Skylander has this quest complete, switch to a Skylander that is working on it still when a piece of fruit appears.

FLAWLESS CHALLENGER

Objective: Complete a non-Story Mode level with full health.

The only requirement for this quest is to complete the level with full health. Taking damage during the level doesn't matter, provided you can return to full health before it's over.

TOTALLY MAXED OUT

Objective: Reach level 20 and purchase all Upgrades for this Skylander.

This quest is tough for your first Skylander, but it becomes easier after you unlock every Legendary Treasure Pedestal, earn the Instant Experience Charm, and collect each Winged Sapphire.

ELEMENTALIST

Objective: Cause 7500 elemental bonus damage.

When your Skylander does elemental bonus damage, their elemental icon appears behind the damage numbers that appear when you attack enemies. Stack up bonus damage with a good Hat, Charms, and the four Legendary Treasures that boost Elemental damage output.

Magic Quests

PUZZLE POWER

Objective: Push a Lazer Puzzle Beam to defeat an enemy.

Bonus Mission Frozen Delight is a great spot to complete this quest, but you must wait until the third Yeti to do it. Lure one of the cyclops enemies across the bridge and push one of the puzzle pieces over it until it turns into XP bubbles.

MAGE RIVALRY

Objective: Defeat a total of 25 Ranged Cyclops.

Each Gazermage and Sleetthrower you defeat counts toward completion of this quest. Beyond appearances across Story Mode, they also show up in Sheep Wreck Islands and the Ghost Traps Bonus Mission.

Fire Quests

MEGA MELTER

Objective: Defeat a total of 25 Ice Golems.

Ice Golems appear in Winter Keep and Cloudbreak Core. Winter Keep is the better spot to hunt for them. Be prepared to run through this level multiple times to complete this quest for each Fire Skylander.

BOMBARDIER

Objective: Defeat a total of 30 enemies with bombs.

Blast Zone has an easy time with Bombardier, but for everyone else, Motleyville is a great level for doing the quest. After defeating Evilized Whiskers, don't take out any enemies until you reach the rail car with the dynamite inside. Use the dynamite to take out the enemies both before and after the gate.

Water Quests

EXTINGUISHER

Objective: Defeat a total of 25 Fire Golems.

Fire Geargolems are the most common encountered throughout Story Mode, and there are a few Fire Golems in the Golem Invasion Bonus Mission Map.

A-FISH-IONADO

Objective: Catch 25 fish with the fishing rod.

There are a few fishing spots in the Story Mode, but the Under Hollow in Woodburrow is the best place to wrap up this quest quickly.

Undead Quests

WITHERER

Objective: Defeat a total of 25 Life Spellpunks.

Life Spellpunks pop up throughout the Story Mode, Arena challenges, and are all over the Golem Invasion Bonus Mission Map.

BACK FROM THE BRINK

Objective: Defeat a boss while at critically low health.

Back from the Brink can be a test of nerves if you try for it intentionally, or a feeling of great relief when you barely defeat a boss while your Skylander's health is blinking red.

Tech Quests

OUT-TECHED

Objective: Defeat Glumshanks in Jungle Rumble without switching Skylanders.

If you need help with defeating Glumshanks with a single Skylander, keep Magic Items handy to restore health, add protection, or deal damage when needed.

PROBLEM SOLVER

Objective: Complete a total of 25 lockpicking puzzles with this Skylander.

The lockpicking puzzles are the Spark Lock Treasure Chests found throughout the Story Mode. There's another Spark Lock Treasure Chest in Woodburrow's The Great Hollow that respawns often.

Life Quests

DEFENDER OF LIFE

Objective: Defeat a total of 25 Undead Spellpunks.

Hunt for Undead Spellpunks (and the Undead Cadet Crushers they summon) in Chapter 14: Fantasm Forest and the Bonus Mission Royal Gems.

FULLY STOCKED

Objective: Defeat a total of 250 enemies while at full health.

This quest is more about being careful while taking down enemies.

Earth Quests

SAVIOR OF THE LAND

Objective: Free the Terrasquid in the Twisty Tunnels without switching Skylanders.

Twisty Tunnels is the eighth chapter of Story Mode. Get through it without changing Skylanders to complete this quest.

UNEARTHER

Objective: Use shovels to dig a total of 25 holes.

Twisty Tunnels asks you to dig a few holes, as does Winter Keep. A few trips through these Story Mode chapters should be enough to dig up 25 holes.

Air Quests

GERONIMO!

Objective: Travel over 250 feet in one fall.

Use the Epic Launch Pad at the top of Treetrunk Peak in Woodburrow to reach the hidden area with the Turkey Hat. Complete the course and return to Woodburrow to complete this quest.

SKYLOOTER

Objective: Collect a total of 500 gold in midair.

Any gold collected while your Skylander is off the ground counts here. That means jumping through a line of valuables counts as much as flying through a line of coins above a bounce pad.

BOSSES

Evil Glumshanks

APPEARS IN: CHAPTER 5: JUNGLE RUMBLE

STAGE 1

There are two hazards to avoid during every stage of the battle against Evil Glumshanks and his improvised Arkeyan tank. The first hazard is Evil Glumshanks. Except for one exception covered in the next paragraph, stay away from it. The other hazard is the spear-lined walls of the arena. Do not touch them at any point!

During the first stage of the fight, Glumshanks puts his headlights on your Skylander and they slowly change color from yellow to red. When the headlights turn red, the tank charges in a straight line across the arena floor. You must not only avoid the charge attack, but you need to bait Glumshanks into driving his tank into one of the panels of spikes. When you are successful, Glumshank's tank loses its Arkeyan armor and is vulnerable to attack. Continue to attack, even while the tank re-armors itself. When the tank is fully re-armored, it sends out a non-damaging pulse to push away nearby objects, including pesky Skylanders!

Continue the pattern of forcing Glumshanks to crash into spikes while avoiding them yourself, attacking his tank when it's vulnerable, and moving to a safe spot in front of spikes again while Glumshank's uses his tank's headlights to line up his attack. After Glumshank loses around one-third of his health, he changes things slightly.

STAGE 2

Glumshanks realizes the spikes are hurting him, so he removes half of them from the walls. The second thing that he does is to launch rockets (watch for the tell-tale red circles on the ground for their target location) before using his headlights to acquire his target.

Your tasks are essentially unchanged during this stage. Avoid incoming rockets, then stand in front of a panel of spears until the tank's headlights turn red. Avoid the charge and lay into the unarmored tank until its armor reforms around it. When Glumshanks is down to one-third health remaining, he calls for reinforcements.

STAGE 3

Glumshanks spawns Arkeyan Knuckledusters for help. These pint-sized terrors are as tenacious as Chompies, but carry a big mace for clubbing Skylanders. To make matters worse, Evil Glumshanks continues to use rockets.

You must now take down the Arkeyan Knuckledusters, avoid the rockets falling from above, and still move in front of the sole set of spikes before the tank's headlights go red. Just to keep things lively, each time you successfully lure Glumshanks into the spikes, he changes which wall is active!

When you deplete Glumshank's health entirely, his coating of darkness is removed and he realizes he's just no Kaos.

Back In Woodburrow

Rufus informs you that Snagglescale has set up a hut near The Airdocks, and has a way to help you improve your skills in battle. Speak with Snagglescale to learn more about Arenas, and even try out the first one! When you are ready to continue the adventure, speak with Tessa about Iron Jaw Gulch.

Baron Von Shellshock & Evilized Whiskers

EVILIZED WHISKERS

Watch the ground for a glowing circle (it looks the same as the ones used by Evilized Kangarats) when Evilzed Whiskers is in the air. When Whiskers slams into the ground, a shockwave spreads out along the ground. Jump over the shockwave, then attack Whiskers while his head is stuck in the ground. When Whiskers is down to three-quarters health, he jumps and lands three times before his head becomes stuck in the ground and you can attack. At 50% health, Whiskers flies off.

The battle against Evilized Whiskers picks up again later in the level after you meet up with Birdwatcher.

Evilized Whiskers begins by bombarding the ground from a perch that's too high for your Skylander to reach. Avoid the target spots on the ground, then dodge three ground slam attacks. After the third ground slam, Whiskers is vulnerable to attack.

The good news for you is that Whiskers begins the fight at around half health. At one-third health, Whiskers mixes things up after you get in your attacks. Instead of returning to his perch immediately, Whiskers fires out an energy beam. Get behind him to avoid being hit by this attack, because it hits hard. Whiskers mixes up his attacks at this point, so be prepared to avoid any of his abilities and strike when he's vulnerable.

BARON VON SHELLSHOCK

Baron von Shellshock is immune to regular attacks most of the time. During the first stage of the battle, the Baron launches various enemies to keep you occupied. He also throws bundles of dynamite at the end of a string of cannonballs. Avoid the cannonballs, then grab the dynamite and throw it at the Baron before the timer reaches zero.

When the dynamite impacts the Baron's vehicle, the vehicle loses a chunk of health, its defenses vanish, and it becomes vulnerable temporarily. Hit it with your best attacks as quickly as possible, but watch out for the enemies the Baron launched earlier. He may be down, but they can keep attacking.

Take out the minions while you're waiting for the next bundle of dynamite, but don't worry about finishing them off if there's dynamite ready for use. This is especially true at the end of the fight. As soon as Baron von Shellshock's health is gone, every enemy assisting him is destroyed instantly.

Fire Viper

STAGE 1

Sharpfin set up two giant crossbows that fire cables at the Fire Viper. You know they are loaded and ready to use when red suction cups are visible at the front of each weapon. To fire a crossbow, you just need to be close enough to get a button prompt to appear over it. Sharpfin will also helpfully leave food items between the crossbows at certain points, so if your Skylander needs a recharge, keep an eye open.

The Fire Viper coughs up fiery mines into the air. A red target circle appears on the ground where one will hit. During the first stage, all you need to do is avoid the circles and fire off both crossbows to bring the Fire Viper's head down to the ground. Don't move too close until after the head touches down. There's a minor shockwave that pushes away anything too close.

The first time you bring down the Fire Viper's head, Sharpfin pops up and points out the crystallized darkness on top of it. Run up to the crystals and deal as much damage as you can. After inflicting a certain amount of damage, the Fire Viper shakes off the suction cups and sends your Skylander to the back of the area, near a pool of damaging goo.

The next thing the Fire Viper does is spray the entire area with fiery breath. Fortunately, two tentacles appear and offer a place to hide from the sweeping breath attack. Repeat the process of using both crossbows and damaging the crystals on top of Fire Viper's head again.

This time after the Fire Viper shakes free, he covers the area in fiery mines that you must avoid. They are not like the ones that explode on contact with the ground. These mines do not go away, even after they crash into your Skylander. Your Skylander takes damage, but the mine sticks around!

Take down the Fire Viper with the crossbows again, and avoid the fiery mines while hiding behind the tentacles during Fire Viper's fiery breath attack. A third successful attack on the crystals atop the Fire Viper's skull initiates the second stage of the battle.

STAGE 2

This stage begins when Fire Viper swallows your Skylander whole! During the trip down the beast's gullet, avoid the violet jets of flame that appear a few times. You'll need every bit of health for the upcoming battle against three Fire Geargolems. You catch a bit of a break as the third Fire Geargolem begins the battle a short distance away, but two at once is bad enough!

Stay on the move as much as possible. Standing still to attack invites one of the other golems to bathe your Skylander in flames, which usually results in the need to change Skylanders on your *Portal of Power*.

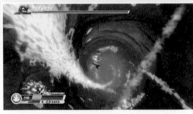

When all three Fire Geargolems are down, the hardest part of the battle is over. All that's left to do is destroy the crystal formation at the back of the chamber. When that's done, you return to Woodburrow, joined by a grateful Ancient Terrasquid.

Back In Woodburrow

Rufus sends you to speak with Tessa, who has set up a turret mini-game above the Trophy Room with Wheellock's help. The turret mini-game is a way to practice your shooting skills. You have a chance to earn gold, especially when you get a perfect wave bonus. The mini-game ends as soon as you hit one mine. When you're done trying out the turret, speak with Sharpfin at The Airdocks.

129

Mesmeralda

Mesmeralda employs three types of puppets during this fight. You encountered two in the previous Story Level, and the new addition, dancing puppets, are the first hazard you must avoid. They project ghostly pink lines across the stage. Stand clear of the lines before the white puppets dash along them. They travel left to right, right to left, and front to back.

After you avoid a few waves of the puppets, two stage lights appear. Each light hits one of the openings in the building on the stage. Look for Mesmeralda's pink eyes to appear in the openings and hit them with the stage light to blind her. She is vulnerable while blinded, which is your opportunity to get in a few shots and reduce her health.

After she recovers, she flies back to the stage and resets the scenery on it, but the building in the set has an extra opening. That is the pattern for each round of this fight. Avoid her minions, blind her with a stage light, then attack her until she recovers and resets the stage.

For the second round, Mesmeralda drops proximity mines during the dancing puppets attack, and continues to drop them when the stage lights appear. There are three lights for three windows this time, so keep watching for her eyes to appear and be ready to attack as soon as she's blinded.

The third round's addition is dancing puppets appearing from two perpendicular directions at closer intervals. The dashing lines for the next batch start to appear before the first batch has faded. She also deploys more proximity mines at a time. There are three stage lights on the stage at the end of this round.

Giant spinning blades make their debut in the fourth round, and the dancing puppets appear in greater numbers. At least the proximity mines are understudies, and off the stage, for this round. There are four stage lights to choose from at the end of this round, and the spinning blade continues to chase your Skylander while you pick a light and attack Mesmeralda.

Mesmeralda adds a second spinning blade to the initial waves of dancing puppets, but she doesn't add any additional stage lights to the end. She also keeps the proximity mines away.

One last round to go! The grand finale begins with a stage filled with dancing puppets and a spinning blade. Mesmeralda gradually adds proximity mines as well. Avoid all the hazards on stage and hit her with one last stage light. When she appears, she drops another spinning blade and a few proximity mines. As each mine explodes, more are added around the stage. When she complains about outside food in the theatre, look around for food in the area if your Skylander is low on health. She's almost down, so don't worry about the food if your Skylander's health is fine. Once you've finished with her it's time to head back to Woodburrow with the Ancient Frosthound.

Back In Woodburrow

Rufus and the Chieftess are overjoyed at the return of the Ancient Frosthound, but Tessa's news tempers the celebration. Speak with Sharpfin when you're ready to travel to Fantasm Forest to learn more.

TESSA
urgent message! Kaos has been spotted near the Fantasm Forest! He's going

Mr. Chompy

APPEARS IN: CHAPTER 15: KAOS' FORTRESS

Trickster found a magical pool in the Mystical Fountains, but Mr. Chompy, a giant Chompy Pastepetal, also claimed it. Mr. Chompy splits into smaller and smaller Chompy Pastepetals as he is struck. Try to focus on one piece at a time. Keep one half as large as possible while taking down the smaller and smaller Chompies spawned by the second half. If you aren't worried about being overwhelmed by numbers, then just keep hammering whatever pieces of Mr. Chompy are in range. After you finish off the last little fragment of Mr. Chompy, Trickster gives you the **Asteroid Hat**.

Kaos' Mom & Bubba Greebs

APPEARS IN: CHAPTER 16: MOTHERLY MAYHEM

DEFEAT KAOS' MOM

As if to show that the rotten apple didn't fall from the gnarled old tree, Kaos' Mom floats safely above the floor, keeping her hands clean while you face her minions. She first sends out evilized creatures to deal with you. These creatures are identical to the ones you faced throughout the Story Mode.

When she runs out of minions, Kaos' Mom vanishes! She is trying to hide within her *Portal of Power*. To reveal her location, remove any Skylanders on your *Portal of Power*. She wasn't expecting you to find her, so she flees back to Kaos' Fortress.

Kaos' Mom returns to her position, floating above the floor. However, two large, green crystals appeared on the floor while everyone was in the

Portal of Power. Kaos' Mom fires a beam at the floor and directs it toward your Skylander. Run behind one of the green crystals so the beam hits it. The crystal absorbs the beam and fires it back at Kaos' Mom, who then flies away to another room.

The next room includes bench seating for an audience, though some of the creatures in the seats join the fight. This round of the fight begins like the last, with evilized enemies attacking in groups while Kaos' Mom stays above the fight on her *Portal of Power*. Watch out for any Life Spell Punks. When one appears, make it your number one target.

After you defeat all the evilized creatures, Kaos' Mom vanishes from her *Portal of Power*. Remove your Skylander from the *Portal of Power* to chase her back into Kaos' Fortress.

When your Skylander is back in the game, Kaos' Mom blasts the ground with her beam attack. Run behind either one of the crystals to deflect it back at her. She flies off again after the beam hits her.

Follow the red carpet, but watch out for glob lobbers on either side. There are a few destructible objects on either side of the hallway at various points along the way.

The red carpet leads from the hallway into the throne room. Kaos' Mom sends out Bubba Greebs, an incredibly large Greeble, to deal with you this time. Bubba Greebs throws various types of Greebles from the balcony. He also throws explosives. You must avoid the red circles on the ground, but watch for a bundle of dynamite to appear on the ground nearby.

Pick up the dynamite and throw it at Bubba Greebs to knock him down to the floor. He sends out a shockwave where he lands, so jump over it and attack him quickly. The Greebles on the floor don't vanish when Bubba Greebs hits the ground, and they won't sit and watch while you attack their large friend. Bubba Greebs continues to throw dynamite until you knock him down, so don't worry about missing an opportunity if a bundle of dynamite goes unused.

After taking some damage, Bubba Greebs recovers and jumps back up to his spot on the balcony. He resumes throwing Greebles and explosives into the lower area, though the types of Greeble change each time you knock him down and damage him.

Once Bubba Greebs runs out of health, Kaos' Mom reappears just long enough to retreat into her *Portal of Power*. Take your Skylander off your *Portal of Power* to return her to the fight.

When everyone is back in the throne room, she fires her beam attack again, but this time there are no crystals! Run away from the beam until Tessa intervenes. Run onto the mirror's surface when it appears and finally defeat Kaos' Mom!

Back In Woodburrow
Rufus and the Chieftess provide an update on Kaos' plans. Speak with Tessa to begin the final fight to save the Skylands from an age of darkness.

Super Evil Kaos

DEFEAT SUPER EVIL KAOS

The first stage of the fight takes place at the feet of Super Evil Kaos. Avoid the shockwaves after he stomps the ground with the Thundersteps of Doom, and attack the crystallized darkness on his toenails. He attacks with both feet, so you must clear the crystals from both.

After half the crystals on his toes have been destroyed, Kaos stomps on the ground twice before letting his foot rest long enough to be attacked. Keep moving from toe to toe when one is depleted of crystals.

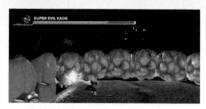

With all the crystals on his toes gone, Super Evil Kaos swallows your Skylander. Attack the crystals on the back of his teeth. You're free to do damage until Kaos opens his mouth and throws in enemies, including a Fire Geargolem.

When you've defeated the enemies, Kaos slams his mouth shut and two shockwaves form from his molars. Jump over both shockwaves and get back to attacking his teeth. Kaos does another bite down, which sends more shockwaves through his mouth.

Kaos throws in another batch of enemies including Ice Geargolem, The group after that has a Tech Geargolem. The next wave of enemies includes both a Tech Geargolem and an Air Geargolem. Keep attacking the teeth and avoiding shockwaves between enemy group appearances. After the final crystal on his teeth is destroyed, your Skylander moves to Kaos' ear canal and into his brain.

Kaos sends minions to defend himself. First up is Glumshanks in his vehicle. It is invulnerable to damage, so just avoid it until it falls off the edge. Up next are enemies you can damage, so take them down as they appear. Grumblebum Thrashers are up first, along with a Boom Boss.

With those enemies out of the way, three shards of crystallized darkness are embedded in the ground. Attack the shards to destroy them, but watch out for the missiles falling from above.

The next wave of enemies is made up of Arkeyan Rip-rotors and Cyclops Gazermages. When you defeat them, three more crystal shards appear. Avoid the incoming missiles and destroy the shards.

The next wave of enemies is a swarm of Kaos sheep. They don't have any range abilities, so keep on the move so they don't overwhelm you with their numbers. Kaos doesn't bother with missiles this time. Instead he sends out Mesmeralda's proximity mine puppets!

Destroying the final three crystals induces a sneeze from Kaos that sends your Skylander out of his head. There's a nearby weapon that's ready to be used against Kaos, but he makes the sprint there as hard as possible.

Every few seconds, Kaos fires a giant purple beam from his hands that destroys everything in its path. He sweeps the beam back down the path toward your Skylander. When it draws near, jump over the beam and hurry ahead.

When your Skylander reaches the cannon, charge it up quickly and end Kaos' latest threat to the Skylands!

Back at Woodburrow

Rufus, Tessa, and Flynn congratulate you on your amazing victory over Kaos. Rufus urges you to visit with Wheellock to learn about Score Mode, and Avril for more information about Timed Attack. You may have defeated Kaos, but there's still plenty more to do!

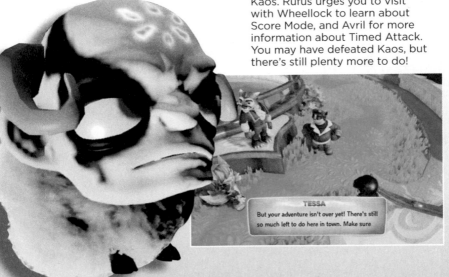

TESSA
But your adventure isn't over yet! There's still so much left to do here in town. Make sure

Sheep Mage

THE SHEEP MAGE

The Sheep Mage changes
into his giant sheep
form and spends most of
his time sucking in and blowing
out air, pushing and pulling your
Skylander and the Sheep Mage's
own cyclops minions, around the
Altar of Worheep.

Stay as far away from the giant sheep
as possible. The spiny orange creatures
that appeared throughout Sheep Wreck Island line the area directly in
front of the Sheep Mage. Take down any cyclopes when the opportunity
presents itself, but staying away from the spiny orange creatures is your
number one priority.

When Blind Beard appears, he tosses a timed bomb that you must
retrieve and throw at the Sheep Mage. When he falls to the ground and
drops the Magic Staff, a few mines spawn and
circle the area. Avoid the mines and attack the
Magic Staff. After a short while, the Sheep Mage
recovers and returns to his position outside the
battle area. The mines are destroyed and more
cyclopes spawn.

The types of cyclopes spawning are
slightly tougher than the first group
faced. Repeat your tactics from
the first stage. Stay clear of the
area directly in front of the Sheep
Mage and take down the cyclopes
when you can. When you use the
timed bomb on the Sheep Mage the
second time, far more mines spawn,
and getting past them is trickier.
Watch for the ones that move and
run through the gaps that appear.
Attack the Magic Staff until the
Sheep Mage recovers and resets
the area.

The next wave of minions includes a
Vortex Geargolem. Don't relax after
you take down the first one. Two
more spawn immediately! Focus
on one enemy at a time until it's
down, then switch to the other one.
When Blind Beard appears with the
third bomb, the mines that appear
around the Magic Staff are set up
similar to the first set, but are more
numerous and move around the
area faster. Attack the Magic Staff
again and destroy it.

Cluck

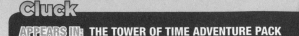

CLUCK

After you place the second gear on the Tower of Time, Cluck takes a more active role in trying to keep everyone out. He drops heavily onto the ground, sending out a shockwave that deals damage. Jump over the shockwave, hit the Time-Freeze switch, and attack Cluck while he's on the ground. Cluck calls for troll reinforcements while he recovers from being attacked, but he still shoots energy spheres into the area. Watch for glowing circles on the ground and keep away from them when they appear.

When the trolls are eliminated, Cluck returns to fight. This time he hits the ground multiple times before he stays down. Use the Time-Freeze switch any time he's on the ground to lock him in place and attack. Just keep track of the shockwaves on the ground. If your Skylander is near one when time flows again, there could be some pain in store. When Cluck is down to about one-quarter health, he decides to tuck tail and run.

The battle against Cluck picks up again after you replace the third gear on the Tower of Time and ride a spinning wood platform from its lowest level to the top.

This fight is similar to the previous one, but this time you must stop time to get through his energy shield. Cluck continues to jump and land and send out shockwaves until you freeze time.

When Cluck is down to about one-third of his total health, he summons Time Spellpunks and discharges a laser blast across the room. When he resumes dropping down from above, he pauses every few jumps and spits energy balls into the air. Orange rings on the ground mark their destination. Take out the Time Spellpunks as soon as they spawn and use the Time-Freeze switch to destroy Cluck's battle suit.

BOSSES

MOUNT CLOUDBREAK

OBJECTIVES

Story Goals

○ Get to Woodburrow

Dares

5 Flynn's Missing Stuff

50 Enemy Goal

0 No Skylanders Defeated

Collections

13 Areas Discovered

3 Treasure Chests

1 Giant Treasure Chest

2 Soul Gems

1 Legendary Treasure

3 Hats

1 Bonus Mission Map

1 Winged Sapphire

1 Story Scroll

Map Key

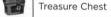	SWAP Zone Challenges
	Treasure Chest
	Giant Treasure Chest
	Pop Thorn Soul Gem
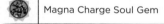	Magna Charge Soul Gem
	Legendary Treasure
	Hat
	Bonus Mission Map
	Winged Sapphire
	Story Scroll
	Dare
	Checkpoint

New Enemies

Chompy

Greeble

Greeble Screwball

Chompy Pod

C

B

C

FINISH

B

A

A

A

START

139

CASCADE GLADE

OBJECTIVES

Story Goals

○ Rescue the Chieftess

Dares

(5) Seed Packets

(50) Enemy Goal

(0) No Skylanders Defeated

Collections

(13) Areas Discovered

(4) Treasure Chests

(1) Giant Treasure Chest

(3) Soul Gems

(1) Legendary Treasure

(3) Hats

(1) Bonus Mission Map

(1) Winged Sapphire

(1) Story Scroll

Map Key

◯	SWAP Zone Challenges
🧰	Treasure Chest
📦	Giant Treasure Chest
	Countdown Soul Gem
	Slobber Tooth Soul Gem
	Rattle Shake Soul Gem
	Legendary Treasure
🎩	Hat
	Bonus Mission Map
	Winged Sapphire
	Story Scroll
⭐	Dare
✅	Checkpoint

New Enemies

Evilized Greeble

Greeble Blunderbuss

Greeble Ironclad

START

Seeker Scope

Seeker Scope

FINISH

MUDWATER HOLLOW

OBJECTIVES

Story Goals

- ◯ Get to the Ancient Flashfin
- ◯ Catch 3 Piranhas
- ◯ Catch the Gear Fish
- ◯ Save the Village
- ◯ De-Evilize the Bog Hog
- ◯ Destroy the Crystals

Dares

- (6) Floaty Life Preserver
- (50) Enemy Goal
- (0) No Skylanders Defeated

Collections

- (26) Areas Discovered
- (6) Treasure Chests
- (1) Giant Treasure Chest
- (3) Soul Gems
- (2) Legendary Treasures
- (2) Hats
- (1) Bonus Mission Map
- (1) Winged Sapphire
- (1) Story Scroll

Map Key

◯	SWAP Zone Challenges
🧰	Treasure Chest
📦	Giant Treasure Chest
⚙	Zou Lou Soul Gem
⚙	Free Ranger Soul Gem
⚙	Bumble Blast Soul Gem
🏆	Legendary Treasure
🎩	Hat
🗺	Bonus Mission Map
🦋	Winged Sapphire
📜	Story Scroll
⭐	Dare
✔	Checkpoint

New Enemies

Grumblebum Thrasher

Life Spell Punk

Grumblebum Rockshooter

Evilized Bog Hog

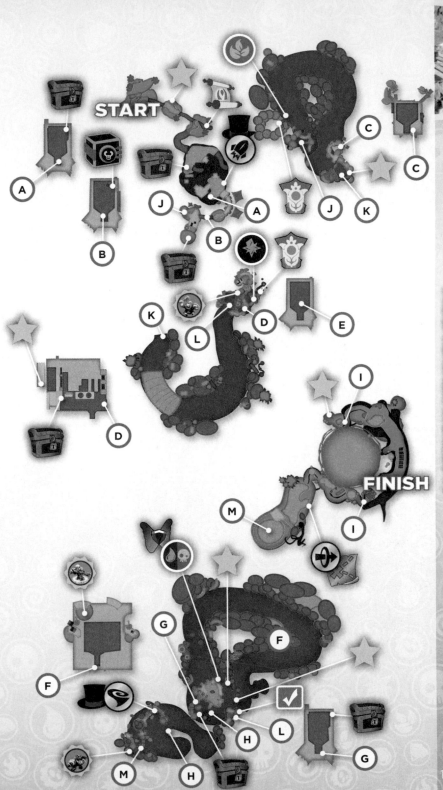

START

FINISH

143

RAMPANT RUINS

OBJECTIVES

Story Goals

○ Un-Evilize the Sugarbats

○ Activate the Stone Monkey

○ Get to the Stone Monkey

Dares

(5) Grave Monkey Totems

(50) Enemy Goal

(0) No Skylanders Defeated

Collections

(12) Areas Discovered

(5) Treasure Chests

(1) Giant Treasure Chest

(2) Soul Gems

(2) Legendary Treasures

(2) Hats

(1) Bonus Mission Map

(1) Winged Sapphire

(1) Story Scroll

Map Key

⬤	SWAP Zone Challenges
📦	Treasure Chest
📦	Giant Treasure Chest
⦿	Roller Brawl Soul Gem
⦿	Star Strike Soul Gem
⬥	Legendary Treasure
🎩	Hat
✖	Bonus Mission Map
🦋	Winged Sapphire
📜	Story Scroll
★	Dare
✔	Checkpoint

New Enemies

Chompy
Rustbud

Arkeyan
Barrelbot

Evilized
Sugarbat

Arkeyan
Rip-Rotor

Arkeyan
Slamshock

Evil
Glumshanks

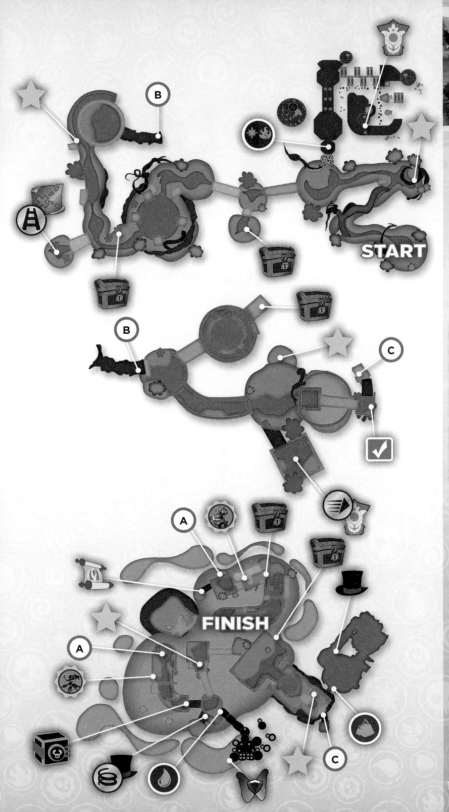

START

FINISH

IRON JAW GULCH

OBJECTIVES

Story Goals

○ Destroy the Airships

Dares

(5) Marshal Wheellock Plushies
(50) Enemy Goal
(0) No Skylanders Defeated

Collections

(15) Areas Discovered
(2) Treasure Chests
(1) Giant Treasure Chest
(3) Soul Gems
(2) Legendary Treasures
(2) Hats
(1) Bonus Mission Map
(1) Winged Sapphire
(1) Story Scroll

Map Key

	SWAP Zone Challenges
	Treasure Chest
	Giant Treasure Chest
	Wind-Up Soul Gem
	Grim Creeper Soul Gem
	Grilla Drilla Soul Gem
	Legendary Treasure
	Hat
	Bonus Mission Map
	Winged Sapphire
	Story Scroll
	Dare
	Checkpoint

New Enemies

Pirate Powderkeg

Fire Geargolem

Pirate Slamspin

Evilized Kangarat

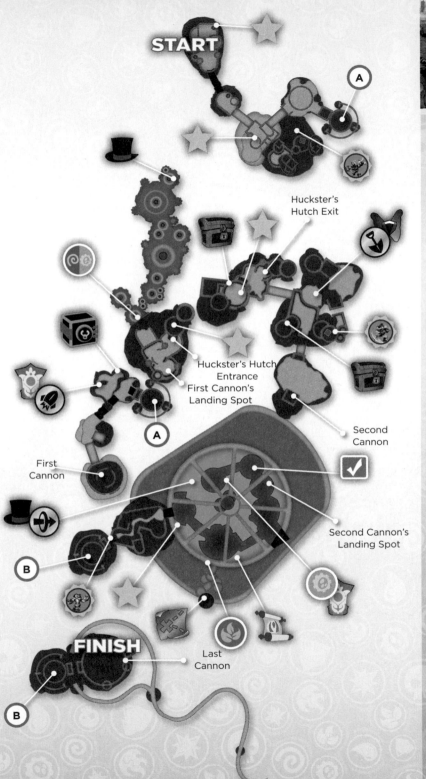

START

A

Huckster's
Hutch Exit

Huckster's Hutch
Entrance
First Cannon's
Landing Spot

A

Second
Cannon

First
Cannon

Second Cannon's
Landing Spot

B

FINISH

Last
Cannon

B

MOTLEYVILLE

OBJECTIVES

Story Goals

- ○ Stop Baron von Shellshock
- ○ De-Evilize Whiskers

Dares

- (5) Toy Trains
- (50) Enemy Goal
- (0) No Skylanders Defeated

Collections

- (24) Areas Discovered
- (5) Treasure Chests
- (1) Giant Treasure Chest
- (3) Soul Gems
- (2) Legendary Treasures
- (2) Hats
- (1) Bonus Mission Map
- (1) Winged Sapphire
- (1) Story Scroll

Map Key

⬤	SWAP Zone Challenges
🧰	Treasure Chest
📦	Giant Treasure Chest
⚙	Boom Jet Soul Gem
⚙	Night Shift Soul Gem
⚙	Scorp Soul Gem
🏵	Legendary Treasure
🎩	Hat
🗺	Bonus Mission Map
🦋	Winged Sapphire
📜	Story Scroll
⭐	Dare
✅	Checkpoint

New Enemies

Chompy Powerhouse	Greeble Heaver	Earth Geargolem

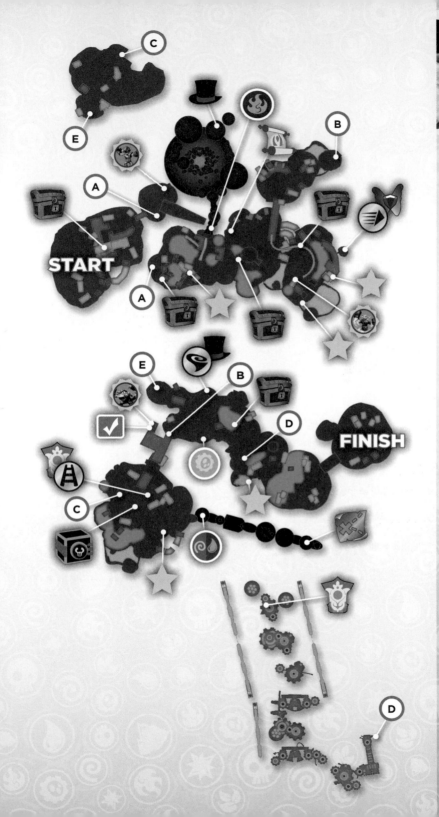

START

FINISH

TWISTY TUNNELS

OBJECTIVES

Story Goals

- **3** Destroy the Evilizer Crystals
- ◯ Get to the Ancient Terrasquid

Dares

- **5** Rubber Duckies
- **50** Enemy Goal
- **0** No Skylanders Defeated

Collections

- **16** Areas Discovered
- **5** Treasure Chests
- **1** Giant Treasure Chest
- **3** Soul Gems
- **2** Legendary Treasures
- **2** Hats
- **1** Bonus Mission Map
- **1** Winged Sapphire
- **1** Story Scroll

Map Key

	SWAP Zone Challenges
	Treasure Chest
	Giant Treasure Chest
	Wash Buckler Soul Gem
	Rip Tide Soul Gem
	Fire Kraken Soul Gem
	Legendary Treasure
	Hat
	Bonus Mission Map
	Winged Sapphire
	Story Scroll
	Dare
	Checkpoint

New Enemies

Cadet Crusher

Boom Boss

Air Spell Punk

Air Geargolem

Fire Viper

START

FINISH

BONEY ISLANDS

OBJECTIVES

Story Goals

- ○ Find Fossil Fuel
- ○ Find More Fossil Fuel
- ○ Help the Caravan Escape
- ○ Return to the Caravan

Dares

- (4) Museum Souvenirs
- (50) Enemy Goal
- (0) No Skylanders Defeated

Collections

- (16) Areas Discovered
- (5) Treasure Chests
- (1) Giant Treasure Chest
- (2) Soul Gems
- (2) Legendary Treasures
- (2) Hats
- (1) Bonus Mission Map
- (1) Winged Sapphire
- (1) Story Scroll

Map Key

⬤	SWAP Zone Challenges
🧰	Treasure Chest
🔲	Giant Treasure Chest
⚙	Dune Bug Soul Gem
⚙	Spy Rise Soul Gem
🏆	Legendary Treasure
🎩	Hat
🗺	Bonus Mission Map
🦋	Winged Sapphire
📜	Story Scroll
⭐	Dare
✅	Checkpoint

New Enemies

Coldspear Cyclops

Cyclops Gazermage

Cyclops Snowblaster

Chompy Frostflower

Loose Cannon

FINISH

START

A

B

A

B

WINTER KEEP

OBJECTIVES

Story Goals

○ Clear Out the South Wall

○ Thaw the Furnace

○ Defend the North Wall

③ Destroy the Blizzard Ballers

○ Take Back the Tower

Dares

④ Lost Mittens

㊿ Enemy Goal

⓪ No Skylanders Defeated

Collections

⑯ Areas Discovered

④ Treasure Chests

① Giant Treasure Chest

② Soul Gems

② Legendary Treasures

② Hats

① Bonus Mission Map

① Winged Sapphire

① Story Scroll

Map Key

⚪	SWAP Zone Challenges
	Treasure Chest
	Giant Treasure Chest
	Stink Bomb Soul Gem
	Rubble Soul Gem
	Legendary Treasure
	Hat
	Bonus Mission Map
	Winged Sapphire
	Story Scroll
⭐	Dare
✔	Checkpoint

New Enemies

Cyclops Sleetthrower

Twistpick Cyclops

Evilized Snowroller

Chompy Blitzbloom

Ice Geargolem

FINISH

START

FROSTFEST MOUNTAINS

OBJECTIVES

Story Goals

- ○ Follow the Illuminator

Dares

- (5) Balloon Animals
- (50) Enemy Goal
- (0) No Skylanders Defeated

Collections

- (18) Areas Discovered
- (7) Treasure Chests
- (1) Giant Treasure Chest
- (2) Soul Gems
- (2) Legendary Treasures
- (2) Hats
- (1) Bonus Mission Map
- (1) Winged Sapphire
- (1) Story Scroll

Map Key

○	SWAP Zone Challenges
	Treasure Chest
	Giant Treasure Chest
	Fryno Soul Gem
	Trap Shadow Soul Gem
	Legendary Treasure
	Hat
	Bonus Mission Map
	Winged Sapphire
	Story Scroll
★	Dare
✓	Checkpoint

New Enemies

Cyclops Brawlbuckler

Evilized Chillydog

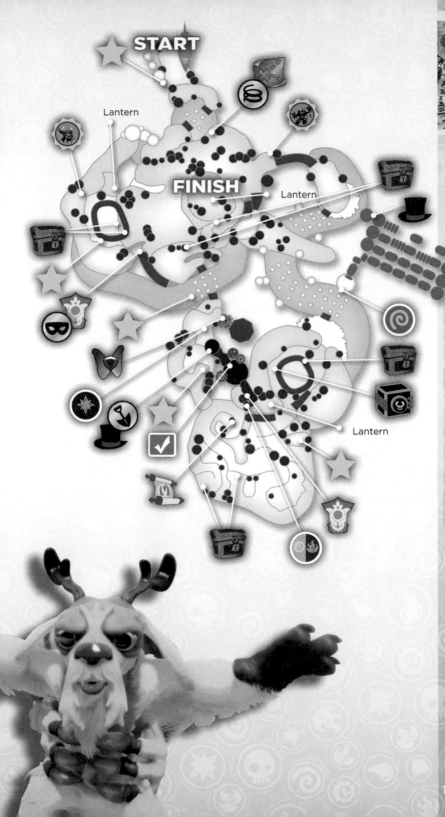

START

Lantern

FINISH

Lantern

Lantern

FANTASM FOREST

OBJECTIVES

Story Goals

- ◯ Put Out the Evilized Fires
- ◯ Save the Ancient Tree Spirit

Dares

- (6) Wooden Dalmatians
- (50) Enemy Goal
- (0) No Skylanders Defeated

Collections

- (16) Areas Discovered
- (4) Treasure Chests
- (1) Giant Treasure Chest
- (3) Soul Gems
- (2) Legendary Treasures
- (2) Hats
- (1) Bonus Mission Map
- (1) Winged Sapphire
- (1) Story Scroll

Map Key

◯	SWAP Zone Challenges
🧰	Treasure Chest
📦	Giant Treasure Chest
⚙	Blast Zone Soul Gem
⚙	Freeze Blade Soul Gem
⚙	Scratch Soul Gem
👑	Legendary Treasure
🎩	Hat
🗺	Bonus Mission Map
🦋	Winged Sapphire
📜	Story Scroll
⭐	Dare
✅	Checkpoint

New Enemies

Chompy
Boomblossom

Undead
Spell Punk

Missile
Mauler

Evilized
Screecher

Tech
Geargolem

START

FINISH

KAOS' FORTRESS

OBJECTIVES

Story Goals

◯ Destroy the Sheepshooters

Dares

(4) Wool Sweater

(50) Enemy Goal

(0) No Skylanders Defeated

Collections

(20) Areas Discovered

(6) Treasure Chests

(1) Giant Treasure Chest

(2) Soul Gems

(2) Legendary Treasures

(1) Hat

(2) Bonus Mission Map

(1) Winged Sapphire

(1) Story Scroll

Map Key

	SWAP Zone Challenges
	Treasure Chest
	Giant Treasure Chest
	Punk Shock Soul Gem
	Doom Stone Soul Gem
	Legendary Treasure
	Hat
	Bonus Mission Map
	Winged Sapphire
	Story Scroll
★	Dare
✔	Checkpoint

New Enemies

Chompy Pastepetal   Mr. Chompy   K-Bot Gloopgunner

K-Bot Splodeshard   K-Bot Mineminer   Magic Spell Punk

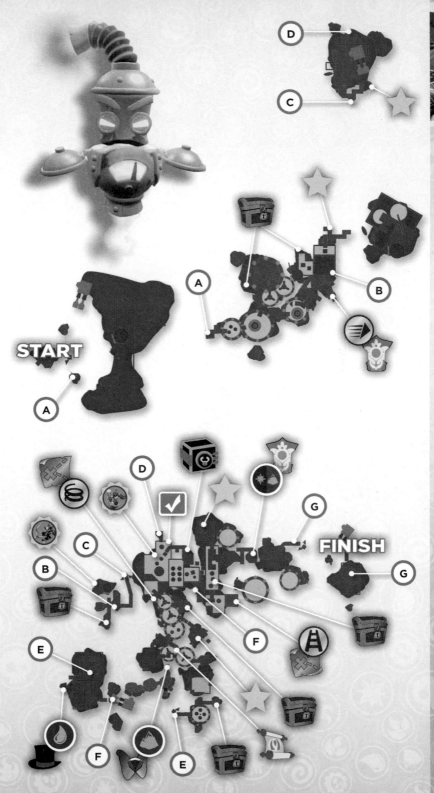

START

FINISH

SHEEP WRECK ISLANDS

OBJECTIVES

Story Goals

- ○ Destroy the Sheep Mage's staff

Dares

- **3** Golden Sheep
- **50** Enemy Goal
- **0** No Skylanders Defeated

Collections

- **16** Areas Discovered
- **3** Treasure Chests
- **1** Giant Treasure Chest
- **0** Soul Gems
- **3** Legendary Treasures
- **3** Hats
- **1** Bonus Mission Map
- **2** Winged Sapphire
- **1** Story Scroll

Map Key

	SWAP Zone Challenges
	Treasure Chest
	Giant Treasure Chest
	Legendary Treasure
	Hat
	Bonus Mission Map
	Winged Sapphire
	Story Scroll
	Dare
	Checkpoint
	Vortex

New Enemies

Vortex Geargolem

Cyclops Coldspear

Cyclops Brawlbuckler

Cyclops Sleetthrower

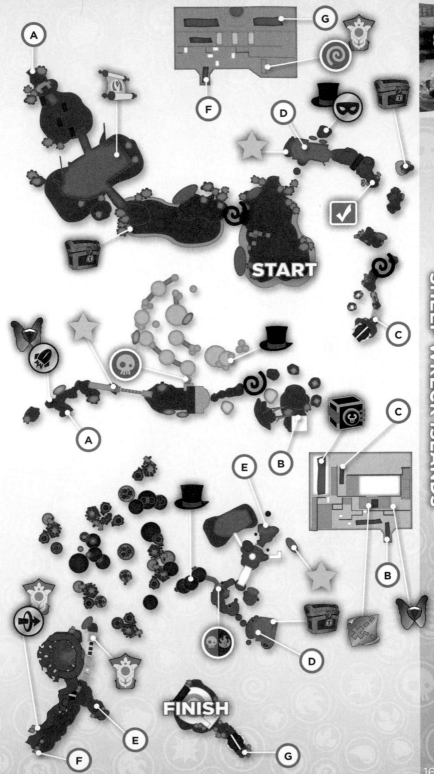

START

FINISH

TOWER OF TIME

OBJECTIVES

Story Goals

- ( ) Place the missing gears in the town center
- ( ) Find the gear in the Steam Works
- ( ) Find the gear in the Wind Works
- ( ) Find the gear in the Water Works
- ( ) Enter the Tower and defeat Cluck

Dares

- (3) Tool Box
- (50) Enemy Goal
- (0) No Skylanders Defeated

Collections

- (9) Areas Discovered
- (3) Treasure Chests
- (1) Giant Treasure Chest
- (0) Soul Gems
- (3) Legendary Treasure
- (2) Hats
- (1) Bonus Mission Map
- (2) Winged Sapphire
- (1) Story Scroll

Map Key

	SWAP Zone Challenges
	Treasure Chest
	Giant Treasure Chest
	Legendary Treasure
	Hat
	Bonus Mission Map
	Winged Sapphire
	Story Scroll
	Dare
	Checkpoint

New Enemies

Time Spell Punk

Clock Geargolem

Boom Boss

Cadet Crusher

Loose Cannon

START

FINISH

WOODBURROW

The **Puma Hat** appears near Woodburrow Gates.

The Rainbow Bridge

Every day between 3 pm and 6 pm (based on your console's time), a bridge appears in the yard and leads to a platform with a **Story Scroll** and a **Treasure Chest**.

AFTER COMPLETING CHAPTER 3: MUDWATER HOLLOW

Ascend the Mushroom Stairway for Hoot Loop's **Soul Gem (Wand of Dreams/Infinite Loop)**. Continue up to Treetrunk Peak and claim the **Winged Sapphire**. Use the Epic Launch Pad to explore a hidden area for the **Turkey Hat**.

AFTER COMPLETING CHAPTER 7: MOTLEYVILLE

Visit The Hollow for a **Story Scroll** and Smolderdash's **Soul Gem (Smolder Dash)**.

AFTER COMPLETING CHAPTER 11: WINTER KEEP

Smash through a stack of boxes at The Dock for the **Sweet Blizzard Bonus Mission Map**.

Map Key

	Treasure Chest
	Hoot Loop Soul Gem
	Smolderdash Soul Gem
	Legendary Treasure
	Legendary Item Pedestals
	Hat
	Bonus Mission Map
	Winged Sapphire
	Story Scroll

Master Eon

Power Pod

Tower of Time Entrance

Sheep Wreck Islands Entrance

Snagglescale's Tent

Tuk's Emporium

Avril

Rainbow Bridge

Wheellock

SWAP ZONE CHALLENGES

Tree Scraping

Flutterfly through the Flashfin Cove!

SWAP Zone Challenges appear throughout the Story Mode, and you must successfully complete them during a Story Level to make them available from the Portal Master screen of the Pause Menu.

Only *SWAP Force* Skylanders with the matching base ability can access SWAP Zone Challenges. Which figure is used for the top half of the *SWAP Force* Skylander doesn't matter when you're trying out SWAP Zone challenges; you must select legs with the correct ability.

Each SWAP Zone challenge has an objective you must complete to clear it. Each type of challenge has its own objective; no two are the same. Each SWAP Zone also requires a special ability activated with the Attack 2 button. The objectives and special abilities are covered in greater detail on the following pages.

Story Level versus Going for Stars versus Score Mode

The zones are identical whether you run them from within a Story Level, in Score Mode, or if you are going for Stars (choose them from the Pause Menu), with minor differences based on what you're looking for in each mode.

During the Story Mode, the coins you collect are added to the total for the current Skylander. Coins do not add to your Score Mode total, and they do nothing for you while going for Stars.

There are three gems that appear in each SWAP Zone Challenge. These gems always appear in the same locations across all three modes. In the Story Mode and SWAP Mode, these gems are red. Gems collected while in Story Mode and Score Mode burst into smaller red gems that you can pick up for extra gold. In Score Mode, the red gems that drop after running a SWAP Zone Challenge are the only items that count toward your score. Always get all three gems in Score Mode!

While you're going for Stars, they are yellow. Picking up all the gems is the second challenge Star for all SWAP Zone Challenges.

GET HELP FROM A FRIEND

A second Skylander on the *Portal of Power* provides a special power to help out with these challenges. The second Skylander can be any playable character. You don't need two *SWAP Force* Skylanders with the same ability.

The second Skylander's portrait appears in the bottom corner of the screen, next to a button and a meter that refills over time. Press the indicated button to activate a special ability. The meter empties and must refill before the ability can be used again. Each SWAP Zone type offers one different ability, which are covered in more detail in the SWAP Zone Challenge sections on the following pages.

Swap Zone Challenges by Type

The following table breaks down the forty-two challenges into the eight base abilities.

TYPE	SKYLANDERS WITH ABILITY	NAME OF CHALLENGES
🔁	Fire Kraken, Rattle Shake	Sunny Heights, Lonely Springs, Parched Heights, Frosty Frolicking, Kaotic Spring
🔁	Spy Rise, Wash Buckler	Tree Top Jaunt, Robot Ramparts, Junkside Climb, Amber Ice Climb, Tower of Falling Goo, Windy Tower
🔁	Grilla Drilla, Rubble Rouser	Spiky Pit, Submerged Sands, Ice Hollows, Glacial Descent, Tick Tock Tunneling
🔁	Blast Zone, Boom Jet	Forest Flyby, Tree Scraping, Storm of Sands, Ice Cold Flying, Fire Flighter, Sheep Strafing
🔁	Stink Bomb, Trap Shadow	Area Fifty Tree, Sunken Sand Base, Nerves of Ice, Fire Fortress, Wool Over Their Eyes
🔁	Freeze Blade, Magna Charge	Woodlands Speedstacle, Frenetic Fog, Drag Stripped, Wind Whipped, Greenlight Raceway
🔁	Doom Stone, Free Ranger	Marbled Gardens, Twisted Towers, Warped Sands, Frozen Top, Spinning Cogs
🔁	Hoot Loop, Night Shift	Going Whoosh, Hourglass Blink, Flash Frost, Ethereal Transfer, Beached Blinkout

Swap Zone Challenges by Story Level

This table shows which SWAP Zone Challenges are available from each Story Level.

STORY LEVEL		SWAP ZONE CHALLENGE	STORY LEVEL		SWAP ZONE CHALLENGE
Mount Cloudbreak	🔁	Tree Top Jaunt	Boney Islands	🔁	Ice Hollows
	🔁	Forest Flyby		🔁	Amber Ice Climb
	🔁	Spiky Pit		🔁	Ice Cold Flying
Cascade Glade	🔁	Sunny Heights	Winter Keep	🔁	Flash Frost
	🔁	Area Fifty Tree		🔁	Wind Whipped
	🔁	Woodlands Speedstacle		🔁	Frozen Top
Mudwater Hollow	🔁	Tree Scraping	Frostfest Mountains	🔁	Nerves of Ice
	🔁	Marbled Gardens		🔁	Frosty Frolicking
	🔁	Going Whoosh		🔁	Glacial Descent
Rampant Ruins	🔁	Robot Ramparts	Fantasm Forest	🔁	Ethereal Transfer
	🔁	Frenetic Fog		🔁	Fire Flighter
	🔁	Lonely Springs		🔁	Fire Fortress
Iron Jaw Gulch	🔁	Hourglass Blink	Kaos' Fortress	🔁	Kaotic Spring
	🔁	Submerged Sands		🔁	Tower of Falling Goo
	🔁	Storm of Sands		🔁	Greenlight Raceway
Motleyville	🔁	Twisted Towers	Sheep Wreck Islands	🔁	Sheep Strafing
	🔁	Junkside Climb		🔁	Beached Blinkout
	🔁	Drag Stripped		🔁	Wool Over Their Eyes
Twisty Tunnels	🔁	Parched Heights	Tower of Time	🔁	Windy Tower
	🔁	Sunken Sand Base		🔁	Spinning Cogs
	🔁	Warped Sands		🔁	Tick Tock Tunneling

During Bounce Challenges, you must pop a Kaos Balloon by landing on it. Your Skylander begins at one end of an area and must bounce between disconnected platforms and other floating objects to reach the Kaos balloon in the same area. Pop three Kaos balloons to complete the challenge. There is always one SWAP Zone Medal on the way to each of the Kaos Balloons.

The most important thing to keep track of during Bounce Challenges is your Skylander's shadow as it appears on each platform. Trust the shadow for your Skylander's location more than how they appear in mid-air.

After a bounce off an object, you can press the Attack 2 button for an extra mid-air bounce. Use your extra bounce wisely. Save it for the highest point in a jump to reach a far away platform and always remember when you still have it should you misjudge a bounce and need a quick save.

To earn the third Star in Bounce Challenges, you must bounce at least one time on every platform. There's no time limit, so be patient while you try to hit all the platforms. There are many levels with platforms that crumble after one use, which means you must carefully plan your route to ensure you have a place to land after each jump.

With a second Skylander active, you get the Triple Jump ability. The second player creates a platform directly under your Skylander, which acts exactly like any other bounce platform, including allowing your Skylander to jump again. Keep this ability available for last-second saves whenever possible. There's never a time when an extra platform is a requirement to reach a platform from any other platform unless you've knocked out a crumbling one.

SUNNY HEIGHTS	Bounce over to this great tourist attraction.

Unlocked: Chapter 2: Cascade Glade

Hazards: Moving platforms

Star Requirements

★	Complete the SWAP Zone
★ ★	Collect all the SWAP Zone Medals
★ ★ ★	Bounce On Every Island

SWAP Zone Medal Locations

1st	Highest platform nearest the Kaos Balloon
2nd	High platform, left side, about halfway to the Kaos Balloon
3rd	High platform, left side, about halfway to the Kaos Balloon

LONELY SPRINGS
Bounce around the Robot Graveyard.

Unlocked: Chapter 4: Rampant Ruins

Hazards: Crumbling platforms

Star Requirements

★	Complete the SWAP Zone
★ ★	Collect all the SWAP Zone Medals
★ ★ ★	Bounce On Every Island

SWAP Zone Medal Locations

1st	Low platform on right, halfway to Kaos Balloon
2nd	High platform on left, use second bounce to reach it, halfway to Kaos Balloon
3rd	High platform on left, close to Kaos Balloon

PARCHED HEIGHTS
Springing around on the squid.

Unlocked: Chapter 7: Twisty Tunnels

Hazards: Moving platforms, crumbling platforms, fire geysers (deals damage but allows jumps after touching, not required for third Star)

Star Requirements

★	Complete the SWAP Zone
★ ★	Collect all the SWAP Zone Medals
★ ★ ★	Bounce On Every Island

SWAP Zone Medal Locations

1st	Highest platform on left side, near Kaos Balloon
2nd	Platform just to the right of Kaos Balloon
3rd	On the right, halfway to the Kaos Balloon

FROSTY FROLICKING
Spring up the mountains and don't slip!

Unlocked: Chapter 12: Frostfest Mountains

Hazards: Air columns (narrow target), crumbling platforms (vanish after one bounce)

Star Requirements

★	Complete the SWAP Zone
★ ★	Collect all the SWAP Zone Medals
★ ★ ★	Bounce On Every Island

SWAP Zone Medal Locations

1st	On the left about halfway from the start to the first air column
2nd	On the right near the second air column
3rd	First air column

KAOTIC SPRING
Don't bounce too high. I think I see the atmosphere.

Unlocked: Chapter 15: Kaos' Fortress

Hazards: Moving platforms, moving goo clouds (coats Skylander and makes them heavier)

Star Requirements

★	Complete the SWAP Zone
★ ★	Collect all the SWAP Zone Medals
★ ★ ★	Bounce On Every Island

SWAP Zone Medal Locations

1st	On the left, halfway to the Kaos Balloon
2nd	On the left, halfway to the Kaos Balloon
3rd	On the right, almost to the Kaos Balloon

CLIMB CHALLENGES

It doesn't get much more basic than Climb Challenges. Start at the bottom of a structure and climb to the top. There are two checkpoints along the way, and each offers extra gold and some food to restore any health lost to falling objects or other hazards.

There are two types of items to watch during your ascent. There are other hazards, but these appear on every level. First, there are the stationary objects. Some are helpful platforms you can use for shielding from the falling objects (more on those next). Others seem helpful, but they also have hazards attached to them, such as spikes. The second type of item is the aforementioned falling objects. Falling objects match the theme of the level (such as acorns when climbing a tree) and they come in three varieties.

The first kind hurt Skylanders, but are blocked by stationary objects. The second type are the harmless fragments of the first type that appear when they are smashed against a stationary object.

Until you learn how to identify the first two objects, assume everything that falls will cause damage!

Some levels also include environmental effects that obscure your vision (clouds, or ships buzzing the level and leaving behind smoke). The final type of falling object are the very large, very heavy items that destroy the platforms you planned on using for shelter. Not every level has them, but they're doubly bad. They harm your Skylander on contact and remove your resting spots.

Wall Dash is an ability that should be saved for lateral or downward movement. Going upward quickly, unless you're trying to reach safety before something hits you, generally leads to trouble.

JUNKSIDE CLIMB

Unlocked: Chapter 7: Motleyville

Hazards: Falling barrels, spinning and moving saw blades, falling mine carts (destroys platforms)

Star Requirements

★	Complete the SWAP Zone
★ ★	Collect all the SWAP Zone Medals
★ ★ ★	No Damage Taken

SWAP Zone Medal Locations

1st	Right side before first checkpoint
2nd	Middle before second checkpoint
3rd	Left side before the finish

AMBER ICE CLIMB

Unlocked: Chapter 10: Boney Islands

Hazards: Ice shards, fossils (destroys platforms), missiles

Star Requirements

★	Complete the SWAP Zone
★ ★	Collect all the SWAP Zone Medals
★ ★ ★	No Damage Taken

SWAP Zone Medal Locations

1st	Right side before first check point
2nd	Middle before second check point
3rd	Left side before the finish

TOWER OF FALLING GOO

Unlocked: Chapter 15: Kaos' Fortress

Hazards: Falling goo, flamethrowers

Star Requirements

★	Complete the SWAP Zone
★ ★	Collect all the SWAP Zone Medals
★ ★ ★	No Damage Taken

SWAP Zone Medal Locations

1st	Left side before first checkpoint
2nd	Right side before second checkpoint
3rd	Middle before the finish

To get the third star in Climb Challenges, you must avoid taking damage. The best way to earn this star is to become familiar with the level. The pattern of items falling is the same each time through a level. Be patient and be careful. Being reckless is for clearing these levels quickly in Story Mode or trying to grab all three SWAP Zone medals!

The second player Skylander ability is Shockwave. Shockwave spreads out from the Skylander doing the climbing and clears off every destructible object and hazard on the screen.

TREE TOP JAUNT

Unlocked: Chapter 1: Mount Cloudbreak

Hazards: Tree nuts, jets obscure vision

Star Requirements

★	Complete the SWAP Zone
★ ★	Collect all the SWAP Zone Medals
★ ★ ★	No Damage Taken

SWAP Zone Medal Locations

1st	Left side before first check point
2nd	Right side before second check point
3rd	Middle before the finish

ROBOT RAMPARTS

Unlocked: Chapter 4: Rampant Ruins

Hazards: Falling boxes, moving platforms, missiles, clouds obscure vision

Star Requirements

★	Complete the SWAP Zone
★ ★	Collect all the SWAP Zone Medals
★ ★ ★	No Damage Taken

SWAP Zone Medal Locations

1st	Left side before first checkpoint
2nd	Right side before second checkpoint
3rd	Left side before the finish

WINDY TOWER

Unlocked: Tower of Time Adventure Pack Level

Hazards: Tree nuts, fan blowing across course, spinning saw blades, clouds obscure vision

Star Requirements

★	Complete the SWAP Zone
★ ★	Collect all the SWAP Zone Medals
★ ★ ★	No Damage Taken

SWAP Zone Medal Locations

1st	Left side before first checkpoint
2nd	Right side before second checkpoint
3rd	Left side before the finish

In Dig Challenges, you move through dark areas where you must jump over gaps, avoid hazards, and get to gems. More than any other challenge, Dig Challenges require learning a pattern through a level to earn all the stars. Digging up the first and second crystals adds 30 seconds to the countdown clock. There's no extra ability in Dig. Digging is your ability!

To get the third Star in Dig challenges, learn the shortest path between crystal locations, and ignore everything else. Don't try to get the second and third stars in the same run. Even with a second player helping, it's incredibly tough to pull off. To buy yourself an extra second or two, don't wait for your Skylander to come into view when a level begins. Start moving forward as soon as the level loads.

The Second player ability is Time Stop. When active, it stops the countdown clock briefly and freezes everything on the screen. To get the most out of each application (it has a considerable recharge time) only use it when the path ahead is clear. That means having no mining carts in the way, and seeing that all spikes are retracted and not blocking the path.

SPIKY PIT
Tunnel down into the Cascade Caves

Unlocked: Chapter 1: Mount Cloudbreak

Hazards: Spike traps

Star Requirements

★	Complete the SWAP Zone
★ ★	Collect all the SWAP Zone Medals
★ ★ ★	Over 53 Seconds Left

SWAP Zone Medal Locations

1st	To the left of the starting point
2nd	To the right of rightmost blue crystal
3rd	To the right (over gaps) of leftmost blue crystal

SUBMERGED SANDS
Everyone likes to play in the sand.

Unlocked: Chapter 6: Iron Jaw Gulch

Hazards: Mining carts

Star Requirements

★	Complete the SWAP Zone
★ ★	Collect all the SWAP Zone Medals
★ ★ ★	Over 53 Seconds Left

SWAP Zone Medal Locations

1st	On the left side, past blue gem closest to start point
2nd	To the right of blue gem in the center of the map
3rd	From the blue gem in the center of the map, move to the back and go left, then climb steps back to the right

ICE HOLLOWS
It's where they keep the fossils.

Unlocked: Chapter 10: Boney Islands

Hazards: Mining carts

Star Requirements

★	Complete the SWAP Zone
★ ★	Collect all the SWAP Zone Medals
★ ★ ★	Over 58 Seconds Left

SWAP Zone Medal Locations

1st	Follow tracks to the right of the starting point (or fall down the gap between first and second blue gems)
2nd	To the left of blue gem in middle of map
3rd	From blue gem at the back of the map, go to the right over gaps

GLACIAL DESCENT
Tunneling through solid ice is not easy. Good thing you're awesome.

Unlocked: Chapter 12: Frostfest Mountains

Hazards: Spiky wall traps

Star Requirements

★	Complete the SWAP Zone
★ ★	Collect all the SWAP Zone Medals
★ ★	Over 58 Seconds Left

SWAP Zone Medal Locations

1st	Go left from the start, all the way back
2nd	From leftmost blue crystal, move toward front then jump left over gap
3rd	All the way in the back, near middle, on the highest row of platforms

TICK TOCK TUNNELING
Can you dig far enough to reach yesterday? That's deep.

Unlocked: Tower of Time Adventure Pack Level

Hazards: Burning rocks

Star Requirements

★	Complete the SWAP Zone
★ ★	Collect all the SWAP Zone Medals
★ ★ ★	Over 48 Seconds Left

SWAP Zone Medal Locations

1st	Directly ahead at start
2nd	Just past (behind) leftmost blue crystal
3rd	From second Medal, go to the right

In Rocket challenges, you guide your Skylander through a designated course marked by rings within an allotted time. You can steer to the left or right by tapping or holding the control stick to the left or right. Pull down on the control stick to spin around and backtrack on the rocket path. Passing through the rings is not mandatory, but they do add five seconds to the timer. That means if you miss a ring and you would lose more than five seconds trying to get back through it, skip it! The final ring on the course does not add any time to the clock.

Your Skylander's extra ability is Boost. Press the Attack 2 button to activate it. Unlike most other abilities, there is no limit on using Boost. It stays active as long as you hold down the button.

To earn the third Star in Rocket Challenges, your Skylander must pass through the course without taking damage. The hazards in Rocket challenges are usually floating mines, so avoid hitting them to get the third Star. Skip trying to get all the Medals on the same run as one where you want to get No Damage Taken. There's always one medal in a dangerous location.

The second player ability is Super Ring. Super Ring briefly causes the rings marking the course to grow to an enormous size. The ability is available often, so don't be shy about putting it to use. It's most helpful when mines surround the ring. The ring pushes the mines as it grows.

FOREST FLYBY
High velocity forest flying!

Unlocked: Chapter 1: Mount Cloudbreak

Hazards: Floating rocks, stationary metal discs, sliding rows of rocks

Star Requirements

★	Complete the SWAP Zone
★ ★	Collect all the SWAP Zone Medals
★ ★ ★	No Damage Taken

SWAP Zone Medal Locations

1st	Moving around rock after fourth ring
2nd	Between second and third ring past first checkpoint
3rd	Left side, near finish ring

TREE SCRAPING
Flutterfly through the Flashfin Cove!

Unlocked: Chapter 3: Mudwater Hollow

Hazards: Connected and electrified balls, stationary metal discs

Star Requirements

★	Complete the SWAP Zone
★ ★	Collect all the SWAP Zone Medals
★ ★ ★	No Damage Taken

SWAP Zone Medal Locations

1st	After fourth ring
2nd	Second ring after second checkpoint, on the right
3rd	Just before finish ring, floating across the course

STORM OF SANDS
Time to do a little bit of refacing.

Unlocked: Chapter 6: Iron Jaw Gulch

Hazards: Stationary mines, moving mines

Star Requirements

★	Complete the SWAP Zone
★ ★	Collect all the SWAP Zone Medals
★ ★ ★	No Damage Taken

SWAP Zone Medal Locations

1st	After third ring, on left
2nd	Past third ring after first check point
3rd	Just before finish ring in mines on the right

ICE COLD FLYING
Not many people get to rocket around in a museum. Don't break anything.

Unlocked: Chapter 10: Boney Islands

Hazards: Frozen mines, spinning rings

Star Requirements

★	Complete the SWAP Zone
★ ★	Collect all the SWAP Zone Medals
★ ★ ★	No Damage Taken

SWAP Zone Medal Locations

1st	In large minefield on left just before first checkpoint
2nd	Between fifth and sixth rings after first checkpoint
3rd	Near the last ring before the finish ring

FIRE FLIGHTER

This is the way to take in the scenery.

Unlocked: Chapter 13: Fantasm Forest

Hazards: Mines, evilized fire

Star Requirements

★	Complete the SWAP Zone
★ ★	Collect all the SWAP Zone Medals
★ ★ ★	No Damage Taken

SWAP Zone Medal Locations

1st	Circling large island clockwise near start
2nd	Spinning around island just past first checkpoint
3rd	After second gate past second checkpoint

SHEEP STRAFING

Off you go into the wild wooly yonder.

Unlocked: Sheep Wreck Islands Adventure Pack Level

Hazards: Stationary metal discs, stationary mines, moving mines

Star Requirements

★	Complete the SWAP Zone
★ ★	Collect all the SWAP Zone Medals
★ ★ ★	No Damage Taken

SWAP Zone Medal Locations

1st	Just before third ring
2nd	Between first and second gates beyond first checkpoint
3rd	Immediately after second gate beyond second checkpoint

👁 SNEAK CHALLENGES

Sneak Challenges technically have two objectives. The first is to activate switches that open up the next area. The final objective is to reach a big red button to destroy the base you infiltrated. Your Skylander is limited to two actions between activating switches and pressing buttons: walking and using stealth. There's no jumping, no dashing, and no attacks of any sort. There are two common hazards while attempting to sneak to the base-destruct button: search lights and laser panels.

Search lights are always red. They sometimes sweep areas, while other times they are stationary and the floor moves through it. If your unstealthed Skylander is spotted by a search light, you must act quickly or fail the challenge (more on this in the next paragraph). Laser panels appear on floors, ceilings, and walls. They fire a short-range laser that damages anything it strikes.

Stealth is your Skylander's secondary ability. Stealth is effective only against the search lights covering areas of each base. Skylanders cannot move while using the Stealth ability in a Sneak Zone. Laser panels don't care about stealth. Their beams harm your Skylander whenever it hits them. Stealthed Skylanders are undetectable by search lights. They pass over your Skylander so long as Stealth is active. Even if your Skylander is detected, going into Stealth quickly enough prevents the search light from ejecting you from the base. You just need to be patient until the threat level has dropped.

To earn the third Star in a Stealth challenge, you must avoid detection. That means never drawing the interest of a search light. If you must use Stealth because a search light grazed your Skylander's toe, it's too late. Being hit by a laser, on the other hand, does not affect your third Star eligibility. It is only the search light that counts.

The second player ability is Lights Out. Lights Out shuts down search lights for a few seconds, but it does nothing for laser panels. Lights Out makes earning a third Star much easier, so invite a friend to help you if you're struggling with it. Save Lights Out for areas near the end of a search light's scanning area. The last thing you want to do is use it in the middle of its path only to have it respawn on top of your Skylander who is an inch from that next platform!

AREA FIFTY TREE
Tiptoe through the tulips. And other foliage.

Unlocked: Chapter 2: Cascade Glade

Hazards: No extra hazards

Star Requirements

★	Complete the SWAP Zone
★ ★	Collect all the SWAP Zone Medals
★ ★ ★	Never Got Spotted

SWAP Zone Medal Locations

1st	To the left of the first security light
2nd	To the right just past first security gate
3rd	To the left just past second security gate

SUNKEN SAND BASE
Don't get caught with sand in your eyes.

Unlocked: Chapter 8: Twisty Tunnels

Hazards: Elevator platforms

Star Requirements

★	Complete the SWAP Zone
★ ★	Collect all the SWAP Zone Medals
★ ★ ★	Never Got Spotted

SWAP Zone Medal Locations

1st	Past first elevator platform
2nd	Ride second elevator platform to highest point, then backtrack
3rd	After second security gate, fall to the right (keep pushing right) between two sets of double lasers to land on a platform

NERVES OF ICE
Don't get spotted. There's weird stuff out there.

Unlocked: Chapter 12: Frostfest Mountains

Hazards: Sliding platforms

Star Requirements

★	Complete the SWAP Zone
★ ★	Collect all the SWAP Zone Medals
★ ★ ★	Never Got Spotted

SWAP Zone Medal Locations

1st	Ride first sliding platform all the way left
2nd	Past first security gate, take sliding platform to the right
3rd	Past second security gate, take sliding platform to the right

FIRE FORTRESS
Stay focused and don't get distracted by... LOOK AT THE PRETTY FLOWERS!

Unlocked: Chapter 13: Fantasm Forest

Hazards: Delayed path formation

Star Requirements

★	Complete the SWAP Zone
★ ★	Collect all the SWAP Zone Medals
★ ★ ★	Never Got Spotted

SWAP Zone Medal Locations

1st	To the right at the start
2nd	To the right of second security switch
3rd	Follow path in front of base destruct switch to the left

WOOL OVER THEIR EYES
Sheep are always up to something. Be wary.

Unlocked: Sheep Wreck Islands Adventure Pack Level

Hazards: Top down view

Star Requirements

★	Complete the SWAP Zone
★ ★	Collect all the SWAP Zone Medals
★ ★ ★	Never Got Spotted

SWAP Zone Medal Locations

1st	After second elevator, go left
2nd	After first security gate, go right
3rd	After second security gate, go straight ahead

Speed challenges require you to guide your Skylander through hazard-filled courses within a certain time limit. Your only control options are pushing the control stick left and right to steer your Skylander in those directions. Pushing forward and back has no effect on your Skylander's speed.

The secondary ability for Speed challenges is Boost. Boost gives your Skylander a quick burst of speed. It only lasts about one second, but it recharges quickly.

The third Star in Speed challenges requires the timer to have a minimum amount of time left after completing the course. To earn the third Star, get into the habit of using Boost as soon as it is available. You can delay it a second if it helps you avoid hitting anything that slows down your Skylander.

The second player ability is Sonic Blast. Sonic Blast emits a destructive wave, clearing most hazards from the path ahead. Some hazards are immune to it, but most stationary hazards are destroyed by Sonic Blast. To get the most out of Sonic Blast, use it at the same time as Boost. Sonic Blast does not have much reach, but it is extended quite a bit when used with a Boost.

WOODLANDS SPEEDSTACLE
Speed through the jungle but watch out for low branches.

Unlocked: Chapter 2: Cascade Glade

Hazards: Stationary hazards, jump ramps

Star Requirements

★	Complete the SWAP Zone
★ ★	Collect all the SWAP Zone Medals
★ ★ ★	Over 10 Seconds Left

SWAP Zone Medal Locations

1st	Sliding across the track halfway to first checkpoint
2nd	After first check point, center of track, jump to reach it
3rd	After second check point, second jump of a double jump, angle to the right

FRENETIC FOG
Cut through the mist at super-duper speeds!

Unlocked: Chapter 4: Rampant Ruins

Hazards: Fog, stationary hazards

Star Requirements

★	Complete the SWAP Zone
★ ★	Collect all the SWAP Zone Medals
★ ★ ★	Over 10 Seconds Left

SWAP Zone Medal Locations

1st	In the food during the jump after the first check point, left side
2nd	In the food during the jump after the second check point, in the middle
3rd	On the right side before shorter hazards

DRAG STRIPPED
Outrun, outlast and race past!

Unlocked: Chapter 7: Motleyville

Hazards: Stationary hazards, moving mines, jump ramps

Star Requirements

★	Complete the SWAP Zone
★ ★	Collect all the SWAP Zone Medals
★ ★ ★	Over 10 Seconds Left

SWAP Zone Medal Locations

1st	On the left behind a barrel
2nd	After first checkpoint, moving back and forth between moving mines
3rd	Above the track after back to back jump ramp rows

WIND WHIPPED
Fleet-feet through the icy sleet.

Unlocked: Chapter 11: Winter Keep

Hazards: Stationary hazards, rolling ice boulders

Star Requirements

★	Complete the SWAP Zone
★ ★	Collect all the SWAP Zone Medals
★ ★ ★	Over 15 Seconds Left

SWAP Zone Medal Locations

1st	On the uphill slope, to the right
2nd	After the first checkpoint, sliding across track in the middle of multiple ice boulders
3rd	After the second checkpoint, Sliding across track after multiple ice boulders, on an uphill slant

GREENLIGHT RACEWAY
Currently traveling at six times the speed of awesome.

Unlocked: Chapter 15: Kaos' Fortress

Hazards: Stationary hazards, moving and bouncing green goo balls, jump ramps

Star Requirements

★	Complete the SWAP Zone
★ ★	Collect all the SWAP Zone Medals
★ ★ ★	Over 14 Seconds Left

SWAP Zone Medal Locations

1st	On the right, between two tall hazards
2nd	On the right, almost to second checkpoint
3rd	Floating over the track on the left after a three-wide jump ramp

SWAP ZONE CHALLENGES

The goal of spin challenges is to destroy a statue of Kaos. Before you reach the platform with the statue of Kaos, however, your Skylander must reach the center of two other platforms. Each platform has a single SWAP Zone medal.

There are a few things complicating this journey. First, Skylanders are harder to control when they start bouncing around, but you can influence their course.Second, your Skylander must remain on the platforms, or the challenge ends immediately. Finally, you must break through layers of bumpers while avoiding hazards tucked in the middle of the layers to reach the center areas.

There are three bumper varieties. The first type are dark gray. These bumpers are the weakest and break down quickly. The yellow bumpers are sturdier and require multiple hits before they break. The bumpers with red and white tops are the sturdiest bumpers. They don't break often, and only after considerable effort on your part.

Super Spin is your Skylander's extra ability. It briefly increases your Skylander's spinning velocity. Be careful about using it. Spinning Skylanders are already challenging to control, and Super Spin magnifies that challenge. One quick burst and your Skylander may end up flying off the edge of the platform!

The third Star for Spin challenges is deceptively easy: don't use Super Spin. Earning this third Star requires a bit more patience than what the other challenges require. They generally ask you to complete things quickly. With no Super Spin, it takes more time!

The second player ability is Multiball. The Multiball acts like a second Skylander, but one you can't control at all. It crashes into objects and caroms around the platform. Save Multiball for clearing explosive hazards, like mines. Just be careful that your eyes stay on your Skylander and not the Multiball when it's active.

MARBLED GARDENS

Take a spin down the river!

Unlocked: Chapter 3: Mudwater Hollow

Hazards: No additional hazards

Star Requirements

★	Complete the SWAP Zone
★ ★	Collect all the SWAP Zone Medals
★ ★ ★	Never Used Super Spin

SWAP Zone Medal Locations

1st	Just to the right of the center
2nd	Right side of platform
3rd	Lower right of platform

TWISTED TOWERS

It's a whirly ride of junk. In a good way.

Unlocked: Chapter 7: Motleyville

Hazards: Mines

Star Requirements

★	Complete the SWAP Zone
★ ★	Collect all the SWAP Zone Medals
★ ★ ★	Never Used Super Spin

SWAP Zone Medal Locations

1st	Top of the platform, just right of center
2nd	Top of the platform, just right of center
3rd	Right side, just above center

WARPED SANDS

Spinning in the Twisty Tunnels might seem redundant but it sure is fun.

Unlocked: Chapter 8: Twisty Tunnels

Hazards: Fan blowing across platforms

Star Requirements

★	Complete the SWAP Zone
★ ★	Collect all the SWAP Zone Medals
★ ★ ★	Never Used Super Spin

SWAP Zone Medal Locations

1st	Right side center, behind rows of bumpers
2nd	Inside the circles of bumpers in the lower right
3rd	Top of platform, left of center, behind rows of bumpers

FROZEN TOP	

Unlocked: Chapter 11: Winter Keep

Hazards: No additional hazards

Star Requirements

★	Complete the SWAP Zone
★ ★	Collect all the SWAP Zone Medals
★ ★ ★	Never Used Super Spin

SWAP Zone Medal Locations

1st	Top left of platform
2nd	Top of platform, slightly left of center
3rd	Top center of platform

SPINNING COGS

Unlocked: Tower of Time Adventure Pack Level

Hazards: No additional hazards

Star Requirements

★	Complete the SWAP Zone
★ ★	Collect all the SWAP Zone Medals
★ ★ ★	Never Used Super Spin

SWAP Zone Medal Locations

1st	Slightly left of center, in the middle of many rows of bumpers
2nd	To the left of the starting point
3rd	Far right center of platform, behind many rows of bumpers

 ## TELEPORT CHALLENGES

Teleport challenges are the least consistent type of challenge. Not because of what is asked of you. You collect three Rune Stones on three different maps to complete each challenge. However, the random nature of the platforms that make up each map keeps each visit to the same Teleport zone a little different.

The general layout of the maps is always the same, but the individual platforms that make up the maps are a little different each time you visit a map. In addition, platforms fall away and are replaced at regular intervals during each map. The change isn't instantaneous (although, after each set of three Rune Stones are collected, you get a bonus round and a fresh set of platforms). A white glow grows around the platform. When it completely surrounds the platform, the platform falls away. If your Skylander is on the platform when it falls, the challenge is over.

Teleport is the only ability your Skylander has for these challenges. It is always available, so you can keep Attack 2 pressed while tapping the control stick in different directions to move between platforms.

To earn the No Damage Taken third Star, learn to recognize hazard platforms and how they work. With some experience, you will know when it is safe to be on certain platforms, when they're about to be dangerous, and when you need to avoid them entirely.

The second player ability is Clean Slate. Clean Slate locks the platform the Skylander is currently standing on, even if it is about to drop away, and causes every other platform to vanish, and be replaced with random new platforms. Save this ability for the times when the platform under the Skylander is about to fall away and has no escape route.

179

GOING WHOOSH

Bug Eyed Blinking around the Bayou!

Unlocked: Chapter 3: Mudwater Hollow

Hazards: Damaging platform, square platform

Star Requirements

★	Complete the SWAP Zone
★ ★	Collect all the SWAP Zone Medals
★ ★ ★	No Damage Taken

SWAP Zone Medal Locations

1st	Appears from lower center
2nd	Appears from top right
3rd	Appears from top right

HOURGLASS BLINK

Home of the great big glass hat.

Unlocked: Chapter 6: Iron Jaw Gulch

Hazards: Damaging platform, square platform, energy blasters

Star Requirements

★	Complete the SWAP Zone
★ ★	Collect all the SWAP Zone Medals
★ ★ ★	No Damage Taken

SWAP Zone Medal Locations

1st	Appears from lower center
2nd	Appears from top right
3rd	Appears from lower right

FLASH FROST

Unlock the secrets of the Winter Keep!

Unlocked: Chapter 11: Winter Keep

Hazards: Damaging platforms

Star Requirements

★	Complete the SWAP Zone
★ ★	Collect all the SWAP Zone Medals
★ ★ ★	No Damage Taken

SWAP Zone Medal Locations

1st	Appears from lower left
2nd	Appears from top right
3rd	Appears from top center

ETHEREAL TRANSFER

Pop in and see the poppies.

Unlocked: Chapter 12: Fantasm Forest

Hazards: Damaging platform, square platform

Star Requirements

★	Complete the SWAP Zone
★ ★	Collect all the SWAP Zone Medals
★ ★ ★	No Damage Taken

SWAP Zone Medal Locations

1st	Appears from center right
2nd	Appears from lower right
3rd	Appears from top left

BEACHED BLINKOUT

It will take sharp-sheared skill to navigate this one.

Unlocked: Sheep Wreck Islands Adventure Pack Level

Hazards: Damaging platform, square platform (can't jump to it), energy blasters (fires from outside active area)

Star Requirements

★	Complete the SWAP Zone
★ ★	Collect all the SWAP Zone Medals
★ ★ ★	No Damage Taken

SWAP Zone Medal Locations

1st	Appears from top center
2nd	Appears from top left
3rd	Appears from center right

BONUS MISSIONS

Bonus Missions are another way for you to earn Stars as a Portal Master. These are quick missions in a confined area. You are sent by Master Eon to help different groups who are dealing with an invasion by Kaos' Forces.

Bonus Mission Maps are found throughout Story Mode and Adventure Pack levels, with a few also for sale from Tuk's Emporium. Completing a challenge rewards you with a Charm.

Many of these missions are challenging, and should be attempted only after your Skylanders are high level and you have purchased most of their upgrades.

You earn Stars based on your total score, and scoring works the same way as other modes that keep track of scoring. You earn points and build your multiplier meter by attacking enemies. The number that appears in the circle near your score is your multiplier, which shows how much more valuable each enemy you defeat, and coin you collect,

is than when the meter is at one. Playing Missions at higher difficulties awards more points. Also, when playing on a higher difficulty, the time limit is longer. You receive extra points for the seconds left on the timer.

TREBLE THEFT	TIME
Map Acquired: Tuk's Emporium for 1000 gold. Requires Portal Master Rank 15.	Easy & Medium: 6:00
	Hard: 8:05
Reward: Body Armor Charm	Nightmare: 15:00
Mission: Bring 5 instruments to the music group	

Score Requirements

★	Earn Over 0 Points
★★	Earn over 150,000 Points
★★★	Earn over 200,000 Points

CHOMPY CHALLENGE	TIME
Map Acquired: After completing Mudwater Hollow.	Easy & Medium: 4:00
	Hard: 5:10
Reward: Elemental Shield Charm	Nightmare: 9:35
Mission: Beat 95 Chompies	

Score Requirements

★	Earn Over 0 Points
★★	Earn over 175,000 Points
★★★	Earn over 250,000 Points

Each musical instrument is suspended above the ground not far from the musician who plays it. There are Battle Gates blocking access to the instruments and you must defeat a variety of trolls to remove the Battle Gate. There is also a gate locked by a musical note near each musician. When you hand over the instrument to the musician, the gate is blown away by the music.

There are many kinds of Chompies to tackle here, and you must take

down 95 of them to complete the challenge. The number of Chompies and Chompy Pods in a given area is limited, and defeating them all opens teleporters. The first area has a single teleporter, but the next three areas each have two. When you choose the correct teleporter, you are sent to an area with more Chompies. If you choose the wrong teleporter, you end up fighting a group of Greebles that you must defeat before the teleporter pad in that area is available for use. The correct teleporters to use are (in order): right, top, and right.

UNDERCOVER GREEBLES

TIME	
Easy & Medium:	4:20
Hard:	5:50
Nightmare:	10:50

Map Acquired: Chapter 15: Kaos Fortress

Reward: Elemental Fortune Charm

Mission: Eliminate 10 Greebles disguised as Sheep.

Score Requirements

★	Earn Over 0 Points
★ ★	Earn over 175,000 points
★ ★ ★	Earn over 250,000 points

Greebles are disguising themselves as sheep to steal items from the archaeologists. There are sheep all over the area, but the imposters are easy to spot when they get up and run on two legs. Move close to them to get them to reveal themselves. You generally face the Greebles one on one, but they sometimes appear in pairs, or supported by other allies, such as Spellpunks. Battle Gates block your progress, which also serve to let you know when a Greeble is nearby.

CURSED STATUES

TIME	
Easy & Medium:	5:00
Hard:	6:45
Nightmare:	12:30

Map Acquired: Chapter 15: Kaos Fortress

Reward: Air Freshener Charm

Mission: Defeat the Greeble Corruptors and destroy 8 statues.

Score Requirements

★	Earn Over 0 Points
★ ★	Earn Over 175,000 Points
★ ★ ★	Earn Over 250,000 Points

There are cursed statues being defended by Greeble Corruptors. You must defeat the Greeble Corruptors and destroy eight statues. Before you can attack a statue, you must take down the Greeble Corruptors. Some statues have more than one Corruptor guarding it. Because time is limited, you should defeat each statue as you come to it and not go looking for another one that is more lightly defended. Some statues have other defenders helping the Greebles as well.

CHOMPY SAUCE

TIME	
Easy & Medium:	5:05
Hard:	6:52
Nightmare:	12:43

Map Acquired: Chapter 14: Fantasm Forest

Reward: Greeble Be Gone Charm

Mission: Mission Shut down 6 valves to stop the spilling Chompy sauce.

Score Requirements

★	Earn Over 0 Points
★ ★	Earn Over 150,000 Points
★ ★ ★	Earn Over 200,000 Points

Greebles are fouling the area inhabited by the elder fish with the Chompy sauce and you must shut down the valves the Greebles are using to pump the sauce into the water. The valves are blocked by Battle Gates, so you must take down the Greeble chefs and other defenders before you can get to it. Life Spellpunks are among the enemies supporting the Greebles, and they should always be your first targets. Opening two valves also causes keys to drop, which are needed to unlock nearby gates. They appear near waterfalls, so watch for them after the announcement that a key has appeared.

FISHY FISHING

TIME	
Easy & Medium:	4:30
Hard:	6:05
Nightmare:	11:15

Map Acquired: Chapter 4: Rampant Ruins

Reward: Rabbit's Foot Charm

Mission: Destroy 5 giant harpoons with bombs.

Score Requirements

★	Earn Over 0 Points
★ ★	Earn Over 150,000 Points
★ ★ ★	Earn Over 230,000 Points

Greebles in the area are using giant harpoons at the Elder Fish sanctuary, and it's harming the local ecosystem. You must find giant bombs and use them to destroy the harpoons. Unfortunately, the bombs you need are blocked by Battle Gates, so you must defeat a number of enemies at each to unlock them. The defenders of the Battle Gates aren't always just Greebles. You must also take on more powerful enemies, like Tech Geargolems. The other problem you face is that you need to cross rolling bridges while carrying some bombs to reach the harpoons. If you're having trouble crossing the bridges while carrying the bombs, try this challenge with one of the flying Skylanders, such as Spyro.

MASTER CHEF	TIME
Map Acquired: Chapter 3: Mudwater Hollow	Easy & Medium: 3:50
Reward: Major Meal Charm	Hard: 5:10
Mission: Fight your way to get to the boss.	Nightmare: 9:35

Score Requirements

★	Earn Over 0 Points
★ ★	Earn Over 200,000 Points
★ ★ ★	Earn Over 350,000 Points

There are a few different types of locked gates to pass through in order to reach the Head Chef in the middle of the map, so be ready for fights at Battle Gates and a search for the key needed for a Locked Gate (sometimes keys are hidden behind Battle Gates!). When the game warns you about a Pumpkin Attack, avoid the red circles on the ground, which indicate where a pumpkin is about to land. Watch for Life Spellpunks during the battle against the Head Chef.

PLANTS VS CAKES	TIME
Map Acquired: Chapter 2: Cascade Glade	Easy & Medium: 5:00
Reward: Four Leaf Clover Charm	Hard: 6:45
Mission: Push 6 cakes to feed the Gobble Pods.	Nightmare: 12:30

Score Requirements

★	Earn Over 0 Points
★ ★	Earn Over 75,000 Points
★ ★ ★	Earn Over 125,000 Points

For this mission, cakes become part of sliding stone puzzles. To feed a cake to a Gobble Pod, you must push the cake on top of the white square directly in front of the Gobble Pod. The only enemies you face during this mission are Greebles, which should not be much of a threat. Enjoy ruining their party!

FRUIT FIGHT	TIME
Map Acquired: Chapter 1: Mount Cloudbreak	Easy & Medium: 5:50
Reward: Tasty Food Charm	Hard: 7:53
Mission: Collect 95 fruits.	Nightmare: 14:35

Score Requirements

★	Earn Over 0 Points
★ ★	Earn Over 100,000 Points
★ ★ ★	Earn Over 230,000 Points

Grabbing individual fruits floating around is the slow way to complete this mission. Look for food boxes (they're marked with an 'X') and wait for the outside attacker (who has been lobbing explosives from the start) to mark your Skylander's location with a red circle. When the explosive hits the food box, all the fruits inside are scattered around, ready to be picked up. When all the fruit in an area has been collected, look for a Battle Gate on a cannon. Defeat the Greebles in the area and use the cannon to travel to another area.

SERPENT ATTACK	TIME
Map Acquired: Tower of Time Adventure Pack Level	Easy & Medium: 3:40
Reward: Elemental Fist Charm	Hard: 4:55
Mission: Find the flute to hypnotize the Sand Monster and hit its three heads.	Nightmare: 9:10

Score Requirements

★	Earn Over 0 Points
★ ★	Earn Over 50,000 Points
★ ★ ★	Earn Over 75,000 Points

When you find a crate with notes coming out of it, break it open to reveal the flute. Play the flute to put the serpent's head to sleep, and then attack it to knock it out. Move on to the next area and repeat the process. The last area is a bit trickier. There are more crates and enemies appear in larger numbers. The task remains the same, however. Reveal the flute, put the Sand Monster's head to sleep, and attack it until its life is depleted. If you're feeling overwhelmed, don't attack the Sand Moster's head while it is asleep. Focus on the enemies to thin their numbers before attacking the Sand Monster.

THIEF ON THE RUN	TIME
Map Acquired: Sheep Wreck Islands Adventure Pack Level	Easy & Medium: 3:30
Reward: Charmed Actions Charm	Hard: 4:45
Mission: Retrieve 75 packages.	Nightmare: 8:45

Score Requirements

★	Earn Over 0 Points
★ ★	Earn Over 150,000 Points
★ ★ ★	Earn Over 230,000 Points

There are two different ways to acquire packages during this mission. The first way is to collect the individual packages that are on the ground. These packages also serve to guide you to the locations of the other source of packages, a Package Thief. The bright red bag slung over their shoulder makes them stand out among the other Greebles who try to stop you during this level. Take out each Package Thief you find to pick up around ten packages at once.

FROZEN DELIGHTS	TIME
Map Acquired: Tuk's Emporium for 1000 gold. Requires Portal Master Rank 25.	Easy & Medium: 3:50
	Hard: 5:10
Reward: Vitamin Supplements Charm	Nightmare: 9:35
Mission: Melt 5 ice creams with the crystal lasers.	

Score Requirements

★	Earn Over 0 Points
★ ★	Earn Over 250,000 Points
★ ★ ★	Earn Over 300,000 Points

This mission is a series of laser crystal puzzles. You must direct the laser to strike the large mounds of ice cream that hold Yeti Elders, and block your path. The enemies on this level are different cyclops types, along with Air Spellpunks. You rarely need to stick around to fight enemies.

SWEET BLIZZARD	TIME
Map Acquired: Behind Sharpfin at Woodburrow's Airdocks, after completing Chapter 11: Winter Keep	Easy & Medium: 4:00
	Hard: 5:25
Reward: Eye Poker Charm	Nightmare: 10:00
Mission: Turn off 5 Ice Cream Machines.	

Score Requirements

★	Earn Over 0 Points
★ ★	Earn Over 100,000 Points
★ ★ ★	Earn Over 250,000 Points

To turn off each Ice Cream Machine, simply interact with it. That's the easy part. The harder part is that many Ice Cream Machines are blocked by Battle Gates, and the enemies and hazards in this Bonus Mission are a step above many others encountered so far. Mesmeralda's proximity mines make an appearance, as do Air Geargolems. Skip the fights that you can, and save your energy for Battle Gates.

FRIGID FIGHT		TIME
Map Acquired: Chapter 12: Frostfest Mountains		Easy & Medium: 4:00
		Hard: 5:25
Reward: Unbridled Energy Charm		Nightmare: 10:00
Mission: Bring 12 ghosts to the appropriate gate.		

Score Requirements

★	Earn Over 0 Points
★ ★	Earn Over 100,000 Points
★ ★ ★	Earn Over 150,000 Points

Guiding ghosts to the appropriate gate is not difficult. The trick is collecting more than one ghost of the same color and avoiding a ghost of a different color. As soon as you touch a ghost with a different color from the ones you already have, you lose all the previous ghosts to pick up the new one. And it's better to collect more than one ghost per trip to the gates because of the time you save. Drop off ghosts at the gates with the matching color to get credit for them. One bit of good news for this Bonus mission: taking damage has no effect on ghosts being carried.

GHOST TRAPS		TIME
Map Acquired: Chapter 11: Winter Keep		Easy & Medium: 4:20
		Hard: 5:50
Reward: Might of the Ancients Charm		Nightmare: 10:50
Mission: Destroy the ghost traps with bombs.		

Score Requirements

★	Earn Over 0 Points
★ ★	Earn Over 150,000 Points
★ ★ ★	Earn Over 240,000 Points

There are nine ghost cages you must destroy with bombs during this Bonus Mission. The bombs are on a timer, so if you are having problems reaching the gates before the bomb explodes, try this mission with a Skylander who has a dashing ability. There are Battle Gates all over the place as well. Most block your progress, but one blocks the bomb you need to destroy the final cage.

ROYAL GEMS		TIME
Map Acquired: Chapter 10: Boney Islands		Easy & Medium: 5:00
		Hard: 6:45
Reward: Wizard Repellant Charm		Nightmare: 12:30
Mission: Defeat 9 armored cyclopes to retrieve the gems.		

Score Requirements

★	Earn Over 0 Points
★ ★	Earn Over 175,000 Points
★ ★ ★	Earn Over 250,000 Points

Each armored cyclops (they're all Brawlbucklers) has at least one helper Spellpunk. The further you get into the Mission, the more Cyclops Brawlbucklers and Spellpunks you face at once. Take down the Spellpunks first. They're generally the greater threat, and the Brawlbucklers are fairly slow. Lead them away from their support, then go after the Spellpunk when the Brawlbuckler misses an attack.

MAGIC CELLS	TIME
Map Acquired: Chapter 8: Twisty Tunnels	Easy & Medium: 3:50
Reward: Electro Magnet Charm	Hard: 5:10
Mission: Collect 95 Blue Energy Cells. Avoid the red cells.	Nightmare: 9:35

Score Requirements

★	Earn Over 0 Points
★ ★	Earn Over 50,000 Points
★ ★ ★	Earn Over 75,000 Points

The good news for this Bonus Mission is that there are few enemy encounters. The bad news is that there wasn't any room for many enemies because there are hazards everywhere! In addition to familiar hazards, you must watch out for the red cells. They don't hurt much, but they briefly lock any Skylander that touches them into place. The larger red hazards that look like pinball bumpers act like them too, throwing Skylanders around, usually into the red cells you were warned to avoid. There are also laser hazards that can only be avoided by jumping over them.

SLEEPY TURTLES	TIME
Map Acquired: Chapter 7: Motleyville	Easy & Medium: 6:00
Reward: Small Shield Charm	Hard: 8:05
Mission: Bring 6 turtles back to their nests.	Nightmare: 15:00

Score Requirements

★	Earn Over 0 Points
★ ★	Earn Over 175,000 Points
★ ★ ★	Earn Over 250,000 Points

Harkening back to early sliding block puzzles, you must push turtles along a path. For this Bonus Mission, you need to move turtles closer to their nests. Move the stone blocks to create a clear path for the turtle first. If there are any Chompies or Chompy Pods in the way, don't worry about destroying them first. Just crush them with the stone blocks.

EGG ROYALE	TIME
Map Acquired: Chapter 6: Iron Jaw Gulch	Easy & Medium: 5:00
Reward: Elemental Outlet Charm	Hard: 6:45
Mission: Bring 6 eggs to the royal nest.	Nightmare: 12:30

Score Requirements

★	Earn Over 0 Points
★ ★	Earn Over 175,000 Points
★ ★ ★	Earn Over 250,000 Points

The eggs you need are scattered around the level, and it's possible to carry more than one at a time. You need to be careful if you try to gather too many eggs at once. If you get hit by anything while carrying an egg, every egg you have is returned back to where you picked it up. To complicate things, some enemies appear on your way to an egg's location, and others wait until after you pick up the egg and are returning it to the nest before they pop up and attack. The path back is never as clear as it seems.

GOLEM INVASION	TIME
Map Acquired: Tuk's Emporium for 1000 gold. Requires Portal Master Rank 35.	Easy & Medium: 5:30
Reward: Element Deflect Charm	Hard: 7:25
Mission: Destroy 12 Golems to free the turtles.	Nightmare: 13:45

Score Requirements

★	Earn Over 0 Points
★ ★	Earn Over 150,000 Points
★ ★ ★	Earn Over 200,000 Points

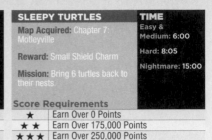

This Bonus Mission helpfully blocks your path when you're near a turtle to free. You face almost every type of Geargolem at some point during this battle, and there are a few fights that pit your Skylander against two Geargolems at the same time. Spellpunks sometimes stick their unwanted noses into fights, so keep an eye open for them to be aiding the Geargolems while hiding behind barriers. Greebles pop up from time to time, but only between Geargolem fights and only to be annoying. You can run past them if you want.

ARENA MODE

There are five total Arena Modes. Two of the modes, Solo Survival and Team Survival, award Stars based on how well you perform on your own and with a partner. The final three modes, Rival Survival, Battle Arena, and Ring Out, pit two players against each other in different styles of player versus player combat.

Completing an Arena Survival challenge for the first time, whether it's Solo or Team, awards a Charm.

SURVIVAL MODE

Survival Mode pits Skylanders under your control against large groups of enemies on small maps. Each challenge is divided into three stages, with a Bonus Stage after the first and second stages. During the Bonus Stage, the Food Thief appears and tries to escape from the arena. He isn't heading for an exit; he appears for a certain time before vanishing. If you take him down, your rewards include food and gold, and plenty of both!

UNLOCKING MAPS

All three Survival modes use the same set of maps, which are made available in groups of four. You must complete the first map in each group to open the second, then the second to open the third, and finally the third map to open the fourth. The first map, Super Hungry Gobble Pods, is available at the conclusion of Chapter 5: Jungle Rumble. Three groups of Survival maps are unlocked by continuing through the Story Mode. To open the final eight Survival maps, you must place the Arkeyan Crossbow figure and the Sheep Wreck Islands figure on your *Portal of Power*. These maps are opened in the same manner as the maps from Story Mode.

SCORING

To earn points and build your multiplier meter, attack enemies and objects. Destroying objects does not award points, but it does help build your meter. Collecting gold items awards points, but does not increase your multiplier meter.

The number that appears in the circle near your score is your multiplier, which shows how much more valuable each enemy you defeat, and coin you collect, is than when the meter is at one. The maximum value of your multiplier is 10. When playing Team Survival, both Skylanders contribute to the multiplier meter, and damage taken by either one lowers the multiplier number. In Rival Survival, each Skylander's progress is tracked individually, with the player with the higher score being declared the winner.

SUPER HUNGRY GOBBLE PODS

Unlocked: Complete Chapter 5: Jungle Rumble.

Reward: Elemental Noms Charm

Score Requirements

★	Earn Over 5000 Points
★ ★	Earn Over 30,000 Points
★ ★ ★	Earn Over 65,000 Points

Enemies

Stage 1	Chompy, Evilized Greeble, Greeble Ironclad
Stage 2	Chompy, Chompy Powerhouse, Greeble Ironclad, Life Spell Punk, Greeble Blunderbuss
Stage 3	Chompy, Chompy Powerhouse, Evilized Greeble, Air Spell Punk, Greeble Ironclad, Life Spell Punk

Super Hungry Gobble Pods is a straightforward brawl against waves of enemies with the added twist of potential allies in the form of the four Gobble Pods in cages around the arena. When a Gobble Pod is free of its cage, it eats nearby enemies, which still count toward your score. The Gobble Pods are returned to their cages, so you may need to free them multiple times. They are indestructible.

POKEY POKEY SPIKES

Unlocked: Complete the Super Hungry Gobble Pods arena.

Reward: Pointy Spear Charm

Score Requirements

★	Earn Over 7500 Points
★ ★	Earn Over 50,000 Points
★ ★ ★	Earn Over 80,000 Points

Enemies

Stage 1	Evilized Greeble, Greeble Heaver, Life Spell Punk, Greeble Slamspin
Stage 2	Evilized Greeble, Greeble Blunderbuss, Greeble Slamspin, Chompy, Earth Geargolem
Stage 3	Evilized Greeble, Greeble Heaver, Earth Geargolem, Chompy Powerhouse, Life Spell Punk

Skylanders are Cursed for Pokey Pokey Spikes, and rain clouds fly over their heads as a reminder. Cursed Skylanders suffer periodic damage, but the good news is that enemies are more likely to drop food when defeated. Spear traps serve as an extra hazard for this arena. During the first two stages, only half the spears are active. However, for the final round all spears are in play.

ANGRY ANGRY PLANTS

Unlocked: Complete the Pokey Pokey Spikes Pods arena.

Reward: Sword Breaker Charm

Score Requirements

★	Earn Over 5000 Points
★ ★	Earn Over 40,000 Points
★ ★ ★	Earn Over 65,000 Points

Enemies

Stage 1	Chompy, Chompy Pastepetal, Chompy Pod, Evilized Greeble, Greeble Heaver, Greeble Slamspin
Stage 2	Evilized Greeble, Chompy Pod, Chompy Powerhouse, Chompy, Greeble Slamspin, Arkeyan Slamshock
Stage 3	Chompy Pod, Chompy, Evilized Greeble, Greeble Heaver, Greeble Slamspin, Chompy Pastepetal, Chompy Powerhouse, Arkeyan Slamshock

Chompy Pods appear at the start of every stage, but they're not the only source of Chompies on this map. Enemies are dropped in from above, climb up from under the ground, and down the tunnels on the sides of the arena.

CHOMP CHOMP CHOMPIES

Unlocked: Complete the Angry Angry Plants arena.

Reward: Delicious Food Charm

Score Requirements	
★	Earn Over 7500 Points
★ ★	Earn Over 50,000 Points
★ ★ ★	Earn Over 80,000 Points

Enemies

Stage 1	Chompy, Grumblebum Rocketshooter, Grumblebum Thrasher
Stage 2	Chompy Rustbud, Grumblebum Rocketshooter, Grumblebum Thrasher
Stage 3	Chompy Powerhouse, Grumblebum Rocketshooter, Grumblebum Thrasher

Your goal in this mission is to keep the pile of fruit in the middle of the arena from being destroyed by the attacking Chompies and Grumblebums. The hardest part of the mission begins when Grumblebum Rocketshooters start to appear. You can't move or shoot through the fruit, which complicates dealing with the ranged attacks of the Rocketshooters. Melee Skylanders, especially slow melee Skylanders, will have a though time here.

SAND-PIT-FALL

Unlocked: Complete Chapter 9: Serpent's Peak.

Reward: Power Blend Charm

Score Requirements	
★	Earn Over 7500 Points
★ ★	Earn Over 50,000 Points
★ ★ ★	Earn Over 80,000 Points

Enemies

Stage 1	Evilized Greeble, Greeble Blunderbuss
Stage 2	Greeble Slamspin, Greeble Blunderbuss, Greeble Ironclad, Fire Geargolem
Stage 3	Fire Geargolem, Greeble Slamspin, Life Spell Punk, Greeble Ironclad

The sinkhole in the middle of the stage spells the end for enemies, but your Skylander takes a hit of damage and is returned to the arena floor. Forcing enemies into the pit still earns points for you, but XP bubbles are likely out of your reach.

SHELLSHOCK'S CURSE

Unlocked: Complete the Sand-Pit-Fall arena.

Reward: Greeble Grapplers Charm

Score Requirements	
★	Earn Over 10,000 Points
★ ★	Earn Over 60,000 Points
★ ★ ★	Earn Over 90,000 Points

Enemies

Stage 1	Arkeyan Barrelbot, Evilized Greeble, Arkeyan Slamshock
Stage 2	Greeble Heaver, Fire Geargolem, Arkeyan Rip-Rotor, Chompy Rustbud, Evilized Greeble
Stage 3	Arkeyan Barrelbot, Life Spell Punk, Chompy Rustbud, Arkeyan Knuckleduster

The Cursed status is back, as is the sinkhole in the middle of the arena floor. Arkeyan Rip-rotors are surprisingly easy to lure into flying over the top of the sinkhole, which still pulls them in at the height of the spin. During the last round, keep on the Life Spell Punks when they spawn. They hug the edges of the arena and heal from the fringes as much as they can.

BEWARE OF THE BIRD

Unlocked: Complete the Shellshock's Curse arena.

Reward: Eight Leaf Clover Charm

Score Requirements

★	Earn Over 10,000 Points
★ ★	Earn Over 60,000 Points
★ ★ ★	Earn Over 90,000 Points

Enemies

Stage 1	Arkeyan Knuckleduster, Chompy Rustbud, Arkeyan Rip-Rotor, Arkeyan Barrelbot, Arkeyan Slamshock
Stage 2	Arkeyan Knuckleduster, Chompy Rustbud, Arkeyan Rip-Rotor, Tech Geargolem
Stage 3	Chompy Rustbud, Arkeyan Rip-Rotor, Tech Geargolem, Arkeyan Knuckleduster, Arkeyan Slamshock

The sinkhole is covered with wood planks for this battle. The Bird flies down and gets its head stuck (after one or two attacks) at the end of each round. Jump in and attack while it is vulnerable. At the end of the second round, it flies to the roof and fires into the arena floor between jumping attacks. During the third round, it pulls its head out of the ground and fires a laser beam from its mouth.

SNAKE IN THE HOLE

Unlocked: Complete the Beware of the Bird arena.

Reward: Health Extender Charm

Score Requirements

★	Earn Over 10,000 Points
★ ★	Earn Over 60,000 Points
★ ★ ★	Earn Over 90,000 Points

Enemies

Stage 1	Evilized Greeble, Greeble Blunderbuss
Stage 2	Greeble Slamspin, Greeble Blunderbuss, Greeble Ironclad
Stage 3	Evilized Greeble, Life Spell Punk, Greeble Slamspin

The sinkhole remains covered for this challenge. A giant snake watches over the arena and spits spiky balls on to the floor (watch out for the red circles) while you're fighting the waves of Greebles. When a horn appears on the arena floor, try to take out as many Greebles as you can and then use the horn to charm the snake. When the snake is charmed, attack it quickly. Repeat this process for all three rounds, until the snake's health bar is depleted.

BOARDING PARTY

Unlocked: Complete Chapter 13: Mesmeralda's Show

Reward: Gourmet Meal Charm

Score Requirements

★	Earn Over 15,000 Points
★ ★	Earn Over 60,000 Points
★ ★ ★	Earn Over 100,000 Points

Enemies

Stage 1	Coldspear Cyclops, Twistpick Cyclops, Missile Mauler
Stage 2	Coldspear Cyclops, Cyclops Gazermage, Cyclops Bucklebrawler
Stage 3	Magic Spell Punk, Missile Mauler, Twistpick Cyclops

Boarding Party is a basic brawler in an arena with no hazards and no obstructions. It takes place on a boat, so enemies appear by climbing over the sides. You can knock them back off the boat at those same spots with a well-timed attack.

ICICLE BOMBING

Unlocked: Complete the Boarding Party arena.

Reward: Ultimate Defense Charm

Score Requirements	
★	Earn Over 15000 Points
★ ★	Earn Over 90,000 Points
★ ★ ★	Earn Over 150,000 Points

Enemies

Stage 1	Coldspear Cyclops, Twistpick Cyclops, Magic Spell Punk, Cyclops Gazermage
Stage 2	Coldspear Cyclops, Twistpick Cyclops, Cyclops Gazermage
Stage 3	Ice Geargolem, Coldspear Cyclops, Twistpick Cyclops, Cyclops Gazermage

There's quite a bit going on in this map. Your Skylander is Cursed, which always makes things more interesting. The bottom half of the map is covered by snow. Finally, a ship flies in the background and it's covered with Cyclops Snowblasters. The Snowblasters fire a stream of ice pellets into the arena as they pass by.

EXPLODING SNOWMEN

Unlocked: Complete the Icicle Bombing arena.

Reward: Kaos Kruncher Charm

Score Requirements	
★	Earn Over 10,000 Points
★ ★	Earn Over 60,000 Points
★ ★ ★	Earn Over 100,000 Points

Enemies

Stage 1	Coldspear Cyclops, Twistpick Cyclops, Missile Mauler,
Stage 2	Coldspear Cyclops, Cyclops Gazermage, Cyclops Bucklebrawler
Stage 3	Cyclops Brawlbuckler, Chompy Frostflower, Magic Spell Punk, Twistpick Cyclops

Each stage is fairly standard until you hit the point where the Food Thief normally makes his appearance. He still appears, but you must first survive a wave of the proximity mines used by Mesmeralda, though they're called ice bombs here. Avoiding the ice bombs becomes increasingly more difficult in each stage. They move across the arena in unison, and you need to keep your Skylander on the move to avoid being blown up.

PERFECT CAPTAIN

Unlocked: Complete the Exploding Snowmen arena.

Reward: Instant Experience Charm

Score Requirements	
★	Earn Over 15,000 Points
★ ★	Earn Over 25,000 Points
★ ★ ★	Earn Over 45,000 Points

Enemies

Stage 1	Coldspear Cyclops, Twistpick Cyclops, Cyclops Gazermage
Stage 2	Chompy Frostflower, Cyclops Brawlbuckler, Cyclops Gazermage
Stage 3	Chompy Frostflower, Cyclops Brawlbuckler, Twistpick Cyclops, Magic Spell Punk

Perfect Captain refers to the fact that your Skylander has only 1 HP for this arena! You must avoid being hit by the enemies on the ship, and you must also avoid the Cyclops Snowblasters firing on the ship as well. The cold hinders your movement if you are hit. Hide behind the higher walls on either end of the ship, and stay on the move. One hit and it's over! Not that you will miss him with only 1 HP, but the Food Thief does not make an appearance in this challenge.

VORTEX BANQUET

Unlocked: Place the Sheep Wreck Islands figure on your Portal of Power.

Reward: Mountain's Resolve Charm

Score Requirements	
★	Earn Over 25,000 Points
★ ★	Earn Over 120,000 Points
★ ★ ★	Earn Over 200,000 Points

Enemies

Stage 1	Coldspear Cyclops, Cyclops Gazermage, Twistpick Cyclops, Vortex Geargolem
Stage 2	Coldspear Cyclops, Cyclops Gazermage, Twistpick Cyclops, Vortex Geargolem
Stage 3	Coldspear Cyclops, Cyclops Gazermage, Twistpick Cyclops, Cyclops Sleetthrower, Vortex Geargolem

The cyclops units carry over their visual theme from Sheep Wreck Islands, but they're the same cyclops you're used to. When a vortex appears in a set of columns in the back of the arena, look for a Vortex Geargolem. You must keep the Vortex Geargolems away from the Vortex when they appear. They don't attack, so you are free to take it down quickly without worrying about defense. If Vortex Geargolems reach three vortices, you fail the challenge.

CYCLOPS MAKEOVER

Unlocked: Complete the Vortex Banquet arena.

Reward: Good Luck Charm

Score Requirements	
★	Earn Over 20,000 Points
★ ★	Earn Over 115,000 Points
★ ★ ★	Earn Over 190,000 Points

Enemies

Stage 1	Coldspear Cyclops, Cyclops Sleetthrower, Twistpick Cyclops, Cyclops Brawlbuckler
Stage 2	Coldspear Cyclops, Cyclops Sleetthrower, Twistpick Cyclops, Magic Spell Punk, Cyclops Brawlbuckler
Stage 3	Twistpick Cyclops, Chompy, Coldspear Cyclops, Cyclops Sleetthrower, Chompy Boomblossom, Cyclops Brawlbuckler

Your Skylander is Cursed for this challenge. When a vortex appears, be on the lookout for a Coldspear Cyclops (they stand out because they're the original green skinned version, and they're larger than the other cyclopes in the area). If the Coldspear Cyclops reaches the vortex, it is upgraded to a Cyclops Brawlbuckler.

SHEEP MAGE RAGE

Unlocked: Complete the Cyclops Makeover arena.

Reward: Mage Masher Charm

Score Requirements	
★	Earn Over 20,000 Points
★ ★	Earn Over 115,000 Points
★ ★ ★	Earn Over 190,000 Points

Enemies

Stage 1	Coldspear Cyclops, Cyclops Gazermage, Vortex Geargolem, Twistpick Cyclops, Small and Giant Blitzbloom Chompy
Stage 2	Coldspear Cyclops, Cyclops Sleetthrower, Vortex Geargolem, Cyclops Brawlbuckler, Chompy Boomblossom, Cyclops Gazermage
Stage 3	Coldspear Cyclops, Vortex Geargolem, Cyclops Brawlbuckler, Cyclops Sleetthrower

Vortex Geargolems spawn at the vortices only, so watch the vortices for trouble. Toward the end of the first round, the Sheep Mage gets involved by spewing thorny objects into the area, and then sucking in and blowing out air. Avoid the thorny objects during the wind storm as best you can. There is no cover, which makes things tougher. After the second round, Chompy Boomblossoms are added to the already dangerous mix, so take them out before they can get close enough to deal damage.

CHUNKY CHOMPIES

Unlocked: Complete the Sheep Mage Rage arena.

Reward: Power Clover Charm

Score Requirements

★	Earn Over 15,000 Points
★ ★	Earn Over 75,000 Points
★ ★ ★	Earn Over 125,000 Points

Enemies

Stage 1	Chompy, Coldspear Cyclops, Vortex Geargolem
Stage 2	Coldspear Cyclops, Chompy Powerhouse, Cyclops Gazermage, Twistpick Cyclops
Stage 3	Coldspear Cyclops, Chompy Blitzbloom, Cyclops Sleetthrower, Chompy Boomblossom

This is a battle primarily against large waves of Chompies followed up by a wave of large Chompies. The Chompies that spawn from the vortices are much larger than other Chompies you fought before. They're much tougher and won't go down easily. The type of Chompy changes with each level, and the big guys always match the little ones.

SAND CASTLE

Unlocked: Place the Arkeyan Crossbow figure on your Portal of Power.

Reward: Cyclops Swatter Charm

Score Requirements

★	Earn Over 15,000 Points
★ ★	Earn Over 50,000 Points
★ ★ ★	Earn Over 100,000 Points

Enemies

Stage 1	Chompy, Cadet Crasher, Loose Cannon, Boom Boss, Missile Mauler
Stage 2	Chompy, Giant Chompy, Cadet Crasher, Loose Cannon, Boom Boss, Missile Mauler
Stage 3	Chompy Boomblossom, Cadet Crasher, Loose Cannon, Boom Boss, Missile Mauler

You must protect the Sand Tower from swarms of tropically themed trolls. The Loose Cannons are the trolls assigned to ignore everything and go after the Sand Tower, so they should be your main targets. Activate the water cannons atop sand castles by sliding them to the front, where they fire water balloons for a bit before they slide back.

BEACH BREACH

Unlocked: Complete the Sand Castle arena.

Reward: Big Pants Charm

Score Requirements

★	Earn Over 5000 Points
★ ★	Earn Over 25,000 Points
★ ★ ★	Earn Over 50,000 Points

Enemies

Stage 1	Chompy, Cadet Crasher, Missile Mauler
Stage 2	Chompy, Giant Chompy, Cadet Crasher, Air Geargolem
Stage 3	Chompy, Giant Chompy, Chompy Boomblossom, Cadet Crasher, Missile Mauler

Your Skylander is Cursed for this challenge. You are back defending the Sand Tower from trolls and Chompies. The trolls are more concerned with attacking your Skylander but the Chompies appear to be devoted to attacking the Sand Tower. Some Chompies that spawn from the surf are a bit larger and tougher than standard Chompies.

TROLL BEACH ATTACK

Unlocked: Complete the Beach Breach arena.

Reward: Impervious Charm

Score Requirements

★	Earn Over 15,000 Points
★ ★	Earn Over 50,000 Points
★ ★ ★	Earn Over 100,000 Points

Enemies

Stage 1	Chompy, Cadet Crusher, Missile Mauler
Stage 2	Chompy Boomblossom, Giant Chompy Boomblossom, Cadet Crusher, Missile Mauler, Air Geargolem
Stage 3	Loose Cannon, Giant Chompy, Cadet Crusher, Missile Mauler, Air Geargolem

Troll Beach Attack is a return to traditional challenges. You must survive three stages of troll and Chompy attacks. No need to defend anything here. The one twist to this level is that the cannons that you were using to help on defense are now trained  on your Skylander! Watch out for red circles appearing on the beach and stay clear to avoid taking damage. At the end of each stage, even the final stage, the cannons blanket the beach with cannonballs. Stay on the move, otherwise your Skylander won't last long.

CHOMPY TSUNAMI

Unlocked: Complete the Troll Beach Attack arena.

Reward: Luck of the Mabu Charm

Score Requirements

★	Earn Over 10,000 Points
★ ★	Earn Over 50,000 Points
★ ★ ★	Earn Over 85,000 Points

Enemies

Stage 1	Chompy, Cadet Crusher, Missile Mauler
Stage 2	Chompy, Chompy Powerhouse, Cadet Crusher, Missile Mauler, Loose Cannon, Boom Boss
Stage 3	Chompy, Chompy Boomblossom, Cadet Crusher, Missile Mauler, Loose Cannon, Air Geargolem

The Chompy Castles that appear in the sand spawn Chompies until they are destroyed. When the castles appear, destroy them quickly or the beach will be overrun with Chompies before you know it.

BATTLE ARENA & RING OUT

Battle Arena and Ring Out share two maps (Rampart Ruins and Fiery Forge) but otherwise have maps unique to them. Both modes have three maps available immediately, even before you start playing the Story Mode. Place the Arkeyan Crossbow figure on your *Portal of Power* to unlock the Treacherous Beach Battle arena.

The Tower of Time figure adds the Ring Out arena, Tic Toc Terrace. The Fiery Forge figure opens an arena of the same name that is available in both modes.

BATTLE ARENA

In Battle Arena, the goal is to reduce the other Skylander's health to zero before the same happens to your Skylander. Power-ups and food appear at random times at different locations on the map, so long as they are turned on for the fight. The other options allow you to change the number of lives each Skylander has (the number of lives left appears near their names), and whether to make two Skylanders of different levels more equal in the arena.

Battle Arena Settings

POWER-UPS	On/Off
FOOD	On/Off
LIVES	1, 3, 5, 7, 9
FAIR FIGHT	On/Off

BATTLE ARENA MAPS

RAMPART RUINS

Unlocked: Available with purchase of game

Rampart Ruins is a compact map that resembles the tops of two castle towers connected by a wooden ramp. Stepping on the teleporters sends your Skylander to the highest point of the opposite tower. The mines blocking the wooden ramp respawn quickly should they be destroyed.

QUICKSAND QUARRY

Unlocked: Available with purchase of game

Quicksand Quarry gets its name from the areas of flowing sand around the map. Skylanders caught in the moving sand are pulled down into it slightly, and suffer reduced movement speed. Skylanders can fall through the hole in the middle of the map (on the quicksand side only) and fall over the edge of the map that isn't protected by a fence. Falling off the map does not count against your life total.

FROZEN OUTPOST

Unlocked: Available with purchase of game

The large spear trap in the center of Frozen Outpost's lower floor is activated by any of the three green pads around it. Once it is triggered, there is a short cooldown before it's ready to use again. The two teleporters on the topmost level send Skylanders to the same spot in the center of the spear trap. The teleporters on the lower level lead to the same spot in the middle of the upper area.

FIERY FORGE

Unlocked: Place the Fiery Forge figure on your Portal of Power

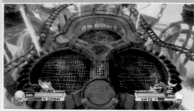

All the action in Fiery Forge takes place either on the narrow walkway looping around the three lava pits, or in the lava pits themselves. Lava appears in the pits often, and either comes up from under a pit, or pours into a pit from above. The lava briefly fills one of the three pits, then drains away.

TREACHEROUS BEACH

Unlocked: Place the Arkeyan Crossbow figure on your Portal of Power

Despite its dangerous-sounding name, Treacherous Beach is relatively quiet for a place where two Skylanders try to knock each other out. The map extends from the tops of both sand castles to the fence in the surf below. Beyond Power-ups and two bounce pads that send Skylanders to the top of the sand castles, there aren't any other environmental items to worry about.

RING OUT

In Ring Out, the goal is to knock the opposing Skylander over the side of the map with a power hit. Each successful attack on your opponent builds a Super Punch meter that appears near your Skylander's name (Skylanders do not have health bars in Ring Out). When the meter is full, the next press of Attack 1 is a Super Punch attack that knocks your opponent's Skylander over the edge if they're close enough.

Power-ups appear at random times at different locations on the map, so long as they are turned on for the fight. The other options allow you to change the number of times each Skylander can be knocked out (the number of lives left appears near their names) before one is declared the winner, and whether to make two Skylanders of different levels more equal in the arena.

Battle Arena Settings

POWER-UPS	On/Off
LIVES	1, 3, 5, 7, 9
FAIR FIGHT	On/Off

RAMPART RUINS

Unlocked: Available with purchase of game

The two castle tops that make up Rampart Ruins appear to be either in the process of being built or being dismantled. There are barely any standing walls, which makes fighting near any edge dangerous. The lack of walls makes Bounce Pads on the level dangerous to use. Try to avoid using them, save as a last resort to escape a Super Punch.

QUICK DRAW CORRAL

Unlocked: Available with purchase of game

Quick Draw Corral is one of the safer arenas in terms of not defeating yourself by falling over the edge unaided. A low wall outlines the outer edge of the walkway around the arena, and it keeps Skylanders contained unless they jump over it or get knocked over it by a Super Punch.

BLOSSOM ISLANDS

Unlocked: Available with purchase of game

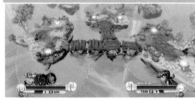

The wooden walkway connecting the three Blossom Islands is the dangerous way to move between the islands. There are six total teleporter locations, with two on each island. However, at most there are only five teleporters active at the same time. The teleporters send Skylanders to the island closest to its location, meaning two islands have two teleporters while the third island has only one. For example, the teleporters on the left and right islands nearer to the top island send Skylanders to the center of the top island.

TIC TOC TERRACE

Unlocked: Place the Tower of Time figure on your Portal of Power

The outer ring and gears of Tic Toc Terrace are perpetually moving. Be careful when moving to the outer ring. The spinning gears and large gaps between the gears make movement between the platforms tricky. The teleporters on the outer ring send Skylanders back to the clock face that makes up the central platform.

FIERY FORGE

Unlocked: Place the Fiery Forge figure on your Portal of Power

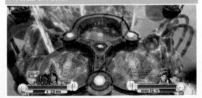

The hazard switch in the center of the map drops the floor out from under the three circular bowls that make up the lowest part of this arena. If the green hazard circle is lit, avoid using the teleporters. They send Skylanders to the center of the areas that lose their floors. The lowest teleporter sends Skylanders to the top bowl. The teleporter on the left sends Skylanders to the right bowl, and the right teleporter goes to the bowl on the left.

ARENA MODE

197

TIME ATTACK MODE

In Time Attack Mode, you earn Stars by completing Story Mode and Adventure Pack levels in under a certain time limit. Each level has its own time requirements for earning Stars, and that information is included on the following pages. Playing on your own and playing with a friend both have the same time requirements.

GET TO THE END AS FAST AS YOU CAN!

00:02.88

pause the timer!

CHANGES IN TIME ATTACK MODE VERSUS STORY MODE

The collectible items on each map (Soul Gems, Legendary Treasures, Hats, and other similar objects) change into objects that freeze the clock for 20-25 seconds. They appear as a blue oval with a clock icon inside. The amount of time the clock is frozen appears in a light blue icon to the left of your timer.

These time-stopping clock icons also appear randomly from destroyed objects and defeated enemies, though these items stop the clock for a much shorter time, about six seconds. Picking up a blue oval item while another one is active adds additional time to the light blue timer.

In-game events, such as Spark Locks, cinematics, or conversations with other characters, pause the clock until the event ends. In all other areas, your timer continues its countdown. That means you should skip every non-essential pick up, SWAP Zone Challenge, and Elemental Gate.

QUICK TIPS FOR MAXIMIZING YOUR SCORE

SKIP EVERYTHING YOU CAN

There is no scoring. There's no bonus for completeness. The only thing that matters is getting to the end. Avoid fights unless defeating enemies is faster than letting them nip at your heels.

FAMILIARITY IS YOUR GREATEST ASSET

Get to know the levels and what you must do and what you can skip. Learn which clock-stopping pick ups are worth the detour to get, and which ones are just too far away to bother with.

USE SKYLANDERS WITH A DASH ABILITY

There are a handful of Skylanders who have an ability that allows them to move through areas faster than others. Get them to level 20, buy all their abilities, and put them to use in Time Attack Mode!

MAGIC ITEMS ARE GREAT

Everything helps when you're trying to get through places quickly. Not just the Winged Boots, but also the Adventure Pack pieces that make Battle Gate encounters go much faster.

Mount Cloudbreak

★	Set a Personal Best Time
★ ★	Cleared in Under: 6:30
★ ★ ★	Cleared in Under: 5:30

Mudwater Hollow

★	Set a Personal Best Time
★ ★	Cleared in Under: 15:00
★ ★ ★	Cleared in Under: 12:00

Jungle Rumble

★	Set a Personal Best Time
★ ★	Cleared in Under: 3:00
★ ★ ★	Cleared in Under: 1:45

Motleyville

★	Set a Personal Best Time
★ ★	Cleared in Under: 12:30
★ ★ ★	Cleared in Under: 11:00

Serpent's Peak

★	Set a Personal Best Time
★ ★	Cleared in Under: 3:00
★ ★ ★	Cleared in Under: 2:30

Winter Keep

★	Set a Personal Best Time
★ ★	Cleared in Under: 16:00
★ ★ ★	Cleared in Under: 14:00

Mesmeralda's Show

★	Set a Personal Best Time
★ ★	Cleared in Under: 4:40
★ ★ ★	Cleared in Under: 4:00

Kaos' Fortress

★	Set a Personal Best Time
★ ★	Cleared in Under: 9:30
★ ★ ★	Cleared in Under: 8:30

Cloudbreak Core

★	Set a Personal Best Time
★ ★	Cleared in Under: 9:30
★ ★ ★	Cleared in Under: 8:20

Tower of Time

★	Set a Personal Best Time
★ ★	Cleared in Under: 22:00
★ ★ ★	Cleared in Under: 20:00

Cascade Glade

★	Set a Personal Best Time
★ ★	Cleared in Under: 6:30
★ ★ ★	Cleared in Under: 4:50

Rampant Ruins

★	Set a Personal Best Time
★ ★	Cleared in Under: 8:00
★ ★ ★	Cleared in Under: 6:00

Iron Jaw Gulch

★	Set a Personal Best Time
★ ★	Cleared in Under: 7:30
★ ★ ★	Cleared in Under: 5:50

Twisty Tunnels

★	Set a Personal Best Time
★ ★	Cleared in Under: 11:30
★ ★ ★	Cleared in Under: 10:00

Boney Islands

★	Set a Personal Best Time
★ ★	Cleared in Under: 14:30
★ ★ ★	Cleared in Under: 11:40

Frostfest Mountains

★	Set a Personal Best Time
★ ★	Cleared in Under: 8:30
★ ★ ★	Cleared in Under: 6:30

Fantasm Forest

★	Set a Personal Best Time
★ ★	Cleared in Under: 25:00
★ ★ ★	Cleared in Under: 20:00

Motherly Mayhem

★	Set a Personal Best Time
★ ★	Cleared in Under: 8:30
★ ★ ★	Cleared in Under: 7:45

Sheep Wreck Islands

★	Set a Personal Best Time
★ ★	Cleared in Under: 18:00
★ ★ ★	Cleared in Under: 16:00

TIME ATTACK MODE

SCORE MODE

In Score Mode, you earn Stars by completing Story Mode and Adventure Pack levels and hitting certain scores. Each level has its own minimum scores for earning Stars, and that information is included on the following pages. Playing on your own and playing with a friend both have the same score requirements.

To earn points and build your multiplier meter, attack enemies and objects. Destroying objects does not award points, but it does help build your meter. Collecting gold items awards points, but does not increase your multiplier meter.

The number that appears in the circle near your score is your multiplier, which shows how much more valuable each enemy you defeat, and coin you collect, is than when the meter is at one. The maximum value of your multiplier is 30. Changing Skylanders during a Score Mode level does not affect your scoring or multiplier. When playing with a friend, both Skylanders contribute to the multiplier meter, and damage taken by either one lowers the multiplier number.

CHANGES IN SCORE MODE VERSUS STORY MODE

The collectible items on each map (Soul Gems, Legendary Treasures, Hats, and other similar objects) change into bonus multipliers. They appear as a blue 1X object. These multipliers also appear randomly from destroyed objects and defeated enemies. A shield power up also appears from time to time. The shield protects your Skylander from losing a multiplier for one hit.

Coins collected during SWAP Zone Challenges do not add to your score. Only the SWAP Zone Medals collected while running a challenge matter. When the medals turn into gems to gather up and the SWAP Zone has been completed, you get a 1X multiplier (it replaces the collectible from completing the challenge) and the gold from gathering the gems.

Spark Locks, whether they're blocking chests or gates, award a big multiplier bonus when you complete the lock with all three bolts.

QUICK TIPS FOR MAXIMIZING YOUR SCORE

TAKE YOUR TIME

There is no time limit in Score Mode, so it's more important to be thorough than it is to be fast. Solve every Spark Lock with three bolts. Complete every SWAP Zone with three gems. Don't skip Elemental gates.

SAVE THE GOLD FOR LAST...

If your multiplier is not maxed out and you run into an area with enemies or objects to destroy, or a bonus multiplier is nearby, don't pick up any gold until after you eliminate everything and build up your multiplier as high as it can be.

...UNLESS THERE'S A CHANCE TO LOSE THE MULTIPLIER

If you're worried about passing through a hazard- or enemy-filled area unharmed, grab everything before you start a fight or run through a dangerous spot.

PLAY IN NIGHTMARE DIFFICULTY

If you're an experienced Portal Master, you can maximize your score by playing in Nightmare Difficulty. Though more challenging, you earn more points.

Mount Cloudbreak

★	Set a Personal Best Score
★ ★	Earn over 100,000 Points
★ ★ ★	Earn over 150000 Points

Cascade Glade

★	Set a Personal Best Score
★ ★	Earn over 40,000 Points
★ ★ ★	Earn over 65,000 Points

Mudwater Hollow

★	Set a Personal Best Score
★ ★	Earn over 100,000 Points
★ ★ ★	Earn over 140,000 Points

Rampant Ruins

★	Set a Personal Best Score
★ ★	Earn over 150,000 Points
★ ★ ★	Earn over 200,000 Points

Jungle Rumble

★	Set a Personal Best Score
★ ★	Earn over 10,000 Points
★ ★ ★	Earn over 19,000 Points

Iron Jaw Gulch

★	Set a Personal Best Score
★ ★	Earn over 120,000 Points
★ ★ ★	Earn over 170,000 Points

Motleyville

★	Set a Personal Best Score
★ ★	Earn over 350,000 Points
★ ★ ★	Earn over 450,000 Points

Twisty Tunnels

★	Set a Personal Best Score
★ ★	Earn over 250,000 Points
★ ★ ★	Earn over 400,000 Points

Serpent's Peak

★	Set a Personal Best Score
★ ★	Earn over 9000 Points
★ ★ ★	Earn over 15,000 Points

Boney Islands

★	Set a Personal Best Score
★ ★	Earn over 250,000 Points
★ ★ ★	Earn over 350,000 Points

Winter Keep

★	Set a Personal Best Score
★ ★	Earn over 200,000 Points
★ ★ ★	Earn over 250,000 Points

Frostfest Mountains

★	Set a Personal Best Score
★ ★	Earn over 150,000 Points
★ ★ ★	Earn over 200,000 Points

Mesmeralda's Show

★	Set a Personal Best Score
★ ★	Earn over 6500 Points
★ ★ ★	Earn over 8500 Points

Fantasm Forest

★	Set a Personal Best Score
★ ★	Earn over 200,000 Points
★ ★ ★	Earn over 400,000 Points

Kaos' Fortress

★	Set a Personal Best Score
★ ★	Earn over 100,000 Points
★ ★ ★	Earn over 150,000 Points

Motherly Mayhem

★	Set a Personal Best Score
★ ★	Earn over 25,000 Points
★ ★ ★	Earn over 40,000 Points

Cloudbreak Core

★	Set a Personal Best Score
★ ★	Earn over 60,000 Points
★ ★ ★	Earn over 90,000 Points

Sheep Wreck Islands

★	Set a Personal Best Score
★ ★	Earn over 300,000 Points
★ ★ ★	Earn over 400,000 Points

Tower of Time

★	Set a Personal Best Score
★ ★	Earn over 350,000 Points
★ ★ ★	Earn over 450,000 Points

SCORE MODE

COLLECTIBLES

In previous installments of the series, collecting everything was a source of pride that conveyed a feeling of accomplishment. After all, not everyone cared to collect every hat when a few had stats that weren't as good as ones they'd already obtained. However, in *Skylanders SWAP Force* being a completionist is vital to increasing your Portal Master rank and creating the most powerful Skylanders possible.

There are five types of collectibles: Hats, Legendary Treasures, Charms, Bonus Mission Maps, and Story Scrolls. The following pages provide more information on each, including how to acquire them all.

Hats

There are 147 hats to collect. Every hat is either found in one of the Story Levels, or purchased at Tuk's Emporium in Woodburrow. You must complete Chapter 2: Cascade Glade and meet certain requirements to purchase some hats.

Each Skylander can wear one hat at a time. Hats convey positive statistical effects while they're worn. To change the hat worn by a Skylander, select the Hats option from the Skylanders Stats screen.

LOCATION / PURCHASE REQUIREMENT

Deely Boppers
Open Tuk's Shop

10 0 0 2 0 0

COST — 500

EFFECT
MAXIMUM HEALTH
SPEED
ARMOR
CRITICAL HIT
CRITICAL HIT MULTIPLIER
ELEMENTAL POWER

HATS FROM STORY MODE

Asteroid Hat
Kaos' Fortress

60 0 0 0 0 0

Aviator's Cap
Sheep Wreck Islands

0 0 0 0 0 30

Beacon Hat
Frostfest Mountains

30 0 0 0 0 15

Beanie
Tower of Time

0 5 0 0 0 20

Bearskin Cap
Boney Islands

10 0 0 5 0 10

Boater Hat
Mudwater Hollow

20 3 0 0 0 0

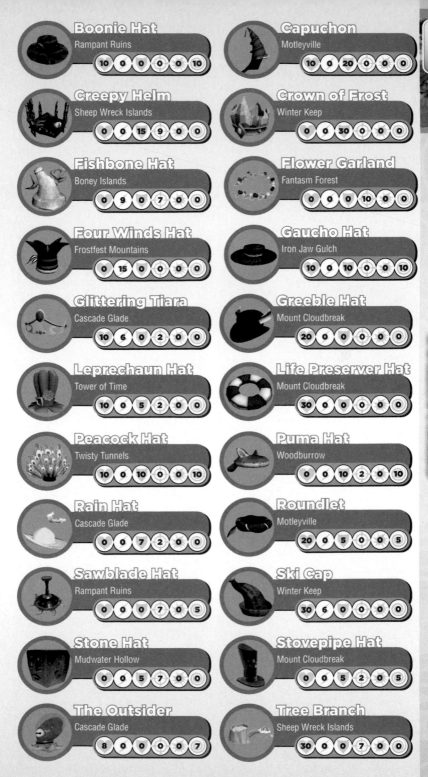

Boonie Hat
Rampant Ruins
10 | **0** | **0** | **0** | **0** | **10**

Capuchon
Motleyville
10 | **0** | **0** | **20** | **0** | **0**

Creepy Helm
Sheep Wreck Islands
0 | **0** | **15** | **9** | **0** | **0**

Crown of Frost
Winter Keep
0 | **0** | **30** | **0** | **0** | **0**

Fishbone Hat
Boney Islands
0 | **9** | **0** | **7** | **0** | **0**

Flower Garland
Fantasm Forest
0 | **0** | **0** | **10** | **0** | **0**

Four Winds Hat
Frostfest Mountains
0 | **15** | **0** | **0** | **0** | **0**

Gaucho Hat
Iron Jaw Gulch
10 | **0** | **10** | **0** | **0** | **10**

Glittering Tiara
Cascade Glade
10 | **6** | **0** | **2** | **0** | **0**

Greeble Hat
Mount Cloudbreak
20 | **0** | **0** | **0** | **0** | **0**

Leprechaun Hat
Tower of Time
10 | **0** | **5** | **2** | **0** | **0**

Life Preserver Hat
Mount Cloudbreak
30 | **0** | **0** | **0** | **0** | **0**

Peacock Hat
Twisty Tunnels
10 | **0** | **10** | **0** | **0** | **10**

Puma Hat
Woodburrow
0 | **0** | **10** | **2** | **0** | **10**

Rain Hat
Cascade Glade
0 | **0** | **7** | **2** | **0** | **0**

Roundlet
Motleyville
20 | **0** | **5** | **0** | **0** | **5**

Sawblade Hat
Rampant Ruins
0 | **0** | **0** | **7** | **0** | **5**

Ski Cap
Winter Keep
30 | **6** | **0** | **0** | **0** | **0**

Stone Hat
Mudwater Hollow
0 | **0** | **5** | **7** | **0** | **0**

Stovepipe Hat
Mount Cloudbreak
0 | **0** | **5** | **2** | **0** | **5**

The Outsider
Cascade Glade
8 | **0** | **0** | **0** | **0** | **7**

Tree Branch
Sheep Wreck Islands
30 | **0** | **0** | **7** | **0** | **0**

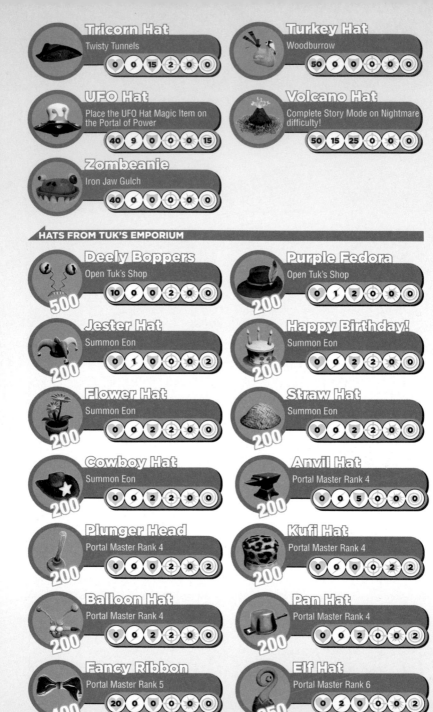

Tricorn Hat
Twisty Tunnels
0 | 15 | 2 | 0 | 0

Turkey Hat
Woodburrow
50 | 0 | 0 | 0 | 0 | 0

UFO Hat
Place the UFO Hat Magic Item on the Portal of Power
40 | 9 | 0 | 0 | 0 | 15

Volcano Hat
Complete Story Mode on Nightmare difficulty!
50 | 15 | 25 | 0 | 0 | 0

Zombeanie
Iron Jaw Gulch
40 | 0 | 0 | 0 | 0 | 0

HATS FROM TUK'S EMPORIUM

Deely Boppers
Open Tuk's Shop
500
10 | 0 | 0 | 2 | 0 | 0

Purple Fedora
Open Tuk's Shop
200
0 | 1 | 2 | 0 | 0 | 0

Jester Hat
Summon Eon
200
0 | 1 | 0 | 0 | 0 | 2

Happy Birthday!
Summon Eon
200
0 | 0 | 2 | 2 | 0 | 0

Flower Hat
Summon Eon
200
0 | 0 | 2 | 2 | 0 | 0

Straw Hat
Summon Eon
200
0 | 0 | 2 | 2 | 0 | 0

Cowboy Hat
Summon Eon
200
0 | 0 | 2 | 2 | 0 | 0

Anvil Hat
Portal Master Rank 4
200
0 | 0 | 5 | 0 | 0 | 0

Plunger Head
Portal Master Rank 4
200
0 | 0 | 0 | 2 | 0 | 2

Kufi Hat
Portal Master Rank 4
200
0 | 0 | 0 | 0 | 2 | 2

Balloon Hat
Portal Master Rank 4
200
0 | 0 | 2 | 2 | 0 | 0

Pan Hat
Portal Master Rank 4
200
0 | 0 | 2 | 0 | 0 | 2

Fancy Ribbon
Portal Master Rank 5
400
20 | 0 | 0 | 0 | 0 | 0

Elf Hat
Portal Master Rank 6
250
0 | 2 | 0 | 0 | 0 | 2

Viking Helmet
Portal Master Rank 6
250
0 | 0 | 0 | 3 | 0 | 0

Fancy Hat
Portal Master Rank 6
250
0 | 1 | 2 | 0 | 0 | 0

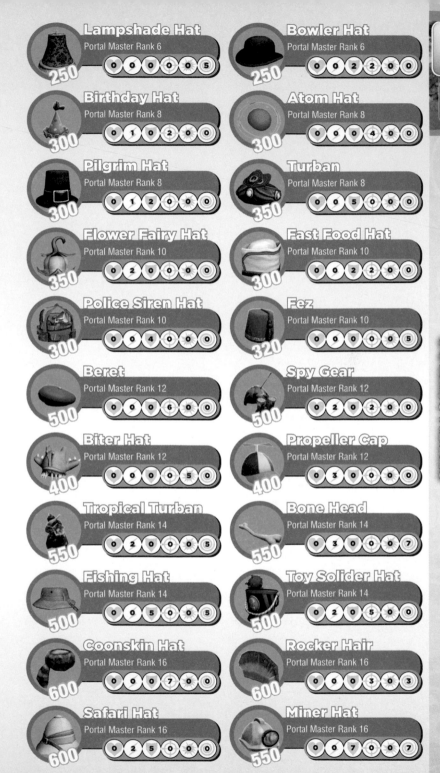

Lampshade Hat
Portal Master Rank 6
250
0 0 0 0 0 5

Bowler Hat
Portal Master Rank 6
250
0 0 2 2 0 0

Birthday Hat
Portal Master Rank 8
300
0 1 0 2 0 0

Atom Hat
Portal Master Rank 8
300
0 0 0 4 0 0

Pilgrim Hat
Portal Master Rank 8
300
0 1 2 0 0 0

Turban
Portal Master Rank 8
350
0 0 5 0 0 0

Flower Fairy Hat
Portal Master Rank 10
350
0 2 0 0 0 0

Fast Food Hat
Portal Master Rank 10
300
0 0 2 2 0 0

Police Siren Hat
Portal Master Rank 10
300
0 0 4 0 0 0

Fez
Portal Master Rank 10
320
0 0 0 0 0 5

Beret
Portal Master Rank 12
500
0 0 0 6 0 0

Spy Gear
Portal Master Rank 12
500
0 2 0 2 0 0

Biter Hat
Portal Master Rank 12
400
0 0 0 0 5 0

Propeller Cap
Portal Master Rank 12
400
0 3 0 0 0 0

Tropical Turban
Portal Master Rank 14
550
0 2 0 0 0 5

Bone Head
Portal Master Rank 14
550
0 3 0 0 0 7

Fishing Hat
Portal Master Rank 14
500
0 0 5 0 0 5

Toy Solider Hat
Portal Master Rank 14
500
0 2 0 5 0 0

Coonskin Hat
Portal Master Rank 16
600
0 0 0 7 0 0

Rocker Hair
Portal Master Rank 16
600
0 0 0 3 0 3

Safari Hat
Portal Master Rank 16
600
0 2 5 0 0 0

Miner Hat
Portal Master Rank 16
550
0 0 7 0 0 7

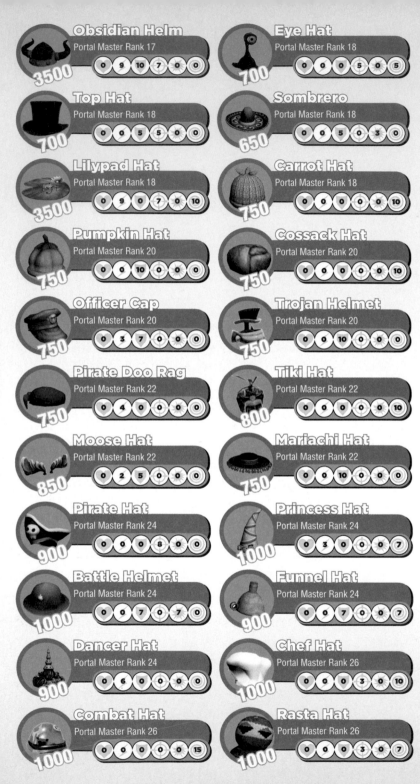

Obsidian Helm
Portal Master Rank 17
0 · 9 · 10 · 7 · 0 · 0
3500

Eye Hat
Portal Master Rank 18
0 · 0 · 0 · 5 · 0 · 5
700

Top Hat
Portal Master Rank 18
0 · 0 · 5 · 5 · 0 · 0
700

Sombrero
Portal Master Rank 18
0 · 0 · 5 · 0 · 3 · 0
650

Lilypad Hat
Portal Master Rank 18
0 · 9 · 9 · 7 · 0 · 10
3500

Carrot Hat
Portal Master Rank 18
0 · 0 · 0 · 0 · 0 · 10
750

Pumpkin Hat
Portal Master Rank 20
0 · 0 · 10 · 10 · 0 · 0
750

Cossack Hat
Portal Master Rank 20
0 · 0 · 0 · 0 · 0 · 10
750

Officer Cap
Portal Master Rank 20
0 · 3 · 7 · 0 · 0 · 0
750

Trojan Helmet
Portal Master Rank 20
0 · 0 · 10 · 0 · 0 · 0
750

Pirate Doo Rag
Portal Master Rank 22
0 · 4 · 4 · 0 · 0 · 0
750

Tiki Hat
Portal Master Rank 22
0 · 0 · 0 · 0 · 0 · 10
800

Moose Hat
Portal Master Rank 22
0 · 2 · 5 · 0 · 0 · 0
850

Mariachi Hat
Portal Master Rank 22
0 · 0 · 10 · 0 · 0 · 0
750

Pirate Hat
Portal Master Rank 24
0 · 0 · 0 · 8 · 0 · 0
900

Princess Hat
Portal Master Rank 24
0 · 3 · 0 · 0 · 0 · 7
1000

Battle Helmet
Portal Master Rank 24
0 · 0 · 7 · 7 · 0 · 0
1000

Funnel Hat
Portal Master Rank 24
0 · 0 · 7 · 0 · 0 · 7
900

Dancer Hat
Portal Master Rank 24
0 · 6 · 0 · 0 · 0 · 0
900

Chef Hat
Portal Master Rank 26
0 · 0 · 0 · 3 · 0 · 10
1000

Combat Hat
Portal Master Rank 26
0 · 0 · 0 · 0 · 0 · 15
1000

Rasta Hat
Portal Master Rank 26
0 · 0 · 0 · 3 · 0 · 7
1000

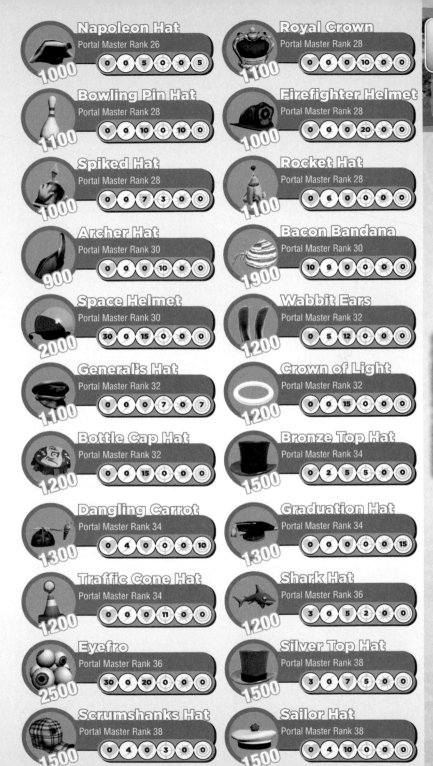

Napoleon Hat — Portal Master Rank 26 — 1000 — 0 0 5 5 0 5

Royal Crown — Portal Master Rank 28 — 1100 — 0 0 0 10 0 0

Bowling Pin Hat — Portal Master Rank 28 — 1100 — 0 0 10 0 10 0

Firefighter Helmet — Portal Master Rank 28 — 1000 — 0 0 0 20 0 0

Spiked Hat — Portal Master Rank 28 — 1000 — 0 0 7 3 0 0

Rocket Hat — Portal Master Rank 28 — 1100 — 0 6 0 0 0 0

Archer Hat — Portal Master Rank 30 — 900 — 0 0 0 10 0 0

Bacon Bandana — Portal Master Rank 30 — 1900 — 10 9 0 0 0 0

Space Helmet — Portal Master Rank 30 — 2000 — 30 0 15 0 0 0

Wabbit Ears — Portal Master Rank 32 — 1200 — 0 5 12 0 0 0

General's Hat — Portal Master Rank 32 — 1100 — 0 0 0 7 0 7

Crown of Light — Portal Master Rank 32 — 1200 — 0 0 15 0 0 0

Bottle Cap Hat — Portal Master Rank 32 — 1200 — 0 0 15 0 0 0

Bronze Top Hat — Portal Master Rank 34 — 1500 — 0 2 5 5 0 0

Dangling Carrot — Portal Master Rank 34 — 1300 — 0 4 0 0 0 10

Graduation Hat — Portal Master Rank 34 — 1300 — 0 0 0 0 0 15

Traffic Cone Hat — Portal Master Rank 34 — 1200 — 0 0 0 11 0 0

Shark Hat — Portal Master Rank 36 — 1200 — 3 0 5 2 0 0

Eyefro — Portal Master Rank 36 — 2500 — 30 0 20 0 0 0

Silver Top Hat — Portal Master Rank 38 — 1500 — 3 0 7 5 0 0

Scrumshanks Hat — Portal Master Rank 38 — 1500 — 0 4 0 3 0 0

Sailor Hat — Portal Master Rank 38 — 1500 — 0 4 10 0 0 0

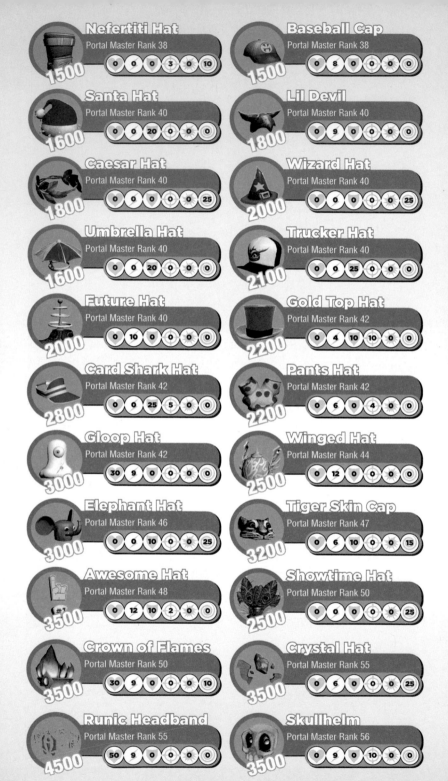

Hat	Rank	Price	Stats
Nefertiti Hat	Portal Master Rank 38	1500	0 9 0 3 0 10
Baseball Cap	Portal Master Rank 38	1500	0 8 0 0 0 0
Santa Hat	Portal Master Rank 40	1600	0 0 20 0 0 0
Lil Devil	Portal Master Rank 40	1800	0 9 0 0 0 0
Caesar Hat	Portal Master Rank 40	1800	0 0 0 0 0 25
Wizard Hat	Portal Master Rank 40	2000	0 0 0 0 0 25
Umbrella Hat	Portal Master Rank 40	1600	0 0 20 0 0 0
Trucker Hat	Portal Master Rank 40	2100	0 0 25 0 0 0
Future Hat	Portal Master Rank 40	2000	0 10 0 0 0 0
Gold Top Hat	Portal Master Rank 42	2200	0 4 10 10 0 0
Card Shark Hat	Portal Master Rank 42	2800	0 0 25 5 0 0
Pants Hat	Portal Master Rank 42	2200	0 6 0 4 0 0
Gloop Hat	Portal Master Rank 42	3000	30 9 0 0 0 0
Winged Hat	Portal Master Rank 44	2500	0 12 0 0 0 0
Elephant Hat	Portal Master Rank 46	3000	0 0 10 0 0 25
Tiger Skin Cap	Portal Master Rank 47	3200	0 6 10 0 0 15
Awesome Hat	Portal Master Rank 48	3500	0 12 10 2 0 0
Showtime Hat	Portal Master Rank 50	2500	0 0 0 0 0 25
Crown of Flames	Portal Master Rank 50	3500	30 9 0 0 0 10
Crystal Hat	Portal Master Rank 55	3500	0 6 0 0 0 25
Runic Headband	Portal Master Rank 55	4500	50 9 0 0 0 0
Skullhelm	Portal Master Rank 56	3500	0 9 0 10 0 0

Unicorn Hat
Portal Master Rank 60

2500 | 0 | 0 | 12 | 10 | 0 | 0

Whirlwind Diadem
Portal Master Rank 60

3500 | 30 | 9 | 10 | 0 | 0 | 0

Knight Helm
Portal Master Rank 65

4700 | 0 | 6 | 15 | 7 | 0 | 15

Cactus Hat
Portal Master Rank 70

4000 | 0 | 9 | 25 | 0 | 0 | 0

Clockwork Hat
Portal Master Rank 75

4000 | 0 | 9 | 0 | 0 | 0 | 25

Teeth Top Hat
Portal Master Rank 75

6000 | 0 | 0 | 25 | 10 | 0 | 20

Great Helm
Portal Master Rank 80

9500 | 0 | 15 | 20 | 3 | 0 | 0

Legendary Treasures

There are 48 Legendary Treasures. Every Legendary Treasure is either found in a Story Level, or purchased at Tuk's Emporium in Woodburrow after meeting certain requirements.

After you complete Chapter 6: Iron Jaw Gulch and speak with Tibbet in Woodburrow's Trophy Room, place Legendary Treasures on the Legendary Pedestals scattered around Woodburrow to boost your Skylanders in various ways. For more information about Legendary Treasures, check out the Improving Your Skylanders section of this guide.

LEGENDARY TREASURES FROM STORY MODE

Amber Treasure
Sheep Wreck Islands
+12 Ranged Armor

Bubble Chest
Mudwater Hollow
+5 Gold Boost

Cascade Bust
Cascade Glade
+5 Elemental Strength Boost

Crooked Currency
Motleyville
+10 Gold Boost

Crystal Fire Hearth
Twisty Tunnels
+5 Elemental Luck Boost

Deputee Badge
Sheep Wreck Islands
+10 Elemental Strength

Elven Arrow
Winter Keep
+3 Critical Hit Multiplier

Endless Cocoa Cup
Frostfest Mountains
+12 Armor

Epic Soap of Froth
Tower of Time
+4 Critical Hit%

Expensive Souvenir
Winter Keep
+5 Critical Hit Multiplier

Geode Glider
Boney Islands
+12 Melee Armor

Glowy Mushroom
Fantasm Forest
+15 Pickup Range

Jolly Greeble
Iron Jaw Gulch
+10 Maximum Health

Luminous Lure
Mudwater Hollow
+10 Ranged Armor

Major Award Monkey
Rampant Ruins
+10 Luck

Masterful Disguise
Kaos' Fortress
+15 Elemental Armor Boost

Moltenskin Scale
Twisty Tunnels
+10 Elemental Food Boost

Mostly Magic Mirror
Mount Cloudbreak
+5 Armor

Navigator Compass
Woodburrow
+5 Ranged Armor

Skylander Scope
Kaos' Fortress
+2 Critical Hit Multiplier

The Bling Grille
Motleyville
+5 Elemental Food Boost

The Brass Tap
Fantasm Forest
+5 Gold Boost

The Monkey's Paw
Rampant Ruins
+5 Food Gain

Tik Tok Neck Clock
Iron Jaw Gulch
+10 XP Boost

Topiary of Doom
Fantasm Forest
+15 Elemental Power

Triassic Tooth
Boney Islands
+2 Speed

Urban Art
Sheep Wreck Islands
+15 XP Boost

Volcano Party Pass
Tower of Time
+10 Melee Armor

Waterfall Decanter
Tower of Time
+5 Armor

Whizzing Whatsit
Complete 36 SWAP Zone Challenges on Nightmare difficulty
+30 Pickup Range

Yeti Teddy
Frostfest Mountains
+5 XP Boost

LEGENDARY TREASURES FROM TUK'S EMPORIUM

Bog Chowder
Portal Master Rank 58
+10 Melee Armor
600

Bonnie Bonsai
Portal Master Rank 37
+15 Luck
900

Boomboom Box
Master Rank 17
+10 Elemental Armor Boost
600

Bottled Warship
Portal Master Rank 23
+3 Critical Hit %
600

Buttering Blade
Portal Master Rank 68
+15 Armor
900

Chieftess Figure
Portal Master Rank 13
+10 Elemental Power
600

Crustaceous Clothes
Master Rank 7
+20 Maximum Health
600

Frozenish Flag
Portal Master Rank 78
+15 Ranged Armor
900

Golden Crunchy
Unlocks after Chapter 3: Mudwater Hollow
+10 Armor
600

Lichen Lantern
Portal Master Rank 9
+5 Melee Armor
300

Mabu Carving
Portal Master Rank 33
+5 Speed
600

 Shiniest Stone
Portal Master Rank 7
+10 Ranged Armor
600

 Snowboulder +1
Portal Master Rank 45
+15 Melee Armor
900

 Sweet Sasparilla
Unlocks after Chapter 3: Mudwater Hollow
+10 Food Gain
600

 Refurbished Engine
Portal Master Rank 27
+10 Elemental Luck Boost
600

 Singing Puppet
Portal Master Rank 55
+15 Ranged Armor
900

 Spyro Duo Balloon
Portal Master Rank 43
+15 Melee Armor
900

Charms

Charms are the one type of collectible not found in Story Levels. You must earn Charms by completing Bonus Mission Maps and Arena challenges. Tuk's Emporium has four Charms for sale as well.

Each Charm is active as soon as you acquire it. All the effects are cumulative and the bonuses from Charms are active at all times.

CHARMS FROM STORY MODE

Air Freshener
Cursed Statues bonus mission
+5 Corrupt Creature Armor

Big Pants
Beach Breach arena
+10 Maximum Health

Body Armor
Treble Theft bonus mission
+4 Armor

Charmed Actions
Thief on the Run bonus mission
+3 Elemental Luck Shot

Cyclops Swatter
Sand Castle arena
+1 Critial Hit Multiplier

Delicious Food
Chomp Chomp Chompies arena
+5 Food Gain

Eight Leaf Clover
Beware of the Bird arena
+4 Luck

Element Deflect
Golem Invasion bonus mission
+5 Golem Armor

Elemental Fortune
Undercover Greebles bonus mission
+2 Elemental Luck Boost

Elemental Fist
Serpent Attack bonus mission
+2 Elemental Strength Boost

Electro Magnet
Magic Cells bonus mission
+5 Pickup Range

Elemental Noms
Super Hungry Gobble Pods arena
+5 Elemental Food Boost

Elemental Shield
Chompy Challenge bonus mission
+2 Elemental Armor Boost

Elemental Outlet
Egg Royale bonus mission
+2 Elemental Power

Eye Poker
Sweet Blizzard bonus mission
+5 Cyclops Armor

Four Leaf Clover
Plants Vs Cakes bonus mission
+2 Luck

Good Luck Charm
Cyclops Makeover arena
+1 Critical Hit %

Gourmet Meal
Boarding Party arena
+5 Gourmet Meal

Greeble Be Gone
Chompy Sauce bonus mission
+5 Greeble Armor

Greeble Grappler
Shellshock Curse arena
+1 Critical Hit Multiplier

Health Extender
Snake in the Hole arena

+50 Maximum Health

Instant Experience
Perfect Captain arena

+5 XP Boost

Luck of the Mabu
Chompy Tsunami arena

+1 Critical Hit %

Major Meal
Master Chef bonus mission

+5 Food Gain

Mountain's Resolve
Vortex Banquet arena

+3 Elemental Armor Boost

Power Blend
Sand-Pit-Fall arena

+1 Critical Hit %

Rabbit's Foot
Fishy Fishing bonus mission

+1 Critical Hit %

Sword Breaker
Angry Angry Plants arena

+5 Melee Armor

Ultimate Defense
Icicle Bombing arena

+6 Armor

Vitamin Supplements
Frozen Delight bonus mission

+15 Elemental Food Boost

Impervious
Troll Beach Attack arena

+5 Ranged Armor

Kaos Kruncher
Exploding Snowmen arena

+1 Critical Hit Multiplier

Mage Masher
Sheep Mage Rage arena

+1 Critical Hit Multiplier

Might of the Ancients
Ghost Traps bonus mission

+3 Elemental Strength Boost

Pointy Spear
Pokey Pokey Spikes arena

+1 Critical Hit %

Power Clover
Chunky Chompies arena

+6 Luck

Small Shield
Sleepy Turtles bonus mission

+2 Armor

Tasty Food
Fruit Fight bonus mission

+5 Food Gain

Unbridled Energy
Frigid Fight bonus mission

+10 Elemental Power

Wizard Repellant
Royal Gems bonus mission

+5 Spell Punk Armor

CHARMS FROM TUK'S EMPORIUM

Life Elixir
Portal Master Rank 19

750 +100 Maximum Health

Golden Abacus
Portal Master Rank 30

750 +5 Gold Boost

Overcharged
Portal Master Rank 39

750 +1 Critical Hit Multiplier

Rocket Propellant
Portal Master Rank 50

750 +1 Speed

Bonus Mission Maps

There are 16 Bonus Mission Maps hidden in Story Levels (one per level), and 3 additional maps are available for purchase from Tuk's Emporium in Woodburrow, after meeting certain requirements.

Chompy Challenge is available once Master Eon unlocks the Bonus Missions.

For more information about completing these challenging maps, turn to the "Bonus Mission Maps" section of this guide.

BONUS MAPS FROM STORY MODE

Undercover Greebles

Kaos' Fortress

Find the Greebles in sheep's clothing and stop them.

Cursed Statues

Kaos' Fortress

Defeat the Greebles and destroy the evil statues.

Chompy Sauce

Fantasm Forest

Close the valves pumping Chompy sauce into the water.

Fishy Fishing

Rampant Ruins

Destroy the giant harpoons in the Elder Fish Sanctuary.

Master Chef

Mudwater Hollow

Defeat the head chef of the Greebles.

Plants Vs Cakes

Cascade Glade

Push 6 cakes to feed the Gobble Pods.

Fruit Fight

Mount Cloudbreak

Collect fruits for the archeologists' expedition.

Serpent Attack

Tower of Time

Free the airship from the sand monster's grasp.

Thief on the Run

Sheep Wreck Islands

Catch the thieves and retrieve the stolen packages.

Sweet Blizzard

Woodburrow

Turn off the Yetis' ice ceam machines.

Frigid Fight

Frostfest Mountains

Bring the wandering ghosts to the right colored gate.

Ghost Traps

Winter Keep

Free the peaceful ghosts from their cages.

Royal Gems

Boney Islands

Defeat the armored Cyclopes to retrieve the royal gems.

Magic Cells

Twisty Tunnels

Recharge the power plant by collecting blue cells.

Sleepy Turtles

Motleyville

Push the sleeping turtles back into their nest.

Egg Royale

Iron Jaw Gulch

Bring the stolen royal eggs to the Queen of the Turtles!

FREE
Chompy Challenge
Unlocks after Chapter 3: Mudwater Hollow

Take out the Chompies and their Chompy Pods.

1000
Treble Theft
Portal Master Rank 15

Retrieve the Kangarats' musical instruments.

1000
Frozen Delight
Portal Master Rank 25

Free the Yetis stuck in ice cream!

1000
Golem Invasion
Portal Master Rank 35

Defeat the Golems and set the turtles free!

Story Scrolls

There are 16 Story Scrolls to collect and each includes an interesting piece of information about the Cloudbreak Isles. Each of the non-boss fight Story Mode Chapters has one Story Scroll hidden in it. Woodburrow has two Story Scrolls that become available as you progress through the Story Mode and uncover new areas within it. Finally, both Adventure Pack levels, Sheep Wreck Islands and Tower of Time, have a Story Scroll.

Kaos' Laboratory
Kaos' Fortress

Greeble Lands
Cascade Glade

Dangerous Profession
Fantasm Forest

Party on the Mountains
Frostfest Mountains

Frozen Galleries
Boney Islands

The Clocktower
Tower of Time

The Great Hollow
Woodburrow

The Platinum Sheep
Sheep Wreck Islands

The Grave Monkey
Rampant Ruins

Motleyville Junk
Motleyville

Enchanted Pool
Woodburrow

The Fire Vipers of Doom
Twisty Tunnels

Whirlwind's Gift
Winter Keep

Magic Recycling
Mudwater Hollow

Magical Pyrotechnics
Mount Cloudbreak

The Glass Hat
Iron Jaw Gulch

ACCOLADES

Accolades measure your progress in completing the game. They track everything from how well you perform in Story Mode Chapters to the size of your Skylanders collection.

Accolades award Stars based on the difficulty in meeting the conditions of a given Accolade. These Stars count toward your Portal Master rank, which in turn unlocks better items and rewards from Tuk's Emporium in Woodburrow.

Challenge Accolades

ACCOLADES	DESCRIPTION	STARS
Full Spark	Complete 20 unique Spark Lock puzzles.	★
Charged Up	Earn 2 Bolts in 20 unique Spark Lock Puzzles	★ ★
Complete Circuit	Earn 3 Bolts in 20 unique Spark Lock Puzzles	★ ★ ★
Knock Knock	Open 50 Single Element Gates in Story Mode.	★ ★
Unhinged	Open 100 Element Gates in Story Mode	★ ★ ★
Safe Passage	Open 40 Dual Element Gates in Story Mode	★ ★
Swap Unlock	Unlock 12 SWAP Zone Challenges.	★
Unswappable	Unlock 24 SWAP Zone Challenges	★ ★
The Full Swap	Unlock 36 SWAP Zone Challenges	★ ★ ★
Big Loot	Open 30 Giant Chests in Story Mode.	★ ★ ★
Maxed Out	Level any Skylander to 20.	★ ★ ★
Ultrapowered!	Purchase every ability upgrade for any Skylander.	★ ★ ★
Buy Now or Bye Now	Purchase every item in Tuk's Emporium	★ ★ ★
Repair the Bridge	Build a bridge to the Elemental Platform.	★ ★ ★
Summon Eon	Progress through Story Mode and summon Eon.	★ ★ ★
Pedestal Pioneer	Unlock all Legendary Treasure Pedestals.	★
Diligent Displayer	Place a Legendary Treasure on every Pedestal	★ ★ ★
Unlock Time Attack	Progress through Story Mode to unlock Time Attack.	★
Unlock Score Mode	Progress through Story Mode to unlock Score Mode.	★
Adventurin' Time	Open all Elemental Gates, SWAP Zones, and Giant Chests in Sheep Wreck Islands. (7 Total)	★ ★
Watching the Clock	Open all Elemental Gates, SWAP Zones, and Giant Chests in the Tower of Time. (7 Total)	★
Dapper Copper	Earn a Bronze Toy Quest Medal for any Skylander.	★
Sliver of Silver	Earn a Silver Toy Quest Medal for any Skylander.	★ ★
Bold Gold	Earn a Gold Toy Quest Medal for any Skylander.	★ ★ ★

Exploration Accolades

ACCOLADES	DESCRIPTION	STARS
Half-A-Dasher	Find 12 Hats hidden in Story Chapters.	★
Haberdasher	Find 24 Hats hidden in Story Chapters.	★ ★
Fasion Ace	Collect 120 Hats.	★ ★ ★

ACCOLADES	DESCRIPTION	STARS
Lucky Find	Open 20 different Treasure Chests in Story Levels.	★
Payday	Open 40 different Treasure Chests in Story Levels.	★ ★
Jackpot	Open 60 different Treasure Chests in Story Levels.	★ ★ ★
Treasure Hunter	Find 12 Legendary Treasures hidden in Story Chapters.	★
Artifact Seeker	Find 23 Legendary Treasures hidden in Story Chapters.	★ ★
Master Collector	Collect 48 Legendary Treasures.	★ ★ ★
Diligent Researcher	Find 6 Story Scrolls in Story Mode.	★
Worldly Scholar	Find 12 Story Scrolls in Story Mode.	★ ★
Literary Master	Find 16 Story Scrolls.	★ ★ ★
Charter Adept	Find 6 Bonus Mission Maps in Story Mode.	★
Cartographer	Find 13 Bonus Mission Maps in Story Mode.	★ ★
Master Georgrapher	Collect 20 Bonus Mission Maps.	★ ★ ★
Power Locator	Find 10 Soul Gems.	★
Soul Gatherer	Find 21 Soul Gems.	★ ★
Spiritual Warden	Find all 32 Soul Gems.	★ ★ ★
Butterfly Catcher	Find 6 Winged Sapphires in Story Mode.	★
Painted Lady Pilferer	Find 12 Winged Sapphires in Story Mode.	★ ★
Monarch Master	Find 18 Winged Sapphires.	★ ★ ★
Charm Bracelet	Collect 22 Charms.	★
Charm Champion	Collect 44 Charms.	★ ★ ★
Woodburrow Wanderer	Discover every area in Woodburrow. (9 Total)	★ ★ ★
Special Specialty	Find every special collectible in Woodburrow. (10 Total)	★ ★ ★

Collection Accolades

ACCOLADES	DESCRIPTION	STARS
Score Four	Add 4 Blue Base Skylanders to your collection.	★
Great Eight	Add 8 Blue Base Skylanders to your collection.	★
Blue Dozen	Add 12 Blue Base Skylanders to your collection.	★
Super Sixteen	Add 16 Blue Base Skylanders to your collection.	★
Double Dozen	Add 24 Blue Base Skylanders to your collection.	★
Blue Thirty-two	Add 32 Blue Base Skylanders to your collection.	★ ★
Indigo Forty	Add 40 Blue Base Skylanders to your collection.	★ ★
Full Blue	Add 48 Blue Base Skylanders to your collection.	★ ★ ★
Mean Green Machine	Add 32 Green Base Skylanders to your collection.	★ ★ ★
Gigantic Hero	Add 8 Giant Skylanders to your collection.	★
Second Wave	Add 30 Orange Base Skylanders to your collection.	★ ★ ★
Supreme Portal Master	Add 80 Skylanders to your collection.	★ ★ ★
Force for Good	Add one SWAP Force Skylander of each SWAP Skill to your collection.	★ ★ ★
Bounce into Action	Add both Bounce SWAP Force Skylanders to your collection.	★
Blast Forward	Add both Rocket SWAP Force Skylanders to your collection.	★
Twist and Turn	Add both Spin SWAP Force Skylanders to your collection.	★
Matched Velocities	Add both Speed SWAP Force Skylanders to your collection.	★
Great Heights	Add both Climb SWAP Force Skylanders to your collection.	★
Tunneling Team	Add both Dig SWAP Force Skylanders to your collection.	★
Shhhhhh!	Add both Sneak SWAP Force Skylanders to your collection.	★
Now You See me	Add both Teleport SWAP Force Skylanders to your collection.	★

1/60

17/53

ACCOLADES

ACCOLADES	DESCRIPTION	STARS
Transmutation	Add one SWAP Force Skylander of each elemental type to your collection.	★
Ambassador	Add one Blue Base Skylander of each elemental type to your collection.	★
Abracadabra	Add 4 Blue Base Magic Skylanders to your collection.	★
Mystic Channeler	Add 10 Magic Skylanders to your collection.	★ ★
Drop in the Ocean	Add 4 Blue Base Water Skylanders to your collection.	★
Sea of Power	Add 10 Water Skylanders to your collection.	★ ★
Gizmo Hero	Add 4 Blue Base Tech Skylanders to your collection.	★
Cutting Edge	Add 10 Tech Skylanders to your collection.	★ ★
Dug Freshly	Add 4 Blue Base Earth Skylanders to your collection.	★
Mountain of Power	Add 10 Earth Skylanders to your collection.	★ ★
Third Degree	Add 4 Blue Base Fire Skylanders to your collection.	★
Blaze of Glory	Add 10 Fire Skylanders to your collection.	★ ★
No Bones About it	Add 4 Blue Base Undead Skylanders to your collection.	★
Six Feet Deep	Add 10 Undead Skylanders to your collection.	★ ★
Floral Foura	Add 4 Blue Base Life Skylanders to your collection.	★
Go Team Green	Add 10 Life Skylanders to your collection.	★ ★
Cloudbreakers	Add 4 Blue Base Air Skylanders to your collection.	★
Storming Through	Add 10 Air Skylanders to your collection.	★ ★
Little Chum	Add a Sidekick to your collection.	★ ★ ★
Stockpile of Magic	Add 4 Blue Base Magic Items to your collection.	★
Wild Blue Yonder	Add 2 Blue Base Adventure Pack Location Pieces to your collection.	★ ★ ★
Legacy of Magic	Add 12 Magic Items to your collection.	★ ★ ★
Glowing	Add a Lightcore Skylander to your collection.	★
Blue Lightning	Add 8 Lightcore Skylanders to your collection.	★ ★
Overbright	Add 16 Lightcore Skylanders to your collection.	★ ★ ★
Big Footprint	Add 30 Series 2 Skylanders to your collection.	★
Reimagined in Blue	Add 6 Blue Base Series 2 Skylanders to your collection.	★
New and Blue	Add 5 Series 3 Skylanders to your collection.	★
Cloubreak Warriors	Add 10 Series 3 Skylanders to your collection.	★
SWAP Cadet	Play with 4 different SWAP Force combinations	★
SWAP Officer	Play with 8 different SWAP Force combinations	★
SWAP Detective	Play with 16 different SWAP Force combinations	★
SWAP Sergeant	Play with 32 different SWAP Force combinations	★ ★
SWAP Lieutenant	Play with 64 different SWAP Force combinations	★ ★
SWAP Commander	Play with 128 different SWAP Force combinations	★ ★
SWAP Chief	Play with 256 different SWAP Force combinations	★ ★ ★
Arm Yourself	Add 2 Blue Base Battle Pieces to your collection.	★ ★ ★

Completion Accolades

ACCOLADES	DESCRIPTION	STARS
Mega Awesome Ending	Complete 17 Story Levels on any difficulty.	★
Digging In	Complete 8 Story Levels on Medium difficulty or harder.	★
Meaty Plot	Complete all Story Levels on Medium difficulty or harder	★ ★
Tough Sample	Complete 6 Story Levels on Hard difficulty or harder.	★
Epic Ballad	Complete 17 Story Levels on Hard difficulty or harder.	★ ★ ★

ACCOLADES	DESCRIPTION	STARS
Rise in Action	Complete 12 Story Levels on Hard difficulty or harder.	★ ★
Fitful Slumber	Complete 4 Story Levels on Nightmare difficulty.	★
Bad Dreams	Complete 8 Story Levels on Nightmare difficulty.	★
Waking Nightmare	Complete 12 Story Levels on Nightmare difficulty.	★ ★
Night Terrorizer	Complete 17 Story Levels on Nightmare difficulty.	★ ★ ★
Twinkle Twinkle	Earn at least 2 Stars on 8 Story Levels	★
Shooting Stars	Earn at least 2 Stars on all Story Levels	★
Meteoric	Earn 3 Stars on 6 Story Levels	★
Superstar	Earn 3 Stars on 12 Story Levels	★
Going Nova	Earn 3 Stars on 17 Story Levels.	★ ★ ★
Navigator of Fun	Complete both Adventure Pack levels on any difficulty.	★
Simple Sojourn	Earn at least 2 Stars on both Adventure Pack Levels.	★
Challenging Journey	Complete both Adventure Pack levels on Medium difficulty or harder.	★
Charting Adventure	Complete both Adventure Pack levels on Hard difficulty or harder.	★
Endless Odyssey	Complete both Adventure Pack levels on Nightmare difficulty.	★ ★ ★
Perfect Journey	Earn 3 Stars on both Adventure Pack Levels	★ ★
Scrapper	Complete 10 Solo Survival Levels on any difficulty.	★
No Equal	Earn 3 Stars on 10 Solo Survival Levels.	★ ★ ★
Champion	Complete 10 Solo Survival Levels on Medium difficulty or harder.	★
Iron Skylander	Complete 10 Solo Survival Levels on Hard difficulty or harder.	★ ★
Gladiator of All Worlds	Complete 10 Solo Survival Levels on Nightmare difficulty.	★ ★ ★
Star of Swords	Earn at least 2 Stars on 10 Solo Survival Levels.	★ ★
Skylands Hero	Complete 18 Bonus Missions on any difficulty.	★
People's Champion	Complete 18 Bonus Missions on Medium difficulty or harder.	★
Epic Warrior	Complete 18 Bonus Missions on Hard difficulty or harder.	★ ★
Immortal Soldier	Complete 18 Bonus Missions on Nightmare difficulty.	★ ★ ★
Force for Justice	Earn at least 2 Stars on 18 Bonus Missions.	★ ★
A Time of Peace	Earn 3 Stars on 18 Bonus Missions.	★ ★ ★
Number Cruncher	Complete 17 Score Mode levels on any difficulty.	★
Point Puncher	Complete 17 Score Mode levels on Medium difficulty or harder.	★
Know the Score	Complete 17 Score Mode levels on Hard difficulty or harder.	★ ★
Exponential Digits	Complete 17 Score Mode levels on Nightmare difficulty.	★ ★ ★
Seeing Stars	Earn at least 2 Stars on 17 Score Mode levels.	★
Number Burst	Earn 3 Stars on all Score Mode Levels	★ ★
Fast Track	Complete 17 Time Attack levels on any difficulty.	★
Speedster	Complete 17 Time Attack levels on Medium difficulty or harder.	★
Dangerous Race	Complete 17 Time Attack levels on Hard difficulty or harder.	★ ★
High Velocity	Complete 17 Time Attack levels on Nightmare difficulty.	★ ★ ★
Silver Medal Run	Earn at least 2 Stars on 17 Time Attack Levels.	★
Go for the Gold	Earn 3 Stars on 17 Time Attack Levels.	★ ★
Challenge Novice	Complete 36 SWAP Zone Challenges on any difficulty.	★
Expert Swapper	Complete 36 SWAP Zone Challenges on Medium difficulty or harder.	★
Tough Customer	Complete 36 SWAP Zone Challenges on Hard difficulty or harder.	★ ★
Zone Crusher	Complete 36 SWAP Zone Challenges on Nightmare difficulty.	★ ★ ★
Advanced Exchange	Earn at least 2 Stars on 36 SWAP Zone Challenges.	★
Unstoppable	Earn 3 Stars on 36 SWAP Zone Challenges	★ ★

ACCOLADES

ACHIEVEMENTS & TROPHIES

Achievements and Trophies are awarded by the console on which you're playing *Skylanders SWAP Force*. Not all consoles award Achievements and Trophies.

Story Mode Achievements

	TITLE	DESCRIPTION	XBOX 360 GAMERSCORE	PS3 TROPHY
	Welcome To Woodburrow	Complete Mount Cloudbreak on any difficulty	25	Bronze
	Chieftess Rescued	Complete Cascade Glade on any difficulty	15	Bronze
	Swamp Secured	Complete Mudwater Hollow on any difficulty	15	Bronze
	Ruins Romped	Complete Rampant Ruins on any difficulty	15	Bronze
	Glumshanks De-Evilized	Complete Jungle Rumble on any difficulty	25	Bronze
	Lawman	Complete Iron Jaw Gulch on any difficulty	15	Bronze
	New Law in Town	Complete Motleyville on any difficulty	15	Bronze
	Squid Squabble	Complete Twisty Tunnels on any difficulty	15	Bronze
	Vexed Viper	Complete Serpent's Peak on any difficulty	25	Bronze
	Cold Caravan	Complete Boney Islands on any difficulty	15	Bronze
	Snowball Fight!	Complete Winter Keep on any difficulty	15	Bronze
	Blizzard Bailout	Complete Frostfest Mountains on any difficulty	15	Bronze
	Puppet Master Pounded	Complete Mesmeralda's Show on any difficulty	25	Bronze
	Woods Wetted	Complete Fantasm Forest on any difficulty	15	Bronze
	Kastle Krashed	Complete Kaos' Fortress on any difficulty	15	Bronze
	Kalamity Averted	Complete Motherly Mayhem on any difficulty	15	Bronze
	Kaos Quashed	Complete Cloudbreak Core on any difficulty	25	Bronze
	Champion of Skylands	Complete all main chapters in Story Mode on any difficulty	100	Gold
	Times are Hard	Complete main chapters in Story Mode on Hard difficulty	150	Gold
	Knight of Nightmares	Complete main chapters in Story Mode on Nightmare difficulty	200	Gold

Miscellaneous Achievements

	TITLE	DESCRIPTION	XBOX 360 GAMERSCORE	PS3 TROPHY
	Boom!	Light the fireworks in Woodburrow	10	Bronze
	Perch Plunge	Dive off the Tree in Woodburrow	10	Bronze
	Newsworthy	Use the mailbox in Woodburrow to see the Message of the Day (Online Only)	15	Bronze
	Golem Graveyard	Defeat 10 Golems	10	Bronze
	NO WAY!!!!!!!!!!!!!!!!!!!	Obtain all other Trophies	—	Platinum

Portal Master Achievements

	TITLE	DESCRIPTION	XBOX 360 GAMERSCORE	PS3 TROPHY
	Race to the Finish	Complete your first Time Attack level	10	Bronze
	Mad Dash	Earn a 3-star rating in any Time Attack level	10	Bronze
	Speed Demon	Earn a 3-star rating in 3 Time Attack levels	15	Bronze
	Fastest One Around	Earn a 3-star rating in 17 Time Attack levels	20	Silver
	Reach for the Sky	Complete your first Score Mode level	10	Bronze
	Racking Up the Points	Earn a 3-star rating in any Score Mode level	10	Bronze
	High Roller	Earn a 3-star rating in 3 Score Mode levels	15	Bronze
	Winning Streak	Earn a 3-star rating in 17 Score Mode levels	20	Silver
	New Challenger	Complete your first Bonus Mission level	10	Bronze
	Up and Coming	Earn a 3-star rating in any Bonus Mission level	10	Bronze
	Rising Star	Earn a 3-star rating in 3 Bonus Mission levels	15	Bronze
	Heroic Champion	Earn a 3-star rating in 5 Bonus Mission levels	20	Silver
	Slings and Arrows	Complete your first Team Survival Arena level	10	Bronze
	Enduring the Onslaught	Earn a 3-star rating in any Team Survival Arena level	10	Bronze
	Coming out Ahead	Earn a 3-star rating in 3 Team Survival Arena levels	15	Bronze

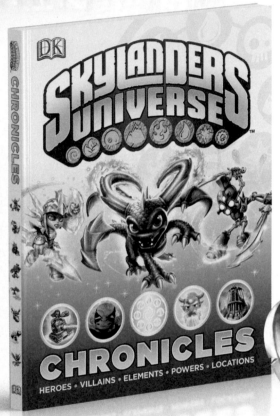

CHARACTER UPGRADE EDITION

Ken Schmidt and V.H. McCarty

DK/BradyGames, a division of Penguin Group (USA).
800 East 96th Street, 3rd Floor
Indianapolis, IN 46240

ISBN: 978-0-7440-1550-8

Printing Code: The rightmost double-digit number is the year of the book's printing; the rightmost single-digit number is the number of the book's printing. For example, 14-1 shows that the first printing of the book occurred in 2014.

17 16 15 14   4 3 2 1

Printed in the USA.

Brady Acknowledgements

BradyGames would like to thank Lindsay Friedman, Alex Gomez, Elías Jiménez, Jeffery Lee, Andrew Lee, Jack Joseph, Ryan Magid, Chris Wassum, Justin Wharton, Danielle Godbout, Scott Moore, Barclay "Buck" Chantel, Brent Gibson, Barry Morales, Pierre-Olivier "POP" Paré, Dominic Morin, Martin Tessier, Raphael Readman, Gabriel Lapointe, Charles Kirouac, Janne Richard, Raphael Corbin, Vincent Auger, Sasan "Sauce" Helmi, and the rest of the team at Activision for the help and support on this project.

BradyGAMES Staff

Vice President and Publisher
Mike Degler

Editor-In-Chief
H. Leigh Davis

Licensing Manager
Christian Sumner

Digital Publishing Manager
Tim Cox

Marketing Manager
Katie Hemlock

Operations Manager
Stacey Beheler

Credits

Senior Development Editor
David B. Bartley

Book Designers
Colin King
Jeff Weissenberger

Production Designers
Areva
Julie Clark